W9-AXI-886

K'ANG-HSI AND THE CONSOLIDATION OF CH'ING RULE 1661-1684

K'ANG-HSI AND THE CONSOLIDATION OF CH'ING RULE 1661-1684

Lawrence D. Kessler

THE UNIVERSITY OF CHICAGO PRESS
Chicago and London

Lawrence D. Kessler is associate professor of history at the University of North Carolina.

The University of Chicago Press, Chicago 60637
The University of Chicago Press, Ltd., London

Printed in the United States of America
80 79 78 77 76 9 8 7 6 5 4 3 2 1

Library of Congress Cataloging in Publication Data
Kessler, Lawrence D
K'ang-hsi and the consolidation of Ch'ing rule, 1661–1684.

Bibliography: p.
Includes index.
1. Ch'ing Sheng-tsu, Emperor of China, 1654–1722.
2. China—History—K'ang-hsi, 1662–1722. I. Title.
DS754.4.C53K47 951'.03'0924 [B] 75-20897
ISBN 0-226-43203-3

For Phyllis, Karen, Warren, and Robert

CONTENTS

CONTENTS

PREFACE

THIS IS A STUDY OF THE EARLY CAREER OF THE K'ANG-HSI EMPEROR (b. 1654; r. 1661–1722)* and the major contribution he made toward the consolidation of Ch'ing rule. I came to this subject through the back door, as it were. While examining the Rebellion of the Three Feudatories, 1673–81, I was struck with the apparent failure of this challenge to Manchu rule to strike a responsive chord among Chinese patriots. Racial animosity toward the alien dynasty had been common in the first few decades after the conquest. Clearly, the Manchus had by this time proved themselves able and legitimate governors of China. How had this achievement been realized?

We know from Franz Michael's pioneering work, *The Origin of Manchu Rule in China* (1942), that rulers of the Manchu state had begun to accommodate themselves to Chinese political and social traditions long before they came through the Great Wall and conquered China. That process, however, had not run its course with the Manchus' entry into Peking in 1644, and for the next eighteen years the new Ch'ing dynasty gave priority to its military tasks. By 1661 the provinces of China proper had been subdued by force of arms. Now the Manchus faced a harder challenge: to "pacify" what they had conquered and to consolidate their grip on the country. The year 1661 is also marked by the death of Shun-

*I shall use the reign title K'ang-hsi (and others) as if it were the emperor's name. The practice, while technically incorrect, has the virtue of conciseness and familiarity. The Chinese characters for names and terms romanized in the text are given in the Glossary.

chih and the succession of his son, K'ang-hsi, to the Dragon Throne.

K'ang-hsi became emperor at the tender age of eight *sui** and underwent an eight-year apprenticeship before he seized the reins of government in 1669 from the regents named by Shun-chih in his will. The heart of this study contrasts the policies and attitudes of the regency and K'ang-hsi and will conclude that consolidation of Ch'ing rule came only after the young emperor had changed the direction of government. By 1684, with the subjugation of Taiwan and the incorporation of that island into the empire, K'ang-hsi had essentially completed his great work as a consolidator. I have not set out to write a complete history of this twenty-four-year period (1661–84); I have investigated only the policies and developments integral to the central theme—K'ang-hsi's contribution to the consolidation of Ch'ing dynastic rule. At times this involves politics, at other times institutional structure, or military strategy, even social policy. By imposing order on these disparate developments, I hope to provide a framework for future research in early Ch'ing history.

I need not say much about my major sources, for there are no surprises, no special material that I consulted. From the list of abbreviations of frequently cited works at the end of this study, it is clear that I rely on the familiar documentary and biographical collections, familiar in title but largely unexploited for the period under study. Since my topic concerns various aspects of imperial policy and its making, these sources are the most appropriate.

Initial research for this study was done in Taiwan under a fellowship granted by the Foreign Area Fellowship Program, and later work was supported by the Research Council of the University of North Carolina. I gratefully acknowledge their generous assistance, but the conclusions, opinions, and other statements in this study are the author's alone.

*Until this century Chinese calculated years, or *sui*, in a way that aged the subject at least a year and perhaps close to two years faster than Western reckoning. A Chinese child was one *sui* at birth and added a *sui* at the passing of each new year (by the Chinese lunar calendar), so that an infant born on the eve of the new year would be two *sui* in the morning. K'ang-hsi's age in *sui* was only a year and three months more than his age by Western calculation, because he was born in the third month. Throughout this study, a person's age will be given in the Western manner unless *sui* are indicated.

PREFACE

I am indebted to a number of scholars for their willing cooperation and valuable assistance in the research and writing of this study; they bear no responsibility for whatever shortcomings it may have. Professor Ping-ti Ho of the University of Chicago, whose broad erudition and painstaking scholarship have been a constant inspiration to me, has been most helpful in all stages of this project. Among the many people at the Institute of History and Philology of Academia Sinica (Taipei) who gave freely of their time and advice, I want to give special recognition to my friend and constant source of information, Professor Hsü Cho-yün, now of the University of Pittsburgh. I also acknowledge the gracious assistance of Li Kuang-t'ao, director of the Institute archives, and the late Wang Pao-hsien, librarian of the Fu Ssu-nien Library, in locating materials useful for my study. Liu Chia-chü and Ho Kuang-mo provided valuable assistance with various problems of research and translation. Others who offered useful comments and criticism on parts of this study are Philip Kuhn, Robert Oxnam, David Roy, Jonathan Spence, Edgar Wickberg, and Jack Wills. I thank them all.

Although they were not directly involved in this project, I must acknowledge the initial stimulation toward Chinese studies I received from Professors H. G. Creel, Edward Kracke, and Earl Pritchard. Special thanks go to Linda Price and Karen Troost for preparing the typed manuscript and to Huan Rosa Tai for providing the Chinese characters in the glossary and bibliography.

Above all, I am indebted to my wife and children for their patience and support through the years of preparing this book, and I gratefully dedicate it to them.

One

INTRODUCTION: THE MANCHU CONQUEST

Although few leaders of the late Ming period could have foreseen the exact nature of the disaster that was soon to overtake them, there certainly were ample signs of dynastic decline. It is not my purpose to examine this decline with any precision and comprehensiveness. Rather, it is important for this study to trace the contours of late Ming, because it is over this terrain that Manchu rulers had to chart a course leading to imperial power in Peking. Also, we are dealing here more with perceptions of problems than with the problems themselves. The Manchu conquerors advertised their rule as a solution to a war-torn and weary China. To gain support for their claims to the Mandate of Heaven, the Manchus had to act to alleviate the accumulated evils of the late Ming period as they and the Chinese perceived them.

The Manchus, however, had to confront more than the lasting problems inherited from the Ming dynasty. As alien rulers, they faced two additional tasks. First, they had to subordinate Manchu tribal interests and institutions to imperial ambitions. Second, they had to construct a dynasty based on the rule of a minority ethnic group and yet acceptable to the Chinese majority. Manchu rulers at least as early as Abahai (Ch'ing T'ai-tsung, 1626–43) began the process of consolidating imperial power and sinicizing their rule. But by the end of the Shun-chih period in 1661 the issues were still alive, and alternative courses of action were still open.

ONE

Ming China and its Discontents

K'ang-hsi on his first Southern Tour in 1684 visited the tomb of Ming T'ai-tsu outside Nanking. After touring the site and noting its state of disrepair, the emperor could not help but speculate on the fall of the previous dynasty. He attributed it to factional struggles and the consequent demoralization of bureaucracy, to the proliferation of taxes and the growth of banditry.[1] In selecting these factors as causative, particularly the matter of factional strife, K'ang-hsi echoed the sentiments of many late Ming and early Ch'ing officials.

For officials of the former dynasty, it must have been comforting to blame the deteriorating situation on factionalism and corruption. Such symptoms of disorder could in time be rectified, or so they thought. Certainly a just and competent emperor could right matters. Yang Lien's famous censorial attack on Wei Chung-hsien in 1624 is a good expression of this reasoning. After detailing the eunuch's "twenty-four great crimes," Yang calls on the emperor (T'ien-ch'i, 1620–27) to take action:

> I beg that the emperor stiffen up and thunder out, so that [Wei] Chung-hsien may be taken in fetters before the ancestral temple. Assemble the major and minor civil and military officials, and order the judicial offices to conduct a careful enquiry, checking item by item the precedents from previous reigns for dealing with eunuchs' misbehavior—having relations within and without, usurping the imperial authority, violating the laws of the ancestors, disrupting court affairs, alienating the hearts of the empire, deceiving the ruler, and turning their backs on imperial grace—so as to deal with [Chung-hsien] according to law, and to quiet the righteous anger of spirits and men. . . . Thereafter there should be an announcement to the empire to explain their crimes and to show that the evil at the ruler's side has indeed been cleared away and that the path of intrigue and influence has indeed been blockaded.
>
> If all this is done and still Heaven's blessings do not return and men's hearts are not pleased—if good order within and peace without do not usher in a new epoch of Great Peace—then I request that you behead me as an offering to Chung-hsien.[2]

With the Ch'ing conquest the Manchus played up the evils of Ming factionalism, both as an attempt to legitimize their rule—contrasting Ch'ing order with Ming disorder—and also as a warning to Manchu and Chinese officials alike to eschew that form of political behavior. To give greater force to their arguments, successive Ch'ing emperors stood on the high ground of Confucian tradition to denounce factionalism.[3] Simply put, Confucians always frowned upon cliques or factions (*tang*), at least in theory. This attitude is based on remarks by the Master himself. Several statements from the Analects can be quoted:

> The gentleman (*chün-tzu*) is proud but not quarrelsome, is sociable but does not belong to a faction (XV, 21).
>
> The gentleman by having a universal outlook is not partial, but the inferior man (*hsiao-jen*) is partial and lacks a universal approach (II, 14).
>
> The gentleman harmonizes well with all men but does not identify with a group; the inferior man unites with others to seek advantage but does not harmonize well (XIII, 23).[4]

The Confucian notion, then, is that the establishment of policy should result from a free and open discussion of the issues, with each man's opinion weighed for its merit and not "because the speaker is what he is."[5] Cliques, factions, or parties, of course, would block the free flow of debate, as members of each group would shape their expression to accord with the agreed-upon position of the group.

A strong challenge to this tradition was issued by Ou-yang Hsiu, the versatile Sung Neo-Confucian. Ou-yang, in defending Fan Chung-yen and his supporters who had been dismissed from government on the charge of factionalism, contended that only superior men (*chün-tzu*) can share the same goals and cooperate with one another for the common good. Inferior men, he argued, can only create momentary associations which fall apart when the realization of private gain is reached. Therefore, if a more or less permanent political grouping appeared, it must be made up of superior men and and should be welcomed by the ruler, not driven out of government service.[6] Ou-yang's essay *P'eng-tang lun* ("On Factions") represented a dissenting opinion in the Confucian tradition. Rarely had anyone realized that defenders of the right needed to act together to be effective. Had his thesis prevailed, perhaps functional power rather than ideological stigma would have accompanied a group of officials bound together for a common cause, and perhaps this group could have been a force against the steady intensification of autocracy in the Ming and Ch'ing dynasties. In the closing decades of the Ming period, the Fu She association developed a rare group consciousness and organization that brought its members some political strength, particularly in the Nanking area, but this revival of scholar-official interest in organizing was aborted by the Ch'ing conquest.[7]

Closely associated with factionalism in the mind of Chinese officials were eunuchs. The Ming dynasty marked the zenith of eunuch power in imperial China. The Tung-lin Academy and party, though not founded on an anti-eunuch basis, foundered in the 1620s in opposition to the eunuch dictator Wei Chung-hsien.[8] The Ming loyalist scholar Huang Tsung-hsi, in his "Plan for a Prince" (*Ming-i tai-fang lu*), consistently attributed to eunuchs the worst excesses of the previous dynasty, and he suggested reducing their numbers drastically. Chinese officials under the new regime did not relax their vigilance against eunuch abuses or a eunuch resurgence. Part of the 1645 impeachment charges against Grand Secretary Feng Ch'üan, for instance, recalled his association with Wei Chung-hsien.[9]

Factional strife and eunuchs may have been the scapegoats of the Ming downfall, but rebel bands and the financial burdens of opposing them were the most pressing concerns of the dynasty and the direct cause of its demise. From the 1630s on, Li Tzu-ch'eng, Chang Hsien-chung, and others led armies whose ranks were swollen with peasants suffering from famines and "extra assessments" (*chia-p'ai*) that reportedly equaled the regular land tax receipts,[10] government soldiers whose pay was in arrears upward of six months, and unemployed postal carriers dismissed when the government curtailed the service due to lack of funds. The local situation was aggravated by a declining bureaucratic quality in the Ch'ung-chen period (1628–43). A recent statistical study of Ming bureaucracy shows a declining percentage of *chin-shih* holding prefectural and county office and a correspondingly higher proportion of lower-degree holders managing these local administrations.[11]

The Manchus, poised on China's northeastern frontier to strike at the faltering Ming dynasty, sought to capitalize on the burgeoning rebel movement. Several times in the 1640s, the Manchus sought an alliance with Li Tzu-ch'eng's forces to topple the Ming dynasty.[12] No alliance was made, but separately each served the other's cause by keeping imperial forces divided and the imperial treasury drained. After 1644, however, when Li sacked Peking and the last Ming emperor hanged himself on Coal Hill overlooking the Forbidden City, the Manchus posed as allies not of Li but of the Chinese people and their way of life against the rebel upstart. The new conquerors particularly appealed to the Chinese ruling circles to protect their political and economic power by fighting Li's peasant armies in cooperation with the Manchus.

Manchu appeals, though, went beyond class lines. Most Chinese, peasant as well as landlord, by now had grown tired of the civil war and its disruption of routine life. As rebel and Ming and Manchu armies pursued one another over the countryside and treated its inhabitants with about equal ferocity, the populace must have lost interest in the chase and wished only for peace. Whoever enforced it earned their recognition as legitimate rulers of China. The Manchus seemed more capable than their rivals of accomplishing this and so gained adherents. As David Nivison has written, "although they came in fact as conquerors, they were able to assume the role of reformers, within the Chinese world order, of Chinese ills."[13]

Finally, one should note a certain uneasiness among late Ming intellectual circles. Their intellectual and political moorings were slipping. A "growing confusion of class roles and concepts" led, on the one hand, to highly individualistic and "selfish" thought and, on the other, to the extension of education and intellectual life beyond the narrow confines of the scholar-official class.[14] Perhaps more importantly, Ming Confucian scholars found it increasingly difficult to follow their traditional calling of public service in face of "the unprecedented concentration of power in the hands of the emperor and its despotic uses by those who acted in his name."[15] To avoid the political and personal dangers that might befall them, many scholars lived in retirement and were politically inactive. But such disengagement created a schizophrenic trap. Confucian scholars could no longer have the comfortable feeling of "good order" associated in their minds with the unity of state and knowledge, of power and truth, of government and the *tao*. Private philosophical positions were divorced from and ran counter to state orthodoxy. With the alien Manchus as masters, Confucian scholars were doubly persuaded to remain aloof from government—for nationalistic as well as politico-philosophical reasons. Their world needed to be made whole again.

Manchu Warriors and Imperial Ambitions

The Manchu military conquest of the frontier and then of China and their subsequent political and social sinicization is an example of the kind of rationalization of rule Weber discussed.[16] What began as the personal, charismatic rule of Nurhaci, a tribal chieftain, developed into a feudal confederacy of Manchu and Mongol tribes through a more centralized feudal state to end up as a bureaucratically managed state along traditional Chinese imperial lines. This transformation of the Manchu state was largely the work of three leaders who themselves never sat on the throne of China: Nurhaci (1559–1626); Abahai (1592–1643), one of Nurhaci's sons and his successor in 1626 as leader of the Manchus; and Dorgon (1612–50), another son of Nurhaci who acted as regent to the first emperor of the Ch'ing dynasty in China.[17] Threats to the supremacy of Manchu imperial interests persisted until the Yung-cheng reign (1723–35), when the Ch'ing dynasty finally became a unitary state.[18] The present discussion, however, will focus only on the pre-1661 period as a background to the contrasting policies of the Oboi regency (1661–69) and K'ang-hsi's early reign (1669–84) examined in this work.

Nurhaci in 1583 inherited the chieftainship of the Chien-chou tribe, one of the three main tribes of the Juchen people who long had occupied the region northeast of Liaotung and who, four centuries earlier, had established a Chin dynasty (1115–1234) over parts of North China. Nurhaci over three decades of fighting and intermarrying extended and consolidated his authority over his own tribesmen, the other Juchen (or Manchu) tribes, and many Mongol tribes. This feudal state Nurhaci was creating was built upon tribal foundations. Conquered peoples and territories were attached to various chieftains or nobles allied with him, but the tribal structure of the conquered people was still preserved.

To transcend tribal loyalties and to centralize feudal authority over his steadily enlarging empire, Nurhaci in 1601 took the first step in creating the Eight Banner system. His followers, regardless of tribal origins, were divided into standardized fighting units of up to 300 able-bodied male adults. These units, called *niru* (a company; later known by its Chinese equivalent, *tso-ling*), were further combined into four larger groupings designated as banners, each distinguished by the yellow, white, red, or blue flag under which it fought. By 1615, the banners were increased to eight, with the new ones identified by borders on their flags, to accommodate the growing number of *niru* formed as a result of new conquests.

The Eight Banner system, however, was much more than a military organization upon which Nurhaci relied to further his conquests. It was also a political, economic, and social organization designed to control and care for the entire population in the Manchu state. And Nurhaci took the Manchus' original basic social units—the *mokun* or clan, and the *gashen* or village—as the organizing principle of his new system. So, while many larger tribal groupings were broken up, their constituent clans and villages with their traditional social and political relationships, were largely preserved in the banners. Some adjustment in size was made to create a more uniform and more militarily functional unit than the *mokun* or *gashen* would permit.[19]

In this fashion, Nurhaci began to integrate the Manchu state and make it more responsive to his direction as he moved toward an open challenge to the Ming dynasty. In 1616, within a year of the completion of the Eight Banners, the Manchu leader declared himself emperor of the Later Chin dynasty. Despite this nomenclature, Nurhaci was not yet ruling in a Chinese imperial style. Feudal elements persisted as he shared power with some of his sons and other younger members of the ruling Aisin-Gioro clan. The most important source of power in the later years of Nurhaci's reign was hereditary command of one of the Eight Banners or of a sizable number of companies within a banner. Clan members in these positions had complete authority over the families and resources of their banner units and could utilize them to build an impregnable economic and military base of power.

Nurhaci honored the four senior banner chiefs—Daisan, Amin, Manggultai and Abahai—with the highest princely rank, *hosoi beile*, and in 1621 ordered them to assist him administratively as rotating prime ministers. In the following year, these four—known as the Four Senior Beile (*ssu-ta beile*)—and the other banner princes (all later informally called *hosoi beile*)[20] formed the Deliberative Council of Princes (*i-cheng wang*) to advise and assist Nurhaci in ruling.[21] The founder of the Manchu state envisioned a collegial rule after his death rather than an imperial system, and all the banner princes were to have an equal voice in policy formation. In April 1622, Nurhaci gave the following instructions to the *hosoi beile*:

> The one who succeeds me should not be one who relies on force. If this type of man becomes ruler, I fear that by relying on the power of his position he would offend Heaven. Furthermore, one man's wisdom is no match for the wisdom of the many. You eight men are the leaders of the Eight Banners, and if you can rule the nation with a common purpose, then nothing will be lost. If among you eight banner chiefs there is one who has talent, virtue and the ability to accept criticism, then he would be the best one to succeed me. If [later] he would not accept criticism and would not honor the *tao*, then he should be replaced with another [among you]. If when he is replaced he is unwilling to submit [to this decision] but causes trouble, then this kind of mischief should not be tolerated. When you eight princes are ruling the country, if any one prince has an idea that would be beneficial to the state, then the other seven ought to discuss this and carry it out. If one himself is not talented but also is unable to support others who are and keeps silent, then he ought to be replaced [as a Beile] by a worthy younger member of the clan. Any reluctance on his part [to being replaced] cannot be tolerated. If any of the eight princes has any reason to travel, he must first tell the whole group and not leave secretly. In the ruler's presence all ought to discuss affairs of state together, promote the virtuous, and reject flatterers; you should not allow only one or two men to approach the ruler [on any matter].[22]

Shortly before he died in 1626, Nurhaci issued another set of instructions on the same subject. He urged the various princes to share equally (wherever possible) the wealth acquired as their state expanded, and to remonstrate with each other if any wrongdoing occurred.[23]

Nurhaci's instructions clearly establish his intention of perpetuating clan rule. He did not seem to recognize any conflict between clan rule and imperial ambitions, although his creation of the Deliberative Council of Princes did lessen the possibility of feudal autonomy of the *hosoi beile* by bringing them into a formal structure of state with mutual responsibilities. He also spoke of choosing someone to succeed him nominally as emperor, but it remained for his son and successor, Abahai, to realize the unsuitability of traditional clan practices in conquering China and ruling a large, multiethnic empire. Nurhaci himself stood in a superior position to the banner princes because of his age and his forceful leadership of the clan, but his successor would not have these natural advantages. The second generation of clan leaders whom Nurhaci chose for high honor and office as *hosoi beile* were now in entrenched positions of power. Nurhaci's successor at best would begin his reign only as primus inter pares.

Nurhaci died without naming a successor but left the choice to the banner princes in accordance with his instructions of 1622. One unofficial source, however, claimed that before he died Nurhaci named his fourteenth son, Dorgon, as heir, with Daisan as regent. Furthermore, he ordered that his sons Ajige, Dorgon, and Dodo—all of the same empress—each be given command of a banner. The Four Senior Beile, fearing the great concentration of power if these blood brothers and their mother controlled three banners, feigned a command from Nurhaci that she should follow the late emperor to the grave.[24] Whatever the situation, the empress Hsiao-lieh did commit suicide and Dorgon was not chosen as the next ruler. Dorgon and Dodo, however, were given banners to control, but not Ajige, who was older and more to be feared than the others.

Daisan led the Four Senior Beile in choosing the youngest of their number, Abahai, as the next ruler. Among all the banner princes, Abahai had the greatest military achievements to his credit and had earned the respect of Manchu and Mongol leaders. So he clearly qualified as "the most talented and virtuous" that Nurhaci envisioned as his successor, even though the former did not specifically name him. Abahai also controlled two banners (the plain and bordered yellow) at the time of his father's death,[25] which added to his relative strength among the other *hosoi beile.* After reportedly declining three times, Abahai accepted the honor and position thrust upon him by the other princes. He joined with fourteen other clan leaders (seven sons, two nephews, and five grandsons of Nurhaci) in swearing a solemn oath to Heaven that they would work together in carrying on the great work of the founder of their state.[26] Abahai's eldest son, Haoge, was included in this oath, which indicates how far the Manchus were in 1626 from establishing any imperial or dynastic principles. Nurhaci's 1622 instructions on collegial rule still dominated the political ethos.

Abahai's march from collective leadership to unitary imperial rule took a decade to complete. The main obstacles to his progress were the remaining senior *beile*, the *hosoi beile's* leadership of the banners, and the wielding of clan influence in the Deliberative Council of Princes. In the initial years of Abahai's reign, Daisan, Amin, and Manggultai continued to take monthly turns as his assistant administrators. But in 1629, he reduced their power by giving this responsibility to younger members of the clan, who would be easier to control. In the following year Abahai imprisoned Amin on a charge of cowardice in battle and gave command of his bordered blue banner to Amin's younger brother, Jirgalang. Not long afterward, Manggultai was also censured for menacing Abahai with his sword. After the deaths in 1633 of Manggultai and in 1635 of his brother Degelei (who shared in Manggultai's control of the plain blue banner), their family was posthumously charged with conspiring to seize the throne from Abahai. In a precedent-setting decision, Abahai placed their banner under his direct control—thus giving him three banners—instead of transferring it to another worthy clan member as Nurhaci had instructed in 1622 and as he had done with Amin's banner in 1630.

Instrumental in this decision was the advice of Chinese scholars, which Abahai deliberately sought in order to justify his modification of collective clan rule. The scholars used the old saying, "a city equal to the nation is the root of disorder," to promote the principle of a centralized imperial state.[27] After Manggultai's censure in 1631, Abahai again relied on Chinese concerns for proper hierarchical ranking to end the practice of the other senior *beile* (only Daisan and Manggultai at this point) sitting alongside him in court facing south. For Manggultai it was an obvious punishment for his misbehavior, but Daisan, when asked by Abahai to comment on this change, had no choice but to recommend its application to himself as well. Thereafter they still sat at his side but below him.[28]

By 1635, then, Abahai commanded three banners, and of the other senior *beile* only Daisan remained. Since he was an early supporter of Abahai, the latter's personal position seemed secure. There still remained the question of general clan influence in the banner system and in some key organs of government. Abahai attacked this problem primarily through increasing bureaucratization of the banners and the court. Immediately after succession to the throne in 1626, he reorganized the banner system by introducing a larger administrative staff and giving it more of the actual command of the banner.[29] The most important of these officials was the *gusai ejen* or banner commander (the title was later converted to *tu-t'ung* in Chinese, or lieutenant-general). Not only were the eight *gusai ejen* meant to serve as representatives of Abahai and the state in the banners; they also diluted the governmental power of the banner princes by serving as Deliberative Ministers (*i-cheng ta-ch'en*). Since they participated in discussions of important state affairs alongside the Deliberative Princes, it is customary after 1626 to speak of this enlarged body of advisers as the Deliberative Council of Princes and Ministers (*i-cheng wang ta-ch'en*) or, more simply, the Deliberative Council. In 1637, three additional representatives of each banner joined the council, thus further strengthening Abahai's control over this supreme deliberative body.[30]

Abahai made a further significant change in the banner system—the creation of separate Mongol and Chinese banners. By 1631, there were two Mongol and one Chinese forces detached from the Manchu banners and operating independently under officers of the same nationality. The Mongol banners expanded to eight in 1635, and the Chinese banners increased to two in 1637, four in 1639, and eight in 1642.[31] A recent study of the creation of the Chinese banners suggests that Abahai's motive in making this step was to reduce the power of the Manchu princes and enlarge his own.[32] It gave him another opportunity to place his own appointees—Chinese and Mongols—in the banners as *gusai ejen*.

Paralleling his reorganization of the banners, Abahai began building the structure of a bureaucratic state following a Chinese model but with some Manchu modifications. In 1629 he established the Literary Office (*wen-kuan*), staffed with Manchus proficient in Chinese, to provide secretarial assistance.[33] In the early years of the Ming dynasty, the bureaucracy was "beheaded" when the post of chancellor (or premier) was abolished, and thereafter the emperor himself became the sole coordinator of government. Because of the emperor's unquestioned need of assistance, a new body of imperial secretaries developed which later came to be formalized as the Grand Secretariat (*nei-ko*). Gradually, grand secretaries acquired an advisory role in decision-making, but their power and prestige never equaled that formerly held by the chancellor.[34] Early Manchu rulers felt the same need of secretarial assistance, but there was the additional problem of translating Manchu documents into Chinese and vice versa.

The Literary Office was reorganized in 1636 into the Three Inner Courts (*nei-san-yüan*), with three courts or bureaus sharing the literary functions formerly performed by the Literary Office alone. The Kuo-shih-yüan recorded, commented on, and issued imperial proclamations; it also collected and compiled historical materials. The Pi-shu-yüan handled correspondence with foreign states, command-edicts (*ch'ih-yü*), and provincial memorials. The Hung-wen-yüan was responsible for the education of the emperor, his sons, and Manchu princes. A grand secretary (*ta-hsüeh-shih*) supervised the work of each bureau, in obvious imitation of the Ming Grand Secretariat. Later, a subchancellor (*hsüeh-shih*) was appointed to assist each of the grand secretaries.[35] Beyond its purely secretarial and literary functions, the Literary Office, and later the Three Inner Courts, served Abahai as a personal staff that was recruited according to ability, not kinship, and that was devoted to his cause—the supremacy of imperial interests over clan interests as represented by the banner princes.[36]

Abahai next established the Six Boards, named after the chief administrative organs of the traditional Chinese state. Banner princes were placed in charge of each board, but their positions were largely nominal. Actual administrative power was wielded by Abahai's appointees at lower levels, many of whom were Mongols or Chinese.[37] Abahai also set up a Censorate in 1636 and a Ministry of Colonial Affairs (*li-fan yüan*) in 1638.

It should be clear by now that Abahai had taken forceful steps to subdue the originally powerful *hosoi beile* and place bureaucratic constraints on them. But the fashioning of imperial power was not finished. As Silas Wu has so aptly stated, "a government superficially patterned on the Ming model was in dangerous tension with the 'state within a state' of Manchu nobility and bannermen. Bureaucrats drawn from this privileged group could exercise hereditary power over both their own clans and their own followers and also over segments of the central bureaucracy."[38] It should be noted that while Abahai was destroying the banner princes' political power, he still maintained the princes' hereditary control over their bannermen and the feudal social relations built into the system—features that were not destroyed until the Yung-cheng period (1723–35).[39]

The selection of a successor to Abahai in 1643 reopened old wounds and revived concern about clan influence. Some princes were promoting Dorgon's candidacy on the belief that Nurhaci had intended him, not Abahai, to succeed in 1626. Dorgon, though, declined out of respect for the late emperor, who had cared for him as a youth and had given him important responsibilities. Others argued that only a son of Abahai should be chosen. Prince Haoge, the eldest son and a famed warrior, was the logical choice. Ajige and Dodo, Dorgon's blood brothers, were unwilling to see a precedent set for limiting the imperial position to Abahai's descendants and suggested instead that Daisan be chosen. The latter declined on account of his advanced age—he was then in his sixties—but offered a compromise solution: Abahai's young son, Fu-lin, should be named, with Dorgon and Jirgalang acting as coregents. Haoge's supporters accepted this arrangement, but some of Dorgon's staunch backers still conspired to make him emperor after the court decision. Dorgon and Daisan exposed them and had them executed.[40] In this manner, a five-year-old became the third ruler of the Manchu state, reigning as the Shun-chih emperor (1644–61).

Because of the emperor's youth, the banner *beile* had an obvious opportunity to aggrandize upon imperial power and undo much of the work of Abahai. But the regents, and particularly Dorgon, continued with the centralization of power and the sinicization of the Manchu political system. Dorgon before 1643 had had personal experience with Chinese-style administration as head of the Board of Civil Appointments in Abahai's government at Sheng-ching (Mukden). He used this strategic position to place his supporters in the newly created bureaucracy. When he became regent, however, he promptly decreed that control of the Six Boards by the banner princes be ended. Later (in 1649) he warned Chinese officials not to tolerate interference by imperial clan members in administrative affairs.[41]

As a counterpart to the sinicization policies he pursued throughout his regency (1643–50),[42] Dorgon centralized power in his own hands. Jirgalang, chosen as coregent in 1643, was quickly reduced to assistant regent and then replaced in 1647 by Dorgon's brother Dodo. When Dodo died in 1649, no one replaced him. In 1648, both Jirgalang and Dorgon's old rival, Haoge, were charged with various offenses and punished.[43] But again, as had Abahai, Dorgon acquired his greatest strength in the banners. In addition to his own banner, the plain white, Dorgon as regent took control of the plain blue banner, one of the three belonging to Abahai, on the grounds that he needed extra protection from his many enemies. He gained a third, the bordered white, in 1649 when Dodo died, with the latter's son Doni in nominal control. Furthermore, one of the regent's henchmen had charge of one of Shun-chih's two yellow banners.[44] Of the remaining original banner princes, two were dead (Daisan of the plain red and Yoto of the bordered red) and the third (Jirgalang of the bordered blue) had been demoted. Clearly, no one could match Dorgon. Just as clearly, the collective sharing of power by banner princes was no longer operative.

Dorgon's personal power as regent overshadowed the imperial position, but his legacy to Shun-chih in 1651 was a strong central bureaucracy coupled with a greatly weakened clan nobility. Ajige and officials of the two white banners serving Doni and Dorbo (another nephew of Dorgon whom the latter adopted as his son and heir) tried to succeed to Dorgon's power, but they badly overplayed their hands. With the aid of Jirgalang and other supporters, Shun-chih regained control of the two yellow banners and added Dorgon's original banner, the plain white. Thereafter, these three banners controlled personally by this emperor and all his successors were designated as the Upper Three Banners (*shang-san ch'i*). Dorgon's other banners were not reassigned to any single prince but placed among the Lower Five Banners (*hsia-wu ch'i*). Whenever a princedom was created, a number of companies from the Lower Five Banners were assigned to it, but with one exception no banner was under the exclusive control of a single family.[45] The absolute sovereignty of the throne had become a fixed principle, replacing Nurhaci's original vision of collective clan rule.

China in 1661

The combination of a centralized, sinicized Manchu state and a receptive Chinese populace facilitated the alien conquest of China in the 1640s and 1650s. But, as a contemporary noted, "seizing the empire is easy, ruling it is difficult."[46] China could be conquered from the saddle, and the Manchus were skilled riders, but it had to be ruled from a throne which capped an elaborate and time-honored system of government. After the Manchus had completed the military phase of their conquest, imperial attention had to shift to political matters. By 1661, armies of the Manchus and their Chinese supporters had swept southward and subjugated each of the eighteen provinces of China proper; the last Ming pretender had fled to Burma where he would later be seized and killed; and the only Ming loyalist leader of any military significance, Cheng Ch'eng-kung (known to Westerners as Koxinga), had abandoned the mainland and occupied Taiwan. While Cheng and his descendants continued to create trouble for Ch'ing rulers—more as an irritant than a real threat—the political and social relationships between ruling Manchus and native Chinese presented far greater and more urgent problems.

In the political sphere, memorialists of the day[47] showed the greatest concern over the continued existence in the south and southwest of three semiautonomous Chinese military leaders—Wu San-kuei in Yunnan and Kweichow, Shang K'o-hsi in Kwangtung, and Keng Chi-mao in Fukien. As long as these feudatory princes ruled large chunks of China outside or above the normal administrative framework of government, Manchu rule was tenuous. At the opposite end of the spectrum of political control, local banditry was still flourishing, feeding off the discontent of the populace caused by natural disasters and the ravages of interdynastic warfare. As one memorialist explained, "when people are suffering, they can either risk death by flouting the law and becoming bandits or face starvation if they do not; so the weak starve but the strong become bandits."[48]

Social conflicts arose out of Manchu efforts to appropriate private land for the use of bannermen, to perpetuate a class of banner slaves, and to change a people's hairstyle for symbolic reasons. The land allotment (*ch'üan-ti*) program was designed both to replace plunder (prohibited by Dorgon in 1644) as a way of supporting banner forces and to reduce friction between Manchus and Chinese by keeping them apart. In the latter respect, the policy failed. Much of the land allotments could come from seized Ming imperial land or deserted estates, but not all of it was located together. This prompted the Manchus to exchange land with Chinese owners and resettle them elsewhere, often not very effectively and on poorer land.[49] Thus, in their desire to keep bannermen and Chinese apart, the Manchu leaders created intense resentment among a large number of dispossessed cultivators. Similarly, in order to prevent ethnic friction, Dorgon ordered the separation of bannermen and Chinese officials, merchants, and commoners in the capital. At great inconvenience, the Chinese were moved out of Peking's inner city to the southern quarter.[50]

The second major source of social conflict between Manchus and Chinese were the laws dealing with fugitive slaves (*t'ao-jen*). Thousands of banner slaves escaped in 1644 after the Manchus had moved into China proper. Since their labor service was considered essential to the economic well-being of bannermen, the government enforced very harsh laws dealing not only with the fugitive but, even more so, with any family that harbored him. While first-time fugitives received whippings when captured, families who concealed them were either executed, or exiled, or their wealth was confiscated and given to a banner.[51] So fearful were Chinese of being accused of harboring a runaway slave that they often refused to help ordinary vagabonds who left their homes in search of work and food. It is even reported that Keng Chung-ming, an early supporter of the Manchus and one of the original feudatory princes, committed suicide when it was discovered that his subordinates were concealing fugitives in his army.[52]

Abuses were natural in the system of apprehending and punishing violators of the fugitive law. The loudest complaint was against those who would falsely accuse a wealthy family of harboring a runaway slave in order to share in the confiscation of the accused's wealth.[53] While the court condemned such perversions of the law's intent, it quickly rebuked any Chinese official questioning the necessity or even the harshness of the fugitive laws. When memorialists in 1654 and 1655 suggested lighter punishments for concealment,[54] the Shun-chih emperor launched into a passionate defense of the law and attacked Chinese as ungrateful and unsympathetic to Manchu problems:

> Both Manchus and Chinese are my subjects, so how could I have any favoritism when it comes to either group's welfare? Recently, [Chinese] memorialists have taken a partisan view of the *t'ao-jen* policy. They do not understand my intentions, knowing only of Chinese difficulties but being unaware of Manchu problems. In the reigns of T'ai-tsu [Nurhaci] and T'ai-tsung [Abahai], Manchu forces endured much in constant warfare. . . . People we captured in war were used to till the land, graze horses, and do other chores. But now, the number of fugitive slaves

> increases daily. Only 10 percent are recaptured, because many traitorous people harbor them. Therefore, we had no choice but to establish very severe laws. This may work a hardship on Chinese, but if we do not crack down, the concealers will become more brazen and the fugitives will multiply. Then who will be our servants? How will we survive? Is there no concern for Manchu hardship?
>
> Emperors of previous dynasties generally ruled only Chinese, but I rule both Manchus and Chinese and must ensure that each group obtains its due. Nothing would please me more than if everyone were prosperous. Not long ago, bandits had seized Peking, and you Chinese knew only bitterness. It was our dynasty that led forces into China to eliminate this suffering and establish peace. . . . Since Manchus rescued Chinese from disaster, Chinese ought to show consideration for Manchus.[55]

Several days after this edict, issued in April 1655, the emperor forbade Chinese from ever again discussing the fugitive laws in their memorials.[56]

A final source of resentment was the required change to a Manchu hairstyle, the queue or pigtail, which Chinese disputed or violated only at the risk of their lives. The conquerors insisted on compliance as a symbol and identification of Chinese submission to Manchu authority. Dorgon's order for the male populace to shave their heads was popularized as *liu-t'ou pu liu-fa, liu-fa pu liu-t'ou,* loosely rendered as "off with your hair, or off with your head!" Although local pockets of individual or group noncompliance existed, and in some instances for several decades,[57] the Manchus ruthlessly imposed the change on thousands of unwilling Chinese, most notably in the southeastern region.[58]

Shun-chih's edict of 1655 quoted above raised another pressing problem of his reign—the sharing of political power between Manchus and Chinese. With the exception of high posts in the central government, where duplicate offices were created, Chinese were competing with Manchus and other bannermen for a limited number of bureaucratic positions. While the emperor, as we have seen, professed to a lack of favoritism, this image of impartiality was occasionally challenged. In 1651, Wei I-chieh, then a metropolitan censor but later to become a grand secretary, urged Shun-chih to stop relying so heavily on bannermen (mostly Chinese at this time, not Manchu) in top provincial appointments.[59] But, after his death, the emperor was accused by Manchu leaders of favoring Chinese over Manchus. These seemingly contradictory evaluations of Shun-chih's personnel policy can be reconciled if we recognize the unique role of Chinese bannermen in the early Ch'ing period.

Chinese bannermen were Chinese by ethnic standards (hence the charge leveled by Manchu leaders) but bannermen by political standards. This is a point that seems too obvious to be worth mentioning, but contemporaries (such as Wei I-chieh) tended to forget the ethnic origin of Chinese bannermen and lumped them together with Manchus and Mongols, designating all of them not even as bannermen but as "Manchus." Indeed, many noncollaborating Chinese considered Chinese bannermen to be racial renegades and no better than Manchus. Chinese bannermen, however, were indispensable to early Ch'ing rulers. Ordinary Chinese were not yet to be trusted, and many of the Manchus did not have the necessary language and governmental skills to be fully utilized. Chinese bannermen suffered neither disability: they could be trusted and they were familiar with the Chinese system of government. Naturally, no language problem existed for them. Furthermore, Manchus were not as trustworthy as Chinese bannermen in the emperor's struggle for political supremacy over influential Manchu princes.

Finally, the new rulers of China faced a serious problem in the alienation of many members of the native intelligentsia. There were an alarming number of Ming loyalists, such as Huang Tsung-hsi and Ku Yen-wu, who refused to join the new regime. Some of them had taken up arms against the Manchus,[60] but by 1661 their energy had been channeled into political and literary opposition. Still, it was dangerous for the Manchus to leave this influential sector of society outside the new political and intellectual order where they might act as magnets to attract anti-Manchu sentiment. This is why one memorialist warned: "We should not worry so much about bandits and natural calamities as about men's ideas and opinions."[61] The Manchus could not afford to let social and political alienation take root and spread.

Here, then, are some of the problems still threatening the stability of the young dynasty—problems requiring mostly political rather than military solutions. Left over from the Ming dynasty were concerns about factionalism and corruption in bureaucracy, the demoralizing effects of eunuch power, the disruption of routine life by banditry and warfare, and a disequilibrium in intellectual circles. The alien character of the dynasty added new dimensions to some of these problems (e.g., factionalism along ethnic lines), but in addition it gave rise to a unique set of conflicts and challenges. The new rulers of China had to transcend their heritage and adjust to the new social and political environment within the Great Wall. If they hoped for a longer rule over China than that exercised by their Juchen ancestors or by their neighboring Mongols, the Manchus had to secure the cooperation of the Chinese elite by respecting their traditions and prerogatives.

On 6 February 1661, the Shun-chih emperor died. His successor, the K'ang-hsi emperor, was only seven years of age. Chosen as regents to guide the young ruler and the empire during his minority were four Manchu elders. Once again, as in 1626 and 1643, the Manchus had reached a critical juncture. The direction of the new dynasty, while seemingly fixed by Dorgon's and Shun-chih's programs of centralization and sinicization, was subject to re-evaluation and possible reversal by conservative clan elements. In fact, a Manchu reaction did flourish during the regency and threaten the dynastic structure fashioned by previous rulers. The policies and programs of the regency, described in the next chapter, are intrinsically important, but they take on added meaning as examples of one possible approach to the problems of the time. An alternative, generally contrasting, and in my opinion more successful approach in achieving consolidation of Ch'ing rule was devised by K'ang-hsi and his advisers after overthrowing the regency in 1669. By knowing the tenor of government and life under the regents, we can even better appreciate the magnitude of K'ang-hsi's achievement.

Two

THE REGENCY

A BOY OF SEVEN CANNOT BE EXPECTED TO UNDERSTAND MUCH ABOUT the intricate workings of a highly refined government structure and the bureaucrats who ran it. K'ang-hsi was no exception, although our knowledge of his later remarkable military and political achievements may lead us to believe he presaged future greatness at an early age.[1] The stage belonged to older and more experienced men in the first years of his reign—the four Manchus chosen as regents by Shun-chih on his deathbed in 1661. The backgrounds of these men tell us something about them—their characters and their ambitions—but our picture of the regents is rather flat until we examine in some detail the policies instituted during their hold on government.[2]

The Four Regents

None of K'ang-hsi's four regents—Soni, Suksaha, Ebilun, and Oboi—was a member of the imperial family. For the first time, Manchus not of the Aisin-Gioro family would be guiding the destiny of the Ch'ing state. The four regents took note of this situation when they first declined—perhaps with false humility—to assume the awesome responsibility entrusted to them by Shun-chih in his "will."[3] Since that document was tampered with by these very same regents, it is possible that the naming of regents itself did not represent the dying emperor's wish. We have no way of knowing. On the other hand, there were good reasons for Shun-chih to select these four men to manage affairs of state during

K'ang-hsi's minority. Each of the regents had helped Shun-chih rid the court of Dorgon's faction. In addition, they had all had outstanding military careers prior to their court service.

The senior member of the regency was Soni, a Manchu of the Heseri clan and enrolled in the plain yellow banner.[4] His father, Sose, and his uncle, Hife, joined the forces of Nurhaci and served as translators in the Literary Office because of their proficiency in Mongol and Chinese as well as the Manchu language. Hife later became one of the first grand secretaries of the Three Inner Courts. Soni also served in the Literary Office, but he won his fame on the battlefield and as a skillful envoy to wavering Mongol allies. During the reign of Abahai, he held several secretarial positions in the Board of Civil Appointments.

Soni became deeply involved in the succession crisis of 1643, in which he originally supported Haoge, thus incurring the enmity of Dorgon, who became regent. In 1645 Dorgon took the first of several reprisals against Soni by stripping him of his second class viscount title. This action marked the culmination of a year-long series of disputes that Soni had had with Dorgon and one of his supporters, Tantai. The latter had impeached Soni's uncle, Hife, who as a result was dismissed from his post as grand secretary. Tantai, in turn, lost his ducal title when impeached by Soni. Finally, Tantai turned on Soni and accused him of several improprieties—fishing and grazing his horse on imperial grounds, and taking a musical instrument from the imperial treasury. Soni was deprived of his title and prohibited from serving in government again.

Tantai and Soni were involved in another case in 1646, but this time both were impeached by a third party, Tulai. Tulai claimed that he wrote Soni about impeaching Tantai but Soni had refused to do so. The latter, in defense, denied any knowledge of the request and thought it absurd that he should be accused of covering up for a man whom only last year he had impeached. Upon investigation, Soni's story was corroborated, and he was exonerated. In addition, he regained his viscount title. Two years later, it was Soni and Tulai who were linked together in the charge that back in 1643 they had conspired to place Haoge on the throne. Soni was spared execution but was fined, stripped of all posts and titles, and sent to guard Abahai's tomb.

This tale of charges and countercharges testifies to the continuing effects of early dynastic banner politics and succession disputes. Soni returned to favor and was called back to court by Shun-chih only in 1651 after the death of Dorgon. For his opposition to the former regent, he was rewarded with an earldom and appointed a senior assistant chamberlain of the Imperial Bodyguard (*shih-wei nei-ta-ch'en*), a minister of the Imperial Household (*tsung-kuan nei-wu-fu ta-ch'en*), and a member of the Deliberative Council (*i-cheng-wang ta-ch'en*).[5] Shun-chih's ultimate gesture of favor toward Soni was to appoint him one of the four regents in 1661.

Suksaha, of the Nara clan, was the son of Suna, who had distinguished himself in campaigns against Korean and Ming armies.[6] The future regent also won glory on the battlefield and was rewarded with a baronage and membership in the Deliberative Council. But again, as in the case of Soni, he performed his greatest service to the Shun-chih emperor by opposing and denouncing Dorgon. Suksaha's role in the disgrace of Dorgon was in fact more remarkable because he was a member of the same banner as Dorgon—the Manchu plain white. Dorgon, as commander of this banner, was thus Suksaha's master. At this stage in the dynasty, the feudal loyalties built into the Eight Banner system had not yet been completely destroyed. Still, after Dorgon's death Suksaha and one of Dorgon's lieutenants provided Shun-chih with the facts he needed to condemn Dorgon as a usurper of imperial prerogatives. Shun-chih rewarded Suksaha by promoting him to captain-general of the Guards division (*hu-chün t'ung-ling*) of his banner.

In 1653 Suksaha was in Hunan to help Hung Ch'eng-ch'ou defeat Sun K'o-wang and other remnants of Chang Hsien-chung's rebel army. The rebels were all killed or driven into southwestern China after several years of fighting. Suksaha's rank was raised to that of a second class viscount, and he was appointed a chamberlain of the Imperial Bodyguards. His opposition to Dorgon and his military merit secured for him a place in the regency in 1661.

The remaining two regents, Ebilun and Oboi, were both members of the Manchu bordered yellow banner. This fact takes on greater significance later during the regency. Ebilun was a member of the Niohuru clan.[7] He inherited the first-class viscount rank from his father, Eidu, and also served as a captain (*tso-ling*) in his banner. Both post and rank were taken away in 1637 because he tried to influence a trial involving his niece, but Ebilun recovered his captaincy and minor hereditary rank as a reward for valorous service in campaigns against the Ming in 1641–42 and against the remnants of Li Tzu-ch'eng's forces in Hupei in 1645–46.

Ebilun again lost his position and rank, and almost his life, in 1648 when he ran afoul of Dorgon. The latter accused Ebilun of being hostile to the princes of the white banners (i.e., Dorgon, Dodo [his younger brother], and Dorbo [Dodo's son who was adopted by Dorgon]) and of placing a contingent of guards outside his gate. The death penalty was recommended, but an imperial edict reduced his punishment to the loss of title and offices and the confiscation of half his possessions. After Shun-chih came to power in 1651, Ebilun's loyalty during Dorgon's regency was rewarded. He recovered his post, was elevated to the rank of duke, and later became a chamberlain of the Imperial Bodyguards and a member of the Deliberative Council. Finally he was named in Shun-chih's will as one of the four regents of K'ang-hsi.

The man who was to become the most powerful of K'ang-hsi's four regents was originally last in order of precedence. Oboi, of the Guwalgiya clan,[8] started out as a lieutenant of the Guards division but had moved up to captain-general of that organization and had acquired the rank of third class viscount by the time the Manchus had entered Peking. He had fought well in campaigns against the Chahar Mongols and against Ming Generals Hung Ch'eng-ch'ou and Wu San-kuei, both of whom later joined the Manchus and were instrumental in the conquest of China.

After the establishment of the dynasty, Oboi continued to accumulate military merit in campaigns against the rebel armies of Li Tzu-ch'eng and Chang Hsien-chung. He served under Ajige in the former campaign and under Haoge in the latter, and in both instances he incurred the hatred of Dorgon for refusing to prefer charges against his commander. In 1645 Dorgon had ordered Oboi and Tantai to denounce Ajige in front of his men, but they refused and were fined. Oboi was twice denounced in 1648 for earlier anti-Dorgon activity. First, he was accused by Tunci, a great-nephew of Nurhaci, of having plotted with Soni, Tantai, Tulai, and others back in 1643 to force the selection of Dorgon's rival, Prince Haoge, as emperor. A few months after this incident, Oboi was charged with contributing some guards to the force Ebilun had gathered to defend himself against Dorgon. In both cases, execution was recommended, but Oboi ended up with a fine in the first instance and was pardoned in the second instance.

Like Soni, Suksaha, and Ebilun, Oboi prospered after 1651 for having opposed Dorgon. The emperor made him a second class duke, a member of the Deliberative Council, a chamberlain of the Imperial Bodyguards, and, finally, a regent of the new emperor.

All four of the regents, then, were Manchu nobles who had reached their positions of power through military achievement and court politics. Only Soni had any background at all in civil office, and he had never held an administrative post higher than 5A. Their lack of involvement in the traditional Chinese administrative machinery was symptomatic of the new regency's national policy. Unlike the first regency under Dorgon, when a great effort was made to accommodate Manchu rule to native Chinese tradition, a sort of Manchu nativism held sway under Oboi and his colleagues.

Nativism has been defined as "any conscious, organized attempt on the part of a society's members to revive or perpetuate selected aspects of its culture."[9] This definition distinguishes nativism from what all societies try to do unconsciously as part of the socialization process. Nativistic movements are not necessarily started by an entire society; certain elements in that society who stand to lose (or have already lost) their favored positions by cultural assimilation and change may in fact take the lead in promoting a revival of native customs and institutions. Furthermore, only certain aspects, never the whole culture, are selected for emphasis and given symbolic importance.[10] The Manchus' Juchen ancestors had experienced such a nativistic movement after establishing the Chin dynasty,[11] and the Oboi regency certainly qualifies as another example. Robert Oxnam in his study concludes that the four Manchu regents of K'ang-hsi shared an "obsession for Manchu dominance" and sought "to create an order in which the Manchu system, Manchu officials, and Manchu ideas held undisputed control":

> The regents emphasized the Manchu elements of the early Ch'ing state and society, while the Chinese elite and Chinese institutions were considered subordinate, sometimes even dangerous, factors. Having conquered on horseback, they sought to rule from horseback. While the regents were in the saddle, they took the Ch'ing state for its last ride towards exclusive Manchu dominance.[12]

But, true to the definition of nativism, the regents were not total reactionaries, "they were willing to consider 'what should be changed' as well as 'what preserved.'"[13]

The beginning of K'ang-hsi's reign demanded statesmanship and a willingness on the part of the ruling group to overcome racial identity and clan interests in order to win Chinese acceptance of their rule. But the regime of Soni, Suksaha, Ebilun, and Oboi did not move in that direction; instead, it pursued a policy of Manchu nativism—a sacrifice of imperial interests to Manchu interests. A discussion of the highlights of the regency will substantiate this point.

The Revival of Manchu Institutions

As Shun-chih approached death in February 1661, he called to his side two of his favorites, Wang Hsi and Margi. Wang was proficient in Manchu and was one of Shun-chih's first daily tutors (*jih-chiang kuan*) and lecturers in the classics (*ching-yen chiang-kuan*).[14] By 1661 he was vice-president of the Board of Rites and chancellor (*chang-yüan hsüeh-shih*) of the Hanlin Academy.[15] Margi, of the Guwalgiya clan (as was Oboi) and the Manchu plain yellow banner, was chosen along with Wang in 1665 as one of the first of Shun-chih's tutors. He was holding the office of subchancellor (*hsüeh-shih*) of the Three Inner Courts when called to Shun-chih's bedside on 4 February 1661.[16]

The emperor informed Wang Hsi and Margi that he was fatally stricken with smallpox and that he wanted to make known his choice of a successor—K'ang-hsi, his third son—and of regents to assist him. As the two men listened to the dying emperor's instructions, Wang was overcome with grief. With difficulty, he regained his composure and began to record a rough draft of the emperor's will. When the bedside audience was finished, Wang retired to polish up his draft. Near daybreak of the fifth, the finished will was submitted to Shun-chih, who approved it and entrusted it to Margi. He left the instruction that, upon his death, Margi and an imperial guardsman, Giyabuja, were first to present the will to the empress dowager, Hsiao-chuang, and afterward to transmit it to the various court nobles and high officials. Shun-chih died that evening, and Margi and Giyabuja acted as they had been instructed.[17]

The will that was made public the next day was reputedly the work of the empress dowager and the four regents. They destroyed

Shun-chih's will, it is claimed, and replaced it with one of their own that would sanction policy changes they contemplated.[18] In the new will—if we accept the idea that it was indeed altered—Shun-chih confessed to and repented of fourteen major errors of his reign.[19] It is this unrelenting self-condemnation—much of it unreasonable and unthinkable in light of the emperor's known predilections,[20] that makes the published will suspect.

Several items in Shun-chih's list of mea culpas showed clearly the intention of the regents to halt the sinicization policies of the deceased emperor. His very first offense was to have strayed from the institutions and practices of his predecessors, Nurhaci and Abahai, and to have gone too far toward adopting Chinese customs. Specifically, Shun-chih admitted his failure to entrust more Manchus with administrative responsibility (the fifth item) and his mistake in reviving eunuch institutions—thereby exposing the government to the same pernicious influences that had wrecked the Ming dynasty (the eleventh item). Within the year the regents took steps to rectify Shun-chih's mistakes by replacing several Chinese-style institutions with Manchu institutions.

The first change came when the Inner Thirteen Yamen (*nei shih-san ya-men*), a eunuch institution, was abolished. In the predynastic period, Nurhaci and Abahai had not established any eunuch institution. Eunuchs existed but they were used for menial chores only.[21] Ming eunuchs were not slaughtered by the Manchus when they entered Peking, so there was always the possibility that they would regain their former prominence if it suited imperial interests. As long as Dorgon was alive and in control of government, eunuch influence was kept to a minimum. First of all, Dorgon did not live within the confines of the palace, where the eunuch pressure was most felt. Then, on a number of occasions, the government took measures to undercut the eunuchs' institutional base of power.[22]

Under Shun-chih's personal rule, however, eunuchs made a recovery as the young emperor sought to strengthen his own, imperial position against the power of the Manchu princes. The Inner Thirteen Yamen was formally established in 1653, and it grew to a formidable institution within a few years. Shun-chih was aware, however, of the dangers that always attended eunuch power in past dynasties. For that reason he carefully stipulated that trustworthy Manchus be appointed to the thirteen yamen as a check on eunuch officials and that the latter could not hold a rank higher than 4. In addition, a series of eight "prohibitions" (*pu-hsü*) were designed to keep eunuchs from becoming involved in court politics.[23] Since Shun-chih was only sixteen at this time, it was suggested that he issued this edict under the influence of a Manchu, T'ung-i, and the leading eunuch, Wu Liang-fu.[24] By the end of Shun-chih's reign, some of the important *chien* of the Inner Thirteen Yamen were called by the more prestigious name of *yüan*.[25]

Shun-chih's tolerance of eunuchs was often opposed by both Manchu and Chinese officials. Chinese who had formerly served under the Ming particularly feared the reappearance of a eunuch secret police.[26] Even Shun-chih himself had misgivings about eunuch influence in 1658 with the uncovering of a huge bribery scandal involving Wu Liang-fu and officials of the outer court. Several of the men implicated in the scandal were cashiered and exiled, but Wu escaped with just a stern warning.[27]

At least one of the future regents of K'ang-hsi had a thorough knowledge of Wu Liang-fu's complicity, because Oboi carried out an investigation of the scandal for Shun-chih.[28] Oboi's attitude toward Wu Liang-fu and the growing power of eunuchs is not hard to guess, and two years later he and the other three regents included a denunciation of eunuchs in Shun-chih's altered will. It is probable that Wu Liang-fu was executed shortly after Shun-chih's death.[29] Then, on 15 March 1661, the Inner Thirteen Yamen was abolished, and Wu and T'ung-i were reviled posthumously for their part in its establishment back in 1653.[30] Throughout K'ang-hsi's reign and the rest of the dynasty, eunuchs were kept in tight rein and never had a chance to recover the influence comparable to that which they once wielded in the 1650s.[31]

Still, there was an evident need for someone to perform the chores and duties that necessitated the rise of eunuchs in the first place. What would be the Ch'ing equivalent for eunuchs? When the imperial edict destroying the Inner Thirteen Yamen proclaimed a return to the practices in use during Nurhaci's and Abahai's time, it clearly meant a return to the *booi* system.[32]

The Manchu word *booi* (*pao-i* in Chinese, bondservant in English) meant "of the house" (*chia-chih* or *chia-ti*), and *booi* were originally household and agricultural servants of Manchu princes and officials. The Manchus considered the labor services provided by *booi* as essential to the economic development and political expansion of the predynastic Manchu state.[33] *Booi* were either people captured in war, or the family of condemned criminals, or men who had voluntarily become slaves (*t'ou-ch'ung*) for a variety of reasons—impoverished men seeking food and shelter, separated men wanting to be reunited with their families already in bondage, unscrupulous men needing protection, or wealthy men trying to avoid confiscation of their property.[34] Their descendants became slaves hereditarily unless manumitted for some special reason.

As Manchu leaders developed imperial ambitions, the private ownership of slaves gave way to more systematic forms of servitude. Some bondservants remained as personal servants of their masters, but bondservants of the emperor and of the Manchu princes controlling a banner were organized in 1615 into standard banner units.[35] To distinguish regular and bondservant units of the banners, the former were now designated *ch'i-fen tso-ling* (banner companies) and the latter were called *pao-i tso-ling* (bondservant companies). Within the new organization bondservants continued to serve their banner prince or emperor in a servant-master relationship. It must be noted, though, that *booi* were servants only to their banner prince; in society at large they could hold office, have personal possessions, and even have slaves of their own.

A further distinction among banner units—and it was a crucial one—was made early in Abahai's reign, although it was not institutionalized until after Dorgon's death. Banners controlled personally by the emperor were designated the Upper Three Banners, and the remaining ones were known as the Lower Five Banners. The *booi* companies of the Upper Three Banners were the household servants of the emperor and managed his affairs. They thus formed the nucleus of what was institutionalized as the Imperial Household (*nei-wu-fu*). According to the latest evidence, bondservant companies of the emperor emerged as a distinct and superior group in 1628, and by 1638 the Imperial Household had an imposing structure to house its offices.[36]

Thus, the Imperial Household existed by the time the Manchus entered Peking in 1644, and it clearly evolved out of the *booi* system. The former supervising officials of the bondservants, known by their Manchu name of *booi amban*, became ministers of the Imperial Household (*tsung-kuan nei-wu-fu ta-ch'en*). The significance of the change in terminology is clear: *booi* overseers of the Upper Three Banners had been elevated from a family level to a state level of operations. In the Upper Three Banners, the former *booi amban* were now the emperor's ministers, and former *booi* were now the emperor's personal servants.

The *booi* system and its outgrowth, the Imperial Household, were institutions native to the Manchus, congenial to the tribal and martial principles of their predynastic society, and instruments of Manchu power. They were the institutions Shun-chih abandoned in 1653 in favor of eunuchs, the traditional servants of Chinese emperors. But Manchu leaders did not take to the new practices, nor did they forget their native institutions. As soon as Shun-chih died, the Manchu regents of K'ang-hsi abolished the eunuch institution and reestablished the Imperial Household, which became a permanent feature of Ch'ing institutional structure. The reconstituted Imperial Household, however, was larger and more complex than earlier, building upon the agencies of the discredited Inner Thirteen Yamen.[37] For Oboi, the Imperial Household was meant to serve Manchu interests against the Chinese,[38] but under K'ang-hsi—when it took final shape—and succeeding emperors, it also served imperial interests against Manchu princes.

A second Manchu institution was revived later in 1661—again as part of the regents' desire to halt the rapid sinicization condoned by Dorgon and Shun-chih. When the new government was being set up in Peking in 1644, Dorgon decided to continue most of the institutions of the Ming period. In line with this policy, the Hanlin Academy was established, but in the following year it was abolished as a distinct organization and incorporated into the Three Inner Courts (*nei-san-yüan*), an outgrowth of the Literary Office established by Abahai.[39] It was not until 1658 that the Three Inner Courts were reorganized into the separate institutions of the Grand Secretariat and the Hanlin Academy, in accordance with Ming governmental practice. An indefinite number of Manchus and Chinese were appointed to the Grand Secretariat, and each was known as the grand secretary of one of the six halls to which he was attached.[40]

After Shun-chih's death, the regents gave up the Hanlin Academy and the Grand Secretariat in favor of a return to the Three Inner Courts. Again, as in the case of abolishing the Inner Thirteen Yamen, the regents justified the new step as being in accordance with Shun-chih's will, where the former emperor expressed regret at having abandoned practices of his forebears and failed to employ Manchus.[41] Under the new arrangement, each of the three bureaus (Kuo-shih-yüan, Pi-shu-yüan, and Hung-wen-yüan) was to be supervised by one Manchu and one Chinese grand secretary. At the outset, however, all eight of the grand secretaries then serving in the Grand Secretariat were transferred to the Three Inner Courts. This meant a temporarily unbalanced lineup of two Manchu and six Chinese grand secretaries, but a third Manchu was to be appointed soon, and three of the positions filled by Chinese were to remain vacant upon the death or transfer of current appointees.[42] In fact, the balance shifted the other way: by the mid-1660s, there were six Manchu secretaries to three Chinese.[43] The Three Inner Courts functioned as a source of Manchu strength throughout the regency, but K'ang-hsi abolished it and reestablished the Grand Secretariat and the Hanlin Academy in 1670.[44] After twenty-seven years of experimentation, the Ch'ing dynasty in the end adopted the Ming form of imperial secretariat.

A final Manchu institution to be elevated in importance by the regents was the Court of Colonial Affairs (*li-fan yüan*), which managed the court's relations with Mongol tribes. In September 1661, the regents declared the Court of Colonial Affairs equal in status to the Six Boards and placed it in the administrative hierarchy right behind the Board of Works and preceding the Censorate.[45]

With the revival of Manchu institutions, important Chinese bureaucratic institutions and practices were altered by the regents to serve their ends. The Deliberative Council, a Manchu innovation, overshadowed to some extent the traditional Six Boards as the policy-making organ, and the regents reduced the size of the Censorate and punished outspokenness by its members.[46] The intimidation of censors was one of the crimes charged to Oboi after his fall in 1669.[47] Oboi and his colleagues also adjusted the personnel evaluation system to reflect their concerns with tax collection and the preservation of order.[48] It was in these two areas of government control that the regents came down so hard on southeasterners in a series of famous "cases."

Attacks on the Chekiang-Kiangnan Elite

In addition to the institutional expressions of Manchu nativism, the regents presented a more aggressive face to the Chinese. Their desire to display Manchu power to dissident southeastern scholars and gentry was clear from the very beginning of the regency. In pursuing their objectives, the regents undoubtedly found willing allies among the top Chinese officials at court—a predominantly northern group. In the early Ch'ing period, natives of four northern provinces—Chihli, Shantung, Honan, and Shansi—monopolized government positions and hence political power. This situation had come about naturally: northerners were the first to submit to the Manchus, and they took advantage of their position to recommend fellow provincials for the numerous openings at court under the new dynasty.[49] Furthermore, 95 percent of the successful candidates on the dynasty's first metropolitan examination in 1646, held when the southern part of China was not yet pacified, came from the same four provinces.[50] Succeeding examinations in Shun-chih's reign redressed the balance of north and south as producers of *chin-shih*, but academic prominence had not yet been converted into political power. In 1661, the northerners who had swamped the court as a result of early recommendation and examination success still held the top positions. For example, of the ten Chinese grand secretaries serving in late 1660 and early 1661, seven were from Chihli, Shantung, or Shansi. Two of those seven had started their careers as 1646 *chin-shih.*[51] The three non-northerners—Hung Ch'eng-ch'ou of Fukien, Chin Chih-chün of Kiangsu, and Hu Shih-an of Szechwan—had submitted to the Manchus either before they came through the Great Wall or as they arrived in Peking.[52] Still, it was only a matter of time before men from Kiangnan and Chekiang, who were already having notable success in the examination system in the late Shun-chih period,[53] would also occupy key government positions. Knowing this, the northerners more likely than not used the political power that was still theirs to support the regents' attacks on southeastern scholar-gentry. This north-south competition for degrees and office, while not the sole determinant of events, was a prominent dimension of early Ch'ing politics, and it was to help shape the events of 1661.

In 1661, there was first of all the famous case of Chuang T'ing-lung, which has been called "the most unjust literary inquisition of the Ch'ing period."[54] It was also precedent-setting: it was the first case of its kind under the Manchus. Chuang T'ing-lung, son of a wealthy Chekiang merchant, had the misfortune, as it turned out, to have come into possession of an unpublished draft history of the Ming dynasty written by Chu Kuo-chen (1557–1632). Chuang decided to revise the draft and add to it, or rather to hire a number of scholars for the task, with the intention of publishing it under his own name. Chuang died (c. 1660) before the work was finished, but under his father's supervision the team of scholars completed their labors, and the book began circulating around Chekiang in late 1660.

The trouble was that Chuang's history of the Ming continued to give Ming reign titles for the years after 1644—that is, reign titles of various Southern Ming pretenders. In addition, the book used the personal names of Manchu rulers (e.g., Nurhaci, instead of Ch'ing T'ai-tsu). Both practices could not but be considered slanderous by the new dynasty, and some readers of the book sought to take advantage of this. Wu Chih-jung, a former magistrate who had been cashiered, was one of these. When the Chuang family in 1661 rebuffed his extortionate demands for money, he reported the contents of the history to the court.

The court, caught in the throes of reaction under the regents and sensitive to slights and expressions of hostility to Manchu rule, decided to deal harshly with the offenders. The purported author, Chuang T'ing-lung, was dead; so his father was arrested and thrown into a Peking jail, where he later died. When the case was closed in 1663, the father's and son's bodies were disinterred and mutilated, their families were bound over to Manchus as slaves, and their possessions were confiscated. Two Manchu commissioners accompanied by several hundred banner troops came to Chekiang in 1662 to investigate the case. As a result, all the scholars involved in preparing the history, the printer, and even purchasers were punished. Over seventy men were executed.[55]

Two of the future great literary figures of the K'ang-hsi period, Ku Yen-wu and Chu I-tsun, came close to being implicated in this case. The former had turned down an invitation to help compile it, and the latter apparently had purchased the book.[56] But two other scholars of note, Wu Yen and P'an Ch'eng-chang, lost their lives for being listed as assistant compilers.[57] The latter had a younger half-brother, P'an Lei, who later became a student of Ku Yen-wu and edited the second edition of Ku's *Jih-chih lu*. In so doing, P'an is said to have made alterations "in order not to offend the susceptibilities of the Manchus"[58]—susceptibilities to which his brother fell victim in 1663. The latter's fate in the Chuang

T'ing-lung case must have influenced P'an Lei's editorial decisions and thus, in part, must have been responsible for the present content of Ku Yen-wu's famous notebook.

Before the regency was over, Ku was involved in another case of literary inquisition. This time he was imprisoned for more than half a year on a charge—false as it turned out—of sponsoring a book containing anti-Manchu sentiment.[59] It was shortly after his release that Ku took on P'an Lei as a student, and the two men's narrow escapes from death in literary purges probably forged a keen bond of friendship between them. As Ch'ien-lung's literary inquisition affected so many men of his time in one way or another,[60] so too did the regents' arbitrary purges touch the lives of early Ch'ing scholars.

At the same time that literary dissent was being punished in Chekiang, thousands of gentry in the neighboring province of Kiangnan met disaster in a crackdown on tax delinquency. Imperial concern over tax arrears was a recurring feature of early Ch'ing administration. Mindful of the late Ming fiscal problems,[61] the Manchu court was tightening up tax-collection procedures. In 1655 the government decreed that all financial commissioners, prefects, and magistrates would be fined and degraded according to the percentage of the tax quota left uncollected in their areas of jurisdiction. These penalties ranged from a forfeiture of six months' salary for a 10 percent tax deficiency to removal from office for arrears of 90 percent or more.[62] A similar sort of sliding scale of punishments for gentry, degree holders, and yamen personnel who consistently failed to pay their taxes went into effect in 1658. Two years later, provincial officials were directed to report the specific amounts of taxes still unpaid by the gentry of their provinces.[63] A series of edicts issued in 1661 shortly after the Shun-chih emperor's death intensified the pressure on provincial and local officials by threatening them with demotion or dismissal for failure to collect their full quota of taxes on time.[64] One local official acting under such pressure initiated the disasters of 1661 in Kiangnan.

Jen Wei-ch'u, the magistrate of Wu-hsien district (Soochow), decided to use harsh measures to collect the delinquent taxes of his district. His zeal in following the court's instructions provoked criticism from local scholars and students. In early March, as scholars and officials gathered at the local Confucian temple to mourn the recent death of the emperor, more than a hundred students took advantage of the governor's presence to press their charges against Jen Wei-ch'u. With conspicuous disregard for the propriety of the situation, the protestors burst in on the governor and angrily demanded the magistrate's dismissal. Eleven student leaders were arrested on the spot and more were taken into custody later—all to await trial in what came to be known as the "Laments in the Temple" case (*k'u-miao an*).[65]

When depositions in the case were taken, Jen claimed that he was under pressure from the governor, Chu Kuo-chih, to make a speedy collection of tax arrears. The governor, in turn, protested that military exigencies demanded a speedy and complete tax collection. Whether the governor acted on his own or had received instructions from Peking is debatable.[66] At any rate, he reported to Peking that the students had abused the magistrate, defiled the late emperor's memory, and obstructed the collection of taxes. When four Manchu officials arrived in Kiangning to investigate—they stayed clear of Soochow for fear of reaction from the populace—the case took a new and fateful turn: the *k'u-miao* protest was lumped together with cases involving prisoners accused of helping the rebel Cheng Ch'eng-kung when he invaded Kiangsu in 1659. A revolt against a magistrate's unorthodox tax-collecting practices was thus transformed into a treasonous attack on the state and dynasty.[67] In the end, eighteen of the *k'u-miao* defendants, including the celebrated literary critic, Chin Jen-jui, were sentenced to death and were beheaded in August 1661.

The *k'u-miao* case was actually only a prelude to the Kiangnan tax arrears case (*tsou-hsiao an*) proper, but it perhaps points to one of the motivating factors for the crackdown on gentry: the failure of the government to eradicate the Ming loyalist naval forces led by Cheng Ch'eng-kung and the sympathy for them that existed in Kiangnan and other southeastern provinces. Chu Kuo-chih had as much reason as the court to be frustrated by the constant coastal attacks of the rebels, because he spent considerable time making defense preparations and devising military strategy to use against Cheng and his followers.[68] It may be that the governor and the court in their frustration took advantage of the *k'u-miao* incident to strike out at the loyalist sympathies of Kiangsu gentry, just as northerners falling behind in academic prominence used the events of 1661 to harass their southern competitors.

This is not to deny, however, the basic interest of the government in tightening up tax collection procedures. Chu Kuo-chih was apparently pressing all local officials to get their taxes collected on time and to report the names of tax defaulters so that he could compile a register for the court.[69] The action taken in the Wu-hsien district was well-known because it led to the *k'u-miao* incident, but other district and prefectural officials felt the pinch as well. Ch'ang-chou prefecture and Lien-ch'uan district can be taken as examples.

When the governor's instructions reached Ch'ang-chou, several hundred gentry had tax deficiencies, and the prefect felt constrained to report their names and the amount they owed to his superior, the governor, because a predecessor had been dismissed for dereliction of duty in tax collection. The impasse was solved by the prefectural director of schools, Kuo Shih-ching, who interceded with the prefect to give the gentry three more days of grace before reporting them to the governor. Kuo then encouraged the gentry, as he had done before, to pay their taxes to prevent another prefect from being cashiered. Kuo's effort succeeded and few men of Ch'ang-chou became involved in the tax arrears case.[70]

Lien-ch'uan district, on the other hand, was hit hard by the investigation. Its total tax deficiency ran into the hundred thousands. A Manchu official came to Lien-ch'uan and compiled a register of 170 gentry who were in arrears of a hundred taels of silver or more. About a thousand more had tax deficiencies of less than a hundred taels. The governor warned the former group that, if they did not pay up quickly, he would send them to Peking for questioning and punishment. Within a week about a hundred thousand taels had been remitted, and only about eight thousand taels remained unpaid. The latter sum was due from families that had died out, but Chu Kuo-chih still insisted on collecting the entire amount. Finally, the Su-Sung circuit censor, Wang Kung-chi, and some of the gentry contributed the requisite amount. In this way all except one of the Lien-ch'uan local elite avoided the rigors and degradation of being sent to Peking. The single exception was Wang Hao, a descendant of the noted Ming scholar and official Wang Shih-chen and a poet of some renown. The court probably singled out as an example someone like Wang Hao from an illustrious family in order to impress and subdue the people of Kiangnan.

The experiences of Ch'ang-chou and Lien-ch'uan must have been repeated through Kiangnan in 1661. The campaign against gentry with tax deficiencies culminated in Chu Kuo-chih's report to Peking on 3 June 1661. The governor submitted a register listing 13,517 gentry and 254 yamen clerks in the four prefectures of Soochow, Sung-chiang, Ch'ang-chou, and Chenkiang, and in the Li-yang district, who had not yet completely paid their taxes. The imperial comment to Chu's memorial was: "Gentry who resist paying their taxes are truly despicable."[71] The Board of Civil Appointments decided that anyone on the governor's list now holding office should be demoted two grades and transferred, while any members of the gentry not in office should be brought to Peking for questioning.[72] Eventually, thousands of officials and gentry members were dismissed, imprisoned, flogged, and deprived of their ranks or titles. A total of 11,346 names was removed from the *sheng-yüan* rolls in the four prefectures and one district noted above.[73]

Many famous scholars, and even a descendant of Confucius,[74] were involved in the Kiangnan tax case of 1661. The poet Wang Hao has already been mentioned. The experiences of Han T'an, Hsü Yüan-wen, Wu Wei-yeh, and Yeh Fang-ai were representative of the broken career patterns and humiliations that scarred the Kiangnan scholarly world at the start of the regency.

Han T'an, of Ch'ang-chou prefecture, was only a *sheng-yüan* in 1661. He was stripped of that degree and remained in obscurity until 1672 when he purchased an Imperial Academy studentship (*chien-sheng*). The following year he placed first on the palace examination for the *chin-shih* degree, and in ensuing years K'ang-hsi chose him to edit and compile a number of important political and literary collections.[75] Hsü Yüan-wen was a younger brother of Hsü Ch'ien-hsüeh, famous scholar and court politician of the later K'ang-hsi period. Like Han T'an, Yüan-wen began his official career with the highest possible qualification, that of *chuang-yüan* for placing first in the palace examination of 1659. This honor entitled him to a middle-ranking post in the Hanlin Academy, a post he lost in the tax arrears case. He later recovered from this setback and went on to become a grand secretary and an important figure in court politics like his elder brother.[76]

Another member of the Kiangnan gentry who lost not only his rank but a lot of property as well in 1661 was the renowned poet Wu Wei-yeh (commonly known by his *hao*, Mei-ts'un). He was a

Ming dynasty *chin-shih* who at first refused to serve the new dynasty, but he relented in the end and held several middle ranking posts in the central government. He also helped edit the sacred injunctions (*sheng-hsün*) of Nurhaci and Abahai. Along with Ch'ien Ch'ien-i and Kung Ting-tzu, Wu formed the group known as the Chiang-tso san-ta-chia (The Three Master Poets of Kiangnan), and all three of them later were targets of Ch'ien-lung's famous literary inquisition.[77] A relative and student of Ch'ien Ch'ien-i, Ch'ien Tseng, lost his *hsiu-ts'ai* degree in 1661 because of tax arrears.[78]

An extreme example of the punitive treatment of Kiangnan scholars was the dismissal from the Hanlin Academy of Yeh Fang-ai. Yeh had the distinction of being the *t'an-hua* (third highest candidate) in the palace examination of 1659 (the year Hsü Yüan-wen placed first), and he had been appointed a Hanlin compiler. Yet in 1661 he was dismissed for a tax deficiency reported to be as little as one *ch'ien* (one-tenth of an ounce of silver). From this incident reputedly came the popular saying: "The *t'an-hua* degree is not worth a cent." Yeh was later employed in his original post, and in 1679 he served as one of the readers for the special *po-hsüeh hung-tz'u* examination held for Chinese scholars.[79] A number of Kiangnan scholars competing in that examination, including P'eng Sun-yü who placed first, had been involved in the tax arrears case of 1661.

From these brief biographical notes, it is clear that the tax case of 1661 did not have a long-lasting effect on Kiangnan gentry and their subsequent careers. But in 1661 great bitterness prevailed throughout Kiangnan. The local elite had met successive disasters in the *k'u-miao* and *tsou-hsiao* cases. Some gentry were actually involved in both incidents. One man was sentenced to death by strangulation in the *k'u-miao* case but was pardoned, only to be dismissed from his post as a result of the *tsou-hsiao* incident.[80] Insult was added to injury when thousands of Kiangnan gentry were herded like cattle to Peking for questioning—driven on, according to one startled observer, in shackles over dusty roads and under a blazing sun, exhausted and dying of thirst.[81]

This attack on the gentry quickly affected the schools of Kiangnan. In Soochow and Sung-chiang prefectures, for instance, the provincial director of education, Hu Tsai-ko, found at most only sixty to seventy students, and sometimes only twenty to thirty, in the schools he visited on his winter tour in 1661, whereas the same schools had over six hundred students at the beginning of the dynasty. As Hu read the skimpy roster of names in each school, he wept to think how Kiangnan's great talent had been reduced to almost nothing.[82] Many observers at the time remarked on the "emptiness" of schools.[83]

The investigation was finally called off by imperial decree in the middle of 1662. Offenders in Peking for questioning or still on the road to the capital were all released and sent home. This decision appeared to a contemporary to be "as refreshing and welcome as a heavy downfall of rain would be to a man trapped in scalding water or a searing fire."[84]

By this time Chu Kuo-chih was no longer governor of Kiangsu. He retired in December 1661 to mourn the death of his father. The new governor, Han Shih-ch'i, won a measure of respect from the people of Kiangnan for clearing a man mistakenly identified as another with a similar name who had a tax deficiency. For this mistake, several officials, including former governor Chu, were said to have been punished, and this made the people rejoice. Actually, Chu was punished for another reason: failure to remain at his post until his replacement arrived.[85] The hatred for Chu was so great in Kiangnan because of his role in the tax arrears case that later authors, it is said, took pleasure in recording his death in 1673 at the hands of Wu San-kuei when the latter revolted against Manchu authority.[86] What is not usually known is that Wu San-kuei's principal adviser and one of the key men around Wu urging him to revolt was Fang Kuang-chen, who had been deprived of his *ling-sheng* (senior licentiate on a government stipend) status in 1661 in the tax case instigated by Chu Kuo-chih.[87] Fang may well have urged on Wu the murder of Chu, then governor of Yunnan, to settle an old score. To the people of Kiangnan it would have been just retribution.

Another, less spectacular, tax arrears case occurred in the neighboring province of Anhwei at the same time, and in Kiangsu province itself, isolated harrassment of tax defaulters was found even after Chu Kuo-chih's *tsou-hsiao an.* One Kiangsu scholar was praised for his perspicuity in giving away over half of the 800 *mou* (a *mou* is about one-sixth of an acre) of land he inherited in late 1661, because shortly afterward a number of his fellow villagers were caught in another tax deficiency case.[88] Finally, in September

1663, all tax arrears dating from 1662 or before were canceled at the request of the Chinese president of the Censorate, Kung Ting-tzu.[89] Kung was one of the Three Master Poets of Kiangnan, and he undoubtedly had the personal plight of his fellow poets Wu Wei-yeh and Ch'ien Ch'ien-i in mind when he submitted his memorial to the throne.

The cancelation of tax arrears in 1663, though, did not end the problem. In 1671 the governor of Kiangsu, Mahu, reported a tax deficiency in Soochow and Sung-chiang prefectures of over two million taels that had built up since the beginning of K'ang-hsi's reign. And in 1679 the government once more had to instruct provincial officials to report on gentry with unpaid taxes so that they might be disciplined.[90] By 1679, however, the court's general attitude toward the scholar-gentry class had changed drastically. The new attitude was best expressed by the special *po-hsüeh* examination held in that year (see chapter 6).

The Maritime Laws of 1661–62

To deal with their one remaining military problem[91]—the Ming loyalist forces led by Cheng Ch'eng-kung—the regents resorted to the draconian measures of evacuating the coastal populations of five provinces and prohibiting coastal trade. These policies, known as *chien-pi ch'ing-yeh* (to fortify the walls and empty the fields) and *hai-chin* (maritime prohibition), were wholly defensive in nature. The Manchus, it must be remembered, were excellent horsemen and archers, but they had no experience in naval warfare and were poor at it. What naval victories they won were due to the efforts of Chinese officers, many of whom had previously served under Cheng Ch'eng-kung. But Manchus were not the only proponents of defensive policies like *chien-pi ch'ing-yeh* and *hai-chin.* These or similar policies were in force in the late Ming dynasty and were regularly proposed by Chinese officials throughout the 1650s and 1660s. Very few men at this time were advocating an aggressive policy, the key feature of which had to be the recruitment and training of a navy. The origin and development of the maritime laws of 1661–62 testify to the widespread acceptance of a defensive strategy.

Even before thought was given to either the *chien-pi ch'ing-yeh* or *hai-chin* policies, the Ch'ing court tried the time-honored approach of offering rank and honor to the rebels as inducement to surrender. Overtures to Cheng Ch'eng-kung and other members of his family were first made in 1652. The government's earliest offers promised to pardon the rebels' past offenses, bestow rank upon them, employ them in hunting down other rebels or pirates, and even gave them control of some customs revenue.[92] This did not satisfy Cheng, who demanded unrestricted control over the four prefectures of Chang-chou and Ch'üan-chou in Fukien, and Ch'ao-chou and Hui-chou in Kwangtung.[93] Even this request was granted in a series of edicts in 1653–54, but Shun-chih refused to yield on the matter of the queue. Cheng, the emperor insisted, must cut his hair and wear the Manchu pigtail as a sign of submission.[94] His father, Cheng Chih-lung, who was then in Peking as a hostage, was even used to send letters to his son urging him to submit.

Neither the emperor's concessions nor the father's pleas had any effect. Cheng Ch'eng-kung steadfastly rebuffed all inducements to submit. On top of it, he continued to accept titles and honors from the Ming court of Chu Yu-lang.[95] Once, in 1654, Cheng pretended to submit only to have the opportunity to collect provisions for his men in Fukien. The Ch'ing court finally despaired of winning him over peacefully, and in the waning days of 1654 sent out a punitive force under Jidu and other Manchu nobles to crush the rebels.[96]

At the same time, steps were taken to impose a ban on coastal trading. A maritime ban was one part of a six-point plan for defeating the rebels recommended in 1654 by Chi K'ai-sheng, a metropolitan censor. The action taken on Chi's memorial is not known, but a similar request by Tuntai, governor-general of Fukien and Chekiang, in 1655 received imperial approval.[97] In the following year, the court adopted *hai-chin* as imperial policy. An edict of 6 August 1656 instructed the governors-general, governors, and regional commanders of the five coastal provinces of Shantung, Kiangnan, Chekiang, Fukien, and Kwangtung, to prohibit any maritime trade under pain of death to the offenders. Furthermore, local officials were ordered to devise ways to obstruct the rebels—building earthen embankments, erecting wooden palisades, and the like.[98]

The reasoning behind the maritime ban and defense preparations was that Cheng was able to survive and resist the Manchus only because merchants and people of the coastal areas were supplying him with essential foodstuffs and military supplies. If the government could cut him off from his sources of supply, then Cheng would fall of his own accord. An implicit feature of this argument, which was sometimes explicitly spelled out, was that the government would not have to wage a naval campaign against the superior forces of the rebels.[99] A few lonely voices spoke up for a vigorous ship-building and naval training program,[100] but this was not attempted until twenty years later.

Despite the stern warning to local officials that negligence in investigating violations of the maritime ban would lead to severe punishment and removal from office, the edict of 6 August 1656 remained a dead letter. The illegal trading and intercourse between the coastal populations and the rebels went on as before. The southeastern regions of the country were generally favorable to Cheng Ch'eng-kung and looked to him to restore the native Ming dynasty. Furthermore, the profit motive led many merchants to sell pine masts, iron utensils, raw silk, iron nails, foodstuffs, and other necessities to the rebels.[101] With the failure first of what today might be called an "open arms" policy toward the rebels and then of the maritime trading ban (*hai-chin*), the Ch'ing court turned to the *chien-pi ch'ing-yeh* approach.[102] The evacuation of coastal populations in wartime was not unique to the early Ch'ing period, but the Manchus were the first to apply it to the entire coastline as a matter of national policy and for an extended period of time (more than twenty years).

The first man to suggest *chien-pi ch'ing-yeh* as imperial policy was Huang Wu, a former subordinate of Cheng Ch'eng-kung. Like many other adherents of Cheng, Huang defected because of the severe military discipline of his leaders.[103] Huang had been entrusted by Cheng with the defense of Hai-ch'eng, a strategic coastal city facing Amoy on the west. In August 1656, Huang surrendered himself, his soldiers, and the city of Hai-ch'eng to the Manchus. This was a great blow to Cheng, because Hai-ch'eng was his main supply depot, where he reputedly had immense stores of armor, shields, guns, gunpowder, and a thirty-year supply of grain. The Manchus rewarded Huang with a ducal title (*Hai-ch'eng kung*)—the title originally offered to Cheng Ch'eng-kung in 1652 and 1653.[104]

Huang Wu, in May 1657, presented a comprehensive "Plan of Maritime Pacification" (*p'ing-hai ts'e*) to deal with the Cheng rebels. His recommendations can be summarized under five headings.[105] First, he requested that Cheng Chih-lung be executed and the Cheng ancestral tombs be destroyed. Second, he suggested a policy of offering generous rewards to rebels who surrendered, and he also urged utilizing the services of defectors, whose skills in naval warfare could be valuable in the struggle against the rebels. Stricter enforcement of the trade ban and increased defense of the seacoast were his third and fourth points. The last and most important recommendation was the removal of coastal populations.

All of Huang's proposals were discussed at court and eventually were carried out. Cheng Chih-lung was degraded in 1657 and executed in 1661,[106] while Huang himself performed the task of desecrating the Cheng family tombs.[107] Huang was also very successful in securing the surrender of many rebels, who were either sent off as colonizers or incorporated into Ch'ing armies.[108] The maritime trade ban and coastal defenses were tightened up in the ensuing years.[109] There was one local instance of coastal evacuation in 1657, but it was not until 1660 after further recommendations by officials such as Wang Ch'i-tso (a junior metropolitan censor), Shih Lang (then a regional commander in Fukien), and Sunahai (president of the Board of War), that the *chien-pi ch'ing-yeh* policy was implemented on a large scale.[110]

The evacuation policy could not have been carried out earlier, because the rebels controlled a good portion of the coastal area. But after Cheng Ch'eng-kung's crushing defeat at Nanking in 1659, the rebels remained confined to the two offshore islands of Amoy and Quemoy. Later, in early 1661, Cheng directed his energies toward driving the Dutch out of Taiwan and establishing his headquarters there. With the coastal areas now relatively free of rebel attacks, the Manchus took this opportunity to "clear the fields and fortify the walls."

The evacuation began in October 1660 in Fukien, where the population of eighty-eight villages in the T'ung-an and Hai-ch'eng districts were removed to the interior at the request of Governor-general Li Shuai-t'ai.[111] From Fukien, the incidence of *chien-pi ch'ing-yeh* spread until by the fall of 1661 the court was referring to the evacuation of the coastal populations of Kiangnan, Chekiang, Fukien, and Kwangtung.[112] Manchu officials were sent to each of these four provinces to supervise the evacuation and to mark off a no-man's land.[113] Removal of population in a fifth province, Shantung, was reported in 1663.[114]

In addition to the shift of coastal populations, the court also issued a new and more forceful trade ban. In a February 1662 edict, the regents spoke of the constant violations of the earlier *hai-chin* decrees. Past infractions would be forgiven, but from the beginning of K'ang-hsi's first year no leniency would be shown. Furthermore, the regents reasoned, "since the coastal population has already been shifted to the interior, investigation of violations should be easy, and officials cannot as before be careless."[115]

Thus, in 1661–62 the *chien-pi ch'ing-yeh* and *hai-chin* policies were adopted by the Manchu rulers as defense strategy against the remaining Ming loyalists. For the next twenty years the trade ban remained in force,[116] and the coastal populations of five provinces were uprooted from their land and forced to abandon their homes and livelihood in order to remove from Cheng Ch'eng-kung and his descendants their sources of supply, support, and manpower.

Not all of the coastal populations, however, suffered equally from the *chien-pi ch'ing-yeh* policy. The two northernmost provinces, Shantung and Kiangnan, remained relatively free of its miseries.[117] In Chekiang the coastal population of Wen-chou, T'ai-chou, and Ningpo were moved inland in 1661, and wooden posts were erected as a boundary. Under the direction of the governor, Chu Ch'ang-tso, the people were resettled on land in the interior, over 90,000 *mou* of land were reclaimed, and the taxes due on the land they had to abandon were remitted. Sentinel mounds were constructed along the coast, and imperial commissioners inspected the depopulated strip five or six times a year.[118] Shang K'o-hsi, one of the three feudatory princes (*P'ing-nan wang*), directed the removal of population in Kwangtung and erected defense fortifications along the coast. Later, through the efforts of Chou Yu-te (governor-general, 1668–70), Wang Lai-jen (governor, 1665–67), and Liu Ping-ch'üan (governor, 1668–74), the removal policy was relaxed, the people were allowed to return to their homes along the coast, and relief measures were instituted.[119]

The province that suffered the most by the *chien-pi ch'ing-yeh* policy was Fukien, where the evacuation of coastal population had begun. In 1663 it was reported that over 8,500 evacuees there had died.[120] Removal in Fukien was closely tied to rebel campaigns along the coast. When Cheng Ching, son of and successor to Cheng Ch'eng-kung, was driven out of Amoy in 1663, the city was destroyed and the population shifted to the interior. In the following year, over 30,000 people of T'ung-shan were evacuated.[121] But during the rebellion of the three feudatories, when Cheng Ching again had a foothold on the mainland, the people of Fukien returned to their homes along the coast. When Ch'ing forces regained control and drove Cheng off the mainland, then the population of the Amoy region was once more removed to the interior.[122]

Westerners corroborated Chinese accounts about the general devastation and misery in Fukien. The Spaniard Diaz spoke of "thousands of towns" burning, with "the fire lasting many days—the clouds of smoke reaching as far as Hia-men [Hsia-men, or Amoy], more than twenty leguas [leagues], and the sun not being visible in all that broad expanse."[123] In October 1662, Constantin Nobel, the Dutch negotiator with the Bort expeditions, was told by Chinese officials that "along the sea-coast we have nothing but ruined cities and villages, where some poor fishermen, with their vessels and nets, with leave of the governors, live to maintain themselves, because all the greatest towns and villages in those parts were by the emperor's orders pulled down to the ground, to prevent the sending of provisions and merchandise to the islands Eymuy [Amoy] and Quemoy." This description by the Chinese of the destruction along the coast was later verified by the Dutch themselves. As they cruised up and down the Fukien coastline, they found many areas devastated—with some of them occupied by followers of Cheng Ching.[124] Christian missions shared in the destruction. The Jesuit Adrien Greslon noted that all the churches along the Fukien coast were destroyed and the little communities of Christians were dispersed by the imperial edict removing the coastal population.[125]

From the accounts of removal in the five coastal provinces, some facts become clear. Removal was undertaken in a zone of land that usually stretched thirty *li* (approximately ten miles) back from the coast.[126] This depopulated strip was marked off in one way or another and was heavily guarded—guarded both against rebel incursions along the coast and against refugees trying to return to their homes. The boundary markers would be either a deep ditch, a wooden stockade, earthen mounds set at regular intervals, or any combination of these.[127] The penalty for crossing back over the boundary was severe punishment or death. Father Navarrete related that "when the time assigned [for removal] was elapsed, they barbarously butchered all that had not obeyed."[128]

In some areas the boundary marker was also used for defense. In these cases it was constructed closer to the sea, and sentinels were stationed along it. The more usual defense installations were forts erected three miles apart and well garrisoned, with lookout towers and earthen mounds for purposes of watch. Watch fires and signal calls were instituted as security aids. Specific measures, such as blocking a harbor with wooden piles, were adopted to meet local exigencies.[129] The coastal areas were frequently inspected by imperial commissioners, who with local officials would take steps to increase or decrease the coastal defenses and to remove or return the coastal populations in accordance with the Manchus' success or failure against the rebels.[130]

There is a great deal of uncertainty as to the types of cities affected by the removal policy. Most Western accounts say the Manchus indiscriminately ordered all population centers evacuated: Diaz referred to "many thousands of towns and cities"; Pauthier and Du Halde listed all cities, towns, bourgs, villages, and fortresses; an anonymous Spanish account of 1663 included even cities of 100,000 and 200,000.[131] Navarrete, however, said that the emperor sent a command down to the authorities of the coastal provinces to "destroy all the open towns and houses that were near the sea." Li Chih-fang, a censor and later to become governor-general of Chekiang, stated in a memorial protesting the removal policy that "since the army, instead of guarding the seacoast, removes the people to the interior, the rebels can march to the interior to the very walls of the cities." Other accounts spoke of removing people from "the fields and huts" or of shifting those who lived "beyond the limit of government garrisons."[132] These latter accounts would indicate that removal did not touch large cities or walled cities but only small farming and fishing villages and individual living units in the countryside. We know, of course, that the population of whole islands, such as Amoy, Quemoy, and Chusan, were removed at one time. Generally, however, it appears that only those areas that were difficult to protect against the rebels' coastal raids were evacuated.

Since a primary reason for developing the maritime laws—both the removal policy and the trading ban—was to remove potential sources of supply from Cheng Ch'eng-kung and his followers, those areas that were evacuated were also destroyed. Homes and even whole towns were razed; the churches and houses of the Christian missions were included in the devastation. Land lay fallow and the fields became wasteland—resembling the effects of a "scorched earth" program.

The removed populace were to receive allotments of land in the interior for supporting themselves in their new environment. Some officials appropriated uncultivated land for use by the refugees and tried in various ways to help settle them. Others apparently did nothing or shifted the burden of responsibility to their subordinates. This prompted the court to remind provincial officials that they must immediately provide arable land and dwelling places for the people to insure their livelihood.[133] The plight of the refugees was eased in other ways: through the remission of taxes, and through officially approved fishing and fuel-gathering expeditions along the coast.[134]

Transfer of Banner Lands

The regency itself was torn by internal dissension throughout its tenure. The two chief antagonists were Suksaha and Oboi. The senior member, Soni, was in bad health and had no stomach for the in-fighting that constantly animated Suksaha and Oboi. Ebilun, for his part, seemed willing to follow the lead of Oboi, who like himself was a member of the bordered yellow banner. Suksaha did not fare well in any comparison with the other regents as to service or rank. Soni had served four rulers—Nurhaci, Abahai, Shun-chih, and now K'ang-hsi, came from a distinguished family, and was a first class earl. Ebilun and Oboi both held the rank of duke (the highest of the nine hereditary ranks). Oboi besides had a long and distinguished military record, while Ebilun's father, Eidu, was one of Nurhaci's most trusted officers. Suksaha at the time of his selection as a regent was only a second class viscount, one rank below the earldom held by Soni. Nor was he from an illustrious family. When it came to a showdown, Suksaha was no match for Oboi.

The issue was joined in 1666 over a matter of great concern to the ruling Manchus—the allocation of banner lands. When land around the capital had been allocated to Manchu nobility, officials, and bannermen in 1644, Dorgon as regent was able to claim for his own banner, the plain white, some of the best land in the extreme northeastern part of Chihli—land that by Manchu tradition of directional precedence should have been reserved for the imperial banners (at that time, the bordered yellow and the plain yellow).[135]

Oboi, of the bordered yellow banner, felt his position was strong enough in 1666 to rectify what many of his fellow bannermen must have considered an old injustice. He began a drive to exchange lands of the bordered yellow and plain white banners in a manner advantageous to the former. Suksaha, of the plain white banner, naturally opposed the move.

A renewed prohibition on the enclosure of land for banner use was decreed in 1664, and even the exchange of banner lands was forbidden except in special circumstances. Flooding was not one of them, but it was on this pretext that Oboi pressed for the exchange of land. On the report of Prince Giyesu that more than 154,000 *shang* (an old Manchu measurement equal to six *mou* and hence about one acre)[136] of banner land had been damaged by flooding and that there was probably even more, as yet unreported, Oboi issued an edict that sent a team of investigators to the affected areas to examine the conditions there.[137]

The commission, consisting of all the banner *tu-t'ung* (Manchu, Mongol, and Chinese), both presidents of the Board of Revenue and its Manchu vice-president, both presidents of the Censorate and its Manchu vice-president, and a junior metropolitan censor from each of the six sections of the Office of Scrutiny, was appointed on 24 February 1666. Reporting its findings exactly one month later to the day, the commission concluded that the bordered yellow banner's land had suffered the greatest damage from flooding. This, of course, is what Oboi wanted to hear, and the vagueness of the commission's report—there were no acreage figures given—leads one to believe that it had no foundation in fact. With the report in hand, Oboi ordered land in Yung-p'ing prefecture, where Dorgon's plain white banner had been located, turned over to the bordered yellow banner. As to the flooded land of the other banners, Oboi was not interested; he let the Board of Revenue ponder that problem.[138]

Once again, as in previous directives issued under the regents, this action was justified in terms of "respecting the practices of our ancestors, T'ai-tsu [Nurhaci] and T'ai-tsung [Abahai]." The more one considers the regency and its policies, the clearer it becomes how useful and important it was to the regents to have Shun-chih's will altered. It provided the regents limitless sanction and authority to halt the sinicization process and restore ancient practices.

The Board of Revenue came up with two alternative plans for

carrying out Oboi's directive. Each envisioned some enclosure of private land in addition to exchanging land of the two banners. Taking parts of each plan, the regents—in reality, Oboi—transferred from the plain white banner to the bordered yellow banner land in an area north of a line between T'ung-chou (39°54′ by 116°41′) and Feng-jun (39°53′ by 118°05′).[139] Adding this territory to the newly enclosed land Oboi's banner received to the northeast of Peking and the land it was promised in Yung-p'ing prefecture, the bordered yellow banner lands would now be located in a broad zone of northern Chihli—from Huai-jou (40°19′ by 116°39′) and Shun-i (40°10′ by 116°40′) districts in Shuntien prefecture in the west to Yung-p'ing prefecture in the east. This would give the bordered yellow banner the honored northern position among banners in reference to the allocation of banner land. Thus Oboi would settle his banner's score with the plain white banner and undo the work of Dorgon at the outset of the dynasty in favor of the latter banner.

Oboi met the first opposition to his plan within the Board of Revenue, whose acting Manchu president, Sunahai, was a member of the plain white banner. Sunahai, who was concurrently a grand secretary, argued that the original land allotments were made twenty years ago and any rearrangement now only would cause untold suffering for bannermen and commoners alike.[140] Not only did Sunahai fail to quash Oboi's proposal when it was first advanced in February, but in the fall of 1666, after the harvest was in, he was chosen, along with the governor-general and governor of Chihli, to supervise the surveying necessary to complete the transfer. No doubt Oboi was setting a trap for Sunahai, hoping that the grand secretary would continue his opposition and thus be forced into a position of disobeying an imperial order.

Sunahai did continue to oppose the shift, and he received strong support from Chu Ch'ang-tso, the governor-general, and Wang Teng-lien, the governor. Both of them submitted memorials to protest the contemplated rearrangement of banner lands and to urge that it be stopped immediately. Chu Ch'ang-tso reported that he had supervised the surveying of land for about a month already, and in all that time he heard a great deal of grumbling from men of the bordered yellow banner supposedly benefiting from the shift. Some were unhappy over leaving their old homes, and others complained that their new land was not as rich as what they formerly had. Some had profited in the exchange—getting better land than they had—and these bannermen, Chu noted, quite naturally were keeping quiet. In general, though, this shift was not necessary for the welfare of the bannermen. Considering also that some commoners were losing land through enclosure, then clearly, Chu felt, the exchange of banner lands was not worth the trouble it created. He realized the risk he was taking in opposing Oboi's project, but he felt duty-bound to report the hardships it was causing and to request an edict stopping it.

The governor sent in a separate memorial on his experiences. Wang Teng-lien encountered similar complaints to those Chu had received from both bannermen and commoners. In addition, he warned that trouble lay ahead. With everyone unhappy over the exchange of land and enclosure of land, many fields were not being prepared or sown, so that next year's harvest would be skimpy. Sunahai added his voice to Chu's and Wang's requests that the project be abandoned.[141]

Oboi, however, was determined to proceed at all costs. He would brook no opposition on this matter. On 15 December 1666, Sunahai, Chu Ch'ang-tso, Wang Teng-lien, and some banner officials were arrested and charged with obstructing the imperial will, failing to perform their duties, and returning to the capital without notice and without completing the transfer of banner lands. The boards of War and of Civil Appointments made the first judgment in the case. On 8 January 1667 they recommended that Sunahai, Chu, and Wang should all be cashiered and turned over to the Board of Punishment for sentencing, while other imperial and banner officials should be degraded or fined. The regents accepted their findings, and the case was proceeding as Oboi had hoped. A week later, the Board of Punishment rendered its verdict. They could find no law covering the crimes attributed to the trio, but they recommended that each be flogged a hundred times and have their possessions confiscated.[142]

K'ang-hsi stepped into the case at this point. He was still only thirteen years old, but he was aware of the enmity between Oboi and prominent officials of the plain white banner, such as Suksaha and Sunahai. K'ang-hsi decided to call in his regents and question them on this matter. Oboi, Soni, and Ebilun all insisted that Sunahai, Chu Ch'ang-tso, and Wang Teng-lien had committed grave offenses and should be executed, not just flogged. Only Suksaha dissented, but K'ang-hsi refused to grant the death sentence. Oboi then took matters into his own hands: he issued an edict that ordered the execution of the three men by strangulation.[143]

Oboi also appointed Pa-ko, Manchu vice-president of the Board of Revenue, to complete the re-allocation of banner lands. He reported back on 23 January on the final disposition of bannermen and banner lands involved in the exchange. A total of 40,600 bordered yellow bannermen were to be relocated on 203,000 *shang* of land—some of it belonging formerly to the plain white banner and some of it being enclosed commoner land. The 22,361 plain white bannermen made homeless in this move were to be settled on 111,805 *shang* of land.[144] A little more than a month later, on 4 March, the Board of Revenue declared that the exchange of banner lands was completed. Then, almost as an afterthought, the board recommended that no further exchange of banner lands be allowed in the future.[145] In accepting this recommendation, Oboi made his intentions clear: the recent exchange of land was not executed for the benefit of the bannermen, but was a naked display of his power. Now that he had carried the day—now that his banner (the bordered yellow) had regained its honored position—further rearrangement was forbidden.

Nor did Oboi's vengeance stop with the execution of the three high officials who actively opposed him. He began a campaign to discredit Dorgon and plain white bannermen, who were his archenemies in the affair just concluded. Ingguldai, a fellow clansman (Tatari) and fellow bannerman (plain white) of Sunahai, was posthumously disgraced in January 1667 for his role in helping Dorgon usurp the bordered yellow banner land for the white banner. Although Ingguldai had long since died (1648), Oboi saw him as an inspiration for Sunahai—Oboi called the latter "a second Ingguldai of the plain white banner." Ingguldai was stripped of his ranks and titles, and his heirs lost the Mongol and Chinese banner slaves previously attached to the family.[146]

At about this time (January 1667), Bahana, one of the Manchu grand secretaries, died, and Oboi refused to grant him a posthumous title or any other honor despite his long career of service to the dynasty. The cause of Oboi's displeasure was an incident of 1651 when Bahana, as lieutenant-general (*tu-t'ung*) of the plain white banner and president of the Board of Revenue, was guilty of favoring his banner at the expense of the bordered yellow banner in distributing supplies.[147] A short while later, Lambu was elevated to *chün-wang* (a prince of blood of the second degree).[148] There were two facts of interest behind this move. One was that Lambu's father, Nikan, was instrumental in the disgrace of Dorgon in 1651. The other was that Lambu's wife was a granddaughter of Oboi. So in one stroke Oboi rewarded a relative and took another swipe at Dorgon.

Oboi's biggest victim was Suksaha, the one regent who opposed him throughout the regency and over the exchange of banner lands. Oboi did not move against Suksaha during the controversy itself, which ran a full year from February 1666 to March 1667, but he did so in the fall of 1667. By then Oboi was able to strengthen the case against his fellow regent with a new incident. Soni had just died,[149] and Oboi was becoming increasingly arrogant; so Suksaha suspected that he might be the next target. Since K'ang-hsi's personal rule had already begun (25 August 1667), Suksaha at the end of August sought to escape the coming storm by relinquishing his governmental responsibilities. Claiming the infirmities of old age, he "prayed that the emperor would send him to guard Shun-chih's tomb so as to prolong his life and repay the emperor's trust." Oboi immediately countered with an edict in which the emperor expressed bewilderment at Suksaha's request and demanded to know "what here at court so threatens your life that guarding the imperial mausoleum would not?"[150] In this way Oboi intimated that Suksaha by his request to retire was expressing disapproval of K'ang-hsi's assumption of personal rule.

Then, in quick succession, Suksaha was arrested (2 September), charged with twenty-four "grave crimes" (4 September), and executed—all over the protests of the emperor.[151] It may be that K'ang-hsi's protests were feigned and that he in fact welcomed the execution of Suksaha because of his apparent unwillingness to relinquish the reigns of government to the young emperor. Still, it appears that Oboi initiated and pursued this case against Suksaha beyond K'ang-hsi's intentions. None of the twenty-four charges spoke directly of Suksaha's opposition to the exchange of banner land; they dwelt instead on his generally uncooperative behavior throughout the regency. But Oboi certainly must have considered Suksaha's elimination as the final step—the crowning achievement—in his campaign against the plain white banner, its members, and its land.

Originally, Suksaha was sentenced to die in the cruelest way possible—a lingering death by mutilation (*ling-ch'ih*)—but in the end, perhaps because of K'ang-hsi's opposition, death by strangulation was prescribed. Numerous relatives and supporters of Suksaha fell with him. Eight were executed, over forty were dismissed from office and some of these were reduced to the status of soldiers, and remaining members of his household became banner slaves.

Oboi was now at the peak of his power, and although K'ang-hsi had reached his majority (fourteen *sui*) and was technically ruling in his own right, Oboi continued to dominate government and dictate policy. Two of the regents, Soni and Suksaha, were gone, and the remaining regent, Ebilun, had always been Oboi's supporter and posed no threat. Forces of opposition were gathering—the most threatening being the person of the emperor himself. We have just seen that K'ang-hsi was growing increasingly disenchanted with the policies and decisions forced on him by Oboi, and the young ruler could not be browbeaten forever. But the time of K'ang-hsi's personal rule was still two years in the future; his apprenticeship had still not run its course.

Three

K'ANG-HSI'S APPRENTICESHIP

WHILE THE REGENTS STEERED THE SHIP OF STATE FOR EIGHT YEARS OF his reign, K'ang-hsi himself remained very much in the background, unseen behind the mask of his position for a number of years. Decisions were made and policies adopted in his name, but surely without his knowledge or interest. He first seems to have emerged as an individual when he was twelve—in the Oboi-Suksaha struggle just described. But within three years K'ang-hsi's personality began to dominate the court as he stepped into and decided an important court issue and then moved boldly to destroy the regency and rule in his own right. From this initial glimpse of an emperor in the making, we can begin to see the outlines of a personal style of rule that would dominate Chinese politics for the next half-century.

The Young Prince and Ruler

K'ang-hsi, third son of Shun-chih, was born on 4 May 1654.[1] Although he was to become the fourth emperor of a dynasty founded by Manchus, K'ang-hsi was less than half-Manchu ethnically. Abahai, his paternal grandfather, had some Mongol blood in his veins, because his mother (Nurhaci's empress Hsiao-tz'u) was the daughter of a Mongol chieftain.[2] K'ang-hsi's paternal grandmother, the empress Hsiao-chuang, was a Mongol princess whose father was descended from Genghis Khan's brother.[3] Thus K'ang-hsi's father was ethnically more Mongol than Manchu. K'ang-hsi's mother, the empress Hsiao-k'ang, was half-Manchu and half-

Chinese. Her father, T'ung T'u-lai, grew up in the service of the Manchus, but his ancestors had long lived in Liaotung and served the Ming dynasty.[4] Nothing is known about Hsiao-k'ang's mother except that she was from the Manchu Gioro clan.[5] If all these strains are reduced to fractions, then K'ang-hsi was one-fourth Chinese (from T'ung T'u-lai), one fourth Mongol (from Empress Hsiao-chuang), one-fourth Manchu (from T'ung's wife), and another fourth a mixture—probably in about equal portions—of Manchu and Mongol (from Abahai). K'ang-hsi's ancestry shows that even early in the dynasty Manchu and Chinese blood was mixing—and in the highest places. Politically, however, the young K'ang-hsi could not be considered anything but a Manchu prince.

The young boy probably had as little experience of a happy, shared family life as any imperial prince.[6] His father, Shun-chih, soon lost interest in the boy's mother and probably in the boy himself, for the emperor had, by the time K'ang-hsi was two, found the great love of his life—the concubine née Donggo. This lady had entered the palace in 1656 at the age of eighteen and immediately became Shun-chih's favorite consort. He wanted to elevate her to the status of empress, but his mother, the dowager empress Hsiao-chuang, and officials opposed the move. Instead, she was designated an imperial consort of the first class (*huang-kuei-fei*). When she died in 1660, the emperor was so grief-stricken that he contemplated suicide and later priesthood, and he himself died within a few months but not without first giving his favorite the posthumous title of Empress Hsiao-hsien.[7]

There is one story—probably apocryphal—about a conversation between Shun-chih and K'ang-hsi. Once, when the latter was five, he and his two brothers visited their father in the palace. Shun-chih asked each of his sons to tell him what his ambition in life was. The youngest, Ch'ang-ning, was only two and could not answer. The eldest, Fu-ch'üan, said that he wanted to be a virtuous ruler. When it was K'ang-hsi's turn to reply, he carried the day by saying he only wanted to grow up and be like his illustrious father.[8] Shun-chih could not help but be immensely pleased with K'ang-hsi's response, but there is no reason to believe that afterward he had anything other than a very formal relationship with his son.

Maternal care was probably just as remote, because K'ang-hsi's mother was only fourteen at the time of his birth.[9] In any case, it was the custom to entrust princes to the care of wet nurses (*ju-mu*) and nurses (*pao-mu*), and K'ang-hsi even lived for a while with his nurses outside the palace in the inner city of the capital.[10] Only one of these nurses is known to us: the *pao-mu* Lady Sun, mother of Ts'ao Yin. Whoever the others were, K'ang-hsi's nurses, and particularly his wet nurse, must have left their imprint on his character and may even have influenced a political decision or two.[11] Their service did not go unrewarded: Lady Sun, her husband, and her son were all honored and rewarded by a grateful K'ang-hsi after he grew up.[12]

Next to his nurses, the prince's most constant companions were eunuchs. K'ang-hsi was born the year after eunuch resurgence reached a peak with the establishment of the Inner Thirteen Yamen. Everywhere the prince went, and in everything he did, palace eunuchs would be in attendance. We have some direct evidence of the young K'ang-hsi's relations with eunuchs—either as a prince or later as emperor—and much can be reconstructed with the help of a later emperor's (Hsüan-t'ung's) reminiscences of his boyhood.

First of all, the basic functions of life—eating and dressing and sleeping—were all accomplished with the aid of eunuchs. Perhaps eating was carried out with the greatest pomp and ceremony. Successive units of eunuch attendants placed strategically around the palace would cry out the imperial desire for food—a crude but effective communications system that would transmit an order to the kitchen in very short time. The food, always prepared and waiting to be delivered, was rushed in on serving tables, tasted by eunuchs first as a precaution, then laid out before the emperor and uncovered. Whether or not K'ang-hsi ate this food is another matter. Hsüan-t'ung (the last Ch'ing emperor) did not: he consumed a second spread prepared specially for him by his empress dowager. But the eunuch kitchens continued to turn out their products nonetheless.[13]

Bedtime for the young K'ang-hsi, as for all children, was probably a time for storytelling, and the eunuchs had no end of them. Ghost stories and stories about the palace and its former inhabitants served not only to entertain—and probably frighten—the prince but also to educate him. Stories, of course, were not confined to the bedtime hour; they probably filled many of the prince's waking hours. K'ang-hsi learned many of the details of late Ming history from eunuchs who had served in the Ming court.[14] Hsüan-t'ung also acknowledged the pedagogical role of eunuchs when he said that while they were his slaves they were also his earliest teachers. He called the chief eunuch his "first teacher in fact if not in name."[15]

When the prince was old enough to romp about and play, the eunuchs served as playmates. Eunuchs also accompanied the emperor on any tour, turning an innocent stroll in the garden into a solemn procession, but imperial playfulness could reduce the procession to chaos.[16]

K'ang-hsi as a child was stricken with the disease most dreaded by Manchus—the smallpox. In the early campaigns of conquest, only Manchu officers who had survived an attack of smallpox were sent on an expedition through Mongol territory, where the disease was thought to be prevalent.[17] Using the same logic, K'ang-hsi's survival of smallpox was given as one of the reasons—perhaps it was the chief reason—why Shun-chih named him heir apparent in his will. So, at the age of seven, K'ang-hsi became ruler of China—in name, not in fact. The real formulators of policy, as we have seen, were the four Manchu regents and, to a lesser extent, the grand empress dowager Hsiao-chuang. K'ang-hsi's own mother, Hsiao-k'ang, died at the age of twenty-three in 1663. She thus never had a chance to wield the considerable influence on policy that she might have possessed by virtue of her position as empress dowager. After her death, the grandmother undertook to raise K'ang-hsi, educate him, and assist him during crises that came up later in his career. While it is said that she never interfered in affairs of state, K'ang-hsi frequently consulted her on matters concerning the Imperial Household.[18]

Perhaps Hsiao-chuang's most important decision was the selection of K'ang-hsi's first empress, Hsiao-ch'eng. Since the latter was the granddaughter of Soni, the senior regent, this marriage had obvious political overtones. It planted the seeds of dissension in the regency and apparently prompted a jealous Oboi to launch his own plans to achieve power.[19] Hsiao-ch'eng and K'ang-hsi were married in 1665, when both were only eleven—she being exactly three months older than he.[20] Hsiao-ch'eng gave birth to two sons: one in 1669 who died in infancy, and the other in 1674. The latter birth was ill-starred: the mother died in childbirth, and the son (Yin-jeng) turned out later to be depraved and probably insane, causing him to lose his status as heir apparent and leading to an intense struggle for the throne among K'ang-hsi's other sons.[21] Neither of K'ang-hsi's other two empresses—one the daughter of the regent Ebilun, the other the daughter of T'ung Kuo-wei—gave birth to any children, but he had numerous offspring by concubines.[22]

More is known about K'ang-hsi's early education than about his other childhood activities. Court historians tell us that he began to read at four. Not only that, but he enjoyed it and would read through the night without tiring. His reading was purposeful: he sampled the dynastic histories, the Confucian classics, and works on government. In a manner that could well serve as a model for modern courses in speed reading, K'ang-hsi would scan ten columns at a glance and still retain its general meaning. The emperor himself repeated this story (or legend) about his early reading habits to one of his tutors, Kao Shih-ch'i, on the first Southern Tour in 1684. Kao had urged K'ang-hsi to stop reading into the night and even the morning hours because it might ruin his health, but the emperor assured him that since the age of four he had read tirelessly and with great enjoyment. After he had become emperor, he continued his studies and had committed to memory the Great Learning (*Ta-hsüeh*) and the Doctrine of the Mean (*Chung-yung*).[23]

Another Ch'ing ruler (Hsüan-t'ung) began his studies early, too, and with fellow students provided to bear the brunt of any criticism provoked by imperial mistakes.[24] Perhaps K'ang-hsi also began his schooling this way, for it is known that he had a number of companions with him as he grew up outside the palace. There is a hint—but it is only a hint—that Ts'ao Yin, son of one of K'ang-hsi's nurses, may have been one of these childhood companions.[25] It is likely that K'ang-hsi also studied with his elder brother: this was the case with the Ch'ien-lung and Hsüan-t'ung emperors.[26]

It is possible that K'ang-hsi at an early age displayed the fondness for learning for which he became famous, but his formal education in the hands of tutors did not begin until after he had arrested Oboi and had begun to rule in his own right. From the very beginning of K'ang-hsi's accession to the throne in 1661 and right up to the eve of Oboi's fall in 1669, censors continually urged that officials be appointed to tutor the emperor in the classics and histories.[27] The response to all of these requests except the last was the same: "It has been noted" (*pao-wen*). Only the last memorialist got a promise of action. His memorial, submitted on 18 May 1669, was praised by K'ang-hsi, who asked the Board of Rites to discuss the matter. Only four days earlier the emperor had ceremoniously visited the

Imperial Academy to encourage students and teachers there to pursue their studies diligently.[28]

K'ang-hsi's words and actions in May 1669 clearly indicated his intention to undertake his studies soon, but a crisis of great moment intervened and set back the beginning of his formal tutoring until 1670. I am referring, of course, to the arrest of Oboi and the great purge of government that followed. K'ang-hsi had his hands full with politics and had no time for his lessons. The breaking of Oboi was actually the emperor's second baptism under fire: before that came the calendar controversy of 1668–69, in which he had his first brush with Western learning and his first taste of personal decision making.

The Calendar Controversy

From the outset, the Ch'ing dynasty based its annual calendar on Western astronomical calculations performed by Jesuits in Peking. The leading missionary in China was the German Jesuit, Adam Schall. He had worked in the Calendrical Bureau under the last Ming emperor, but he served the new rulers equally well.[29] After impressing Dorgon with the accuracy of Western methods in precisely plotting the course of an eclipse of the sun, Schall, on 23 December 1644, was given authority to supervise the work of the Imperial Board of Astronomy (*ch'in-t'ien-chien*). He was later named director of the board (*chien-cheng*), which carried a ranking of 5A, and was repeatedly honored by Shun-chih and by the regents of K'ang-hsi.[30]

As might be expected, Muslim and Chinese functionaries in the board who saw their position weaken as Schall's star rose fought against the Jesuits and their methods. One of the Muslim officials, Wu Ming-hsüan, enlisted the services of an eccentric, xenophobic commoner from Kiangnan, Yang Kuang-hsien.[31] The latter was in the habit of directly petitioning the throne (*k'ou-hun*)[32] on what he considered were dangers to the nation. From about 1659 on, Yang mounted a sustained attack, in writings and memorials to the throne, against Schall, his religion, and his calendrical calculations. By 1664 his campaign had succeeded. In mid-September he presented to the Board of Rites all the evidence he had collected on the treasonous activities of Schall and his associates—both Western and Chinese—and asked the board to warn the regents and request action.

Yang's evidence, as given in his essay *Chai-miu lun*, consisted of a number of diverse themes. Foremost among Schall's crimes was his propagation of a heretical religion that was seducing the people. Worse still, the Jesuits had churches ("thirty in all") and followers ("over a million") scattered throughout the land and in the capital which they utilized as a vast spy network. They must be preparing rebellion, thought Yang.[33] The charge of rebellion—groundless and absurd as it might appear—would certainly have touched a raw nerve in the regents. The provinces had not been subdued too long ago, and remnants of Ming loyalist forces still roamed the seas along the southeastern coast. The regents might be skeptical of Yang's insinuations, but they could not afford to ignore them.

Another piece of evidence that Yang interpreted as a Jesuit attempt to undermine imperial authority was the phrase *i hsi-yang hsin-fa* written on the cover of the calendars they drew up. It only meant that the calendar in question had been calculated according to the new methods introduced by the missionaries, but Yang read into the phrase a deeper, seditious meaning.[34] A calendar was one of the symbols of imperial authority and a mainstay of the Confucian world order; tributaries had to accept and use the current Chinese calendar as a sign of submission to Chinese suzerainty.[35] For the Manchus, concerned also about their legitimacy in Chinese eyes, it was doubly important to establish a correct, unimpeachable calendar. So any suggestion that threw into doubt the recognized superiority of the Chinese calendar—even one concerning merely the method of calculation and not the calendar itself or its ideological function—could be interpreted as treasonous. On top of this, the calendar Schall presented for the K'ang-hsi period only contained two hundred years. This was an indiscretion that outraged Chinese sensibilities about infinite reigns.[36]

The final concern of Yang Kuang-hsien was to point out the heretical pamphlet written by a Chinese convert at the direction of Father Schall. This work, entitled *T'ien-hsüeh chuan-kai*, traced the origin of the Christian Church in China back to the time of Fu-hsi, a Chinese culture hero whom that author identified as a leader of one of the lost tribes of Israel. This would make Chinese descendants of Hebrews—surely an odious idea to the Chinese—and reduce the Chinese classics to mere commentaries on the heretical religion, a God-worshiping religion (*T'ien-hsüeh*) that had died out in the Chou period but which was being revived by the Jesuit missionaries.[37]

Yang Kuang-hsien submitted a second treatise to the Board of Rites, this one entitled *Hsüan-tse i.* It accused the Jesuits, and Schall in particular, of a serious misapplication of *feng-shui.* Schall in 1658 had used the wrong set of geomantic principles, it alleged, to select (*hsüan-tse*) the date and site for the burial of Prince Jung, the infant son of Shun-chih's favorite consort. Schall's purpose in making inauspicious selections, according to Yang, was to cast spells upon the young prince's parents. Hsiao-hsien's death in September 1660, followed by Shun-chih's death five months later, seemed evidence enough to Yang.[38]

The government placed Yang under surveillance while it pondered a course of action. On 24 September 1664, the Board of Rites and the Board of Civil Appointments were ordered to try Schall on the charges brought by Yang.[39] From the boards, the case was passed on to the Deliberative Council, whose members carefully questioned both Schall and Yang and investigated the charges one by one. The councillors admitted that astronomy was not their forte and that they found it hard to determine which side was correctly calculating the calendar. But they knew one thing: some of Schall's methods varied from China's traditional procedures. They also knew that Schall's two-hundred-year calendar and his geomantic selections were acts of grave impropriety. Standing on tradition and superstition, the Deliberative Council on 30 April 1665 handed down sentences of death by dismemberment for Schall and seven associates in the Board of Astronomy, and decapitation for five of their relatives (including Schall's adopted son, P'an Chin-hsiao).

The harsh sentences did not fit in with the recently announced general amnesty, which followed the 16 April earthquake in Peking. In reviewing the sentences, the regents (on behalf of K'ang-hsi) felt that Schall deserved a lesser punishment because of his old age—he was then seventy-four—and his long service to the dynasty. Two of his Chinese associates were also singled out for special consideration because of their previous success in choosing imperial mausoleum sites. The Deliberative Council dutifully reconsidered their recommendations and on 17 May reduced the sentences of Schall, the two Chinese geomancers, and Schall's adopted son to flogging and exile. The death sentences of the other nine stood. The edict finally disposing of the case was even more lenient: five of the seven board officials were to be decapitated, but everyone else was pardoned. Schall and the others were not sent into exile.[40]

The Jesuits, however, did not get through this ordeal without setbacks. All the missionaries were rounded up and sent to Macao—banished from the empire. Only the four Jesuits then in Peking—Schall, Ferdinand Verbiest, Louis Buglio, and Gabriel de Magalhaens—were exempted.[41] Schall died not long after and was succeeded by Verbiest as head of the Peking mission and chief expert on astronomy. But it would be several years before his knowledge was pressed into service by the court, because a second consequence of the trial was the replacement of Jesuits and Western methods in the Board of Astronomy by Yang Kuang-hsien and traditional methods.

Yang's knowledge of astronomy was minimal, and he tried to be relieved of his job as director of the board, but his pleas were ignored. What little he knew about calendars and astronomy he had learned from Wu Ming-hsüan, whom he brought into the board as his assistant. Neither of them was confident of his ability and sent up several memorials asking for help.[42] Yang and Wu blundered along this way until 1668, when K'ang-hsi decided to carry out his own investigation of the conflicting methods.

Personal rule by K'ang-hsi officially began on 25 August 1667. He was aged fourteen *sui* at this time, and, since Shun-chih had begun to rule at that age, it seemed proper to everyone at court that K'ang-hsi should follow his father's precedent. Still, K'ang-hsi was not running the government or making decisions. He disapproved of the roughshod way Oboi had run over opposition to his project to transfer banner lands, but he was powerless to stop the regent at the time. It is easy to imagine that the young emperor nursed his wounds and silently prepared himself for a struggle with Oboi. Perhaps he saw in the calendar controversy an opportunity to try his hand at personal decision making, a chance to experience the dangers of court politics, a time to test the winds of change.

K'ang-hsi stepped into the calendar controversy on 5 October 1668. Wu Ming-hsüan asked the Board of Rites to seek expert opinion on the calendars which he and other astronomers had constructed because there were discrepancies among them. The board decided that Wu's calendar was the most accurate and should be put into use in K'ang-hsi's ninth year (1670); the calendar for the coming year had already been issued and need not be recalled. K'ang-hsi was not satisfied with the casual and slipshod handling of the matter and ordered Wu to prepare a calendar for his eighth year (1669), which he wanted to examine personally.[43] After pursuing it and growing more and more suspicious of the men in charge of the Board of Astronomy,[44] he sought the opinion of Father Verbiest.

The Flemish Jesuit received a copy of Wu Ming-hsüan's calendar for K'ang-hsi's eighth year on 29 December 1668 (it was only the twenty-sixth day of the eleventh month by the lunar calendar). He studied it carefully for one month and found a number of errors in it. For instance, he thought an intercalary month should not be added after the twelfth month. Wu's calendar also contained two vernal equinoxes (*ch'un-fen*) and two autumnal equinoxes (*ch'iu-fen*) and numerous other errors. Verbiest also pointed out that Wu had not taken into consideration the varying time zones in the empire but had calculated everything on the basis of Peking alone. Then, to clinch his case with a little appeal to national pride, he asked how the emperor, whose virtue and power had spread far and wide to attract scores of nations as tributaries and users of the Chinese calendar, could tolerate an inaccurate one.[45]

Verbiest's memorandum was submitted to K'ang-hsi on 27 January 1669. The latter promptly called for a joint conference of the Deliberative Council with other high level officials to weigh the charges. They, in turn, sought the appointment of a blue-ribbon committee to conduct a public verification of the two antagonists—Verbiest and Yang Kuang-hsien—and their methods—Western and traditional. K'ang-hsi named twenty men, headed by Grand Secretary Tuhai, to serve on the committee.[46]

The committee, in conjunction with the director of the Board of Astronomy, Mahu, checked on the accuracy of each side's calendar for the eighth year in predicting two of the solar periods that had just passed, *li-ch'un* ("the arrival of spring") and *yü-shui* ("the day of the rains"), and in calculating the phases of Jupiter and Mars in that period. In all instances, Verbiest's prediction had been substantiated by the actual occurrences, whereas Wu Ming-hsüan's calculations were incorrect. Yang, Wu, and the traditional methods were discredited; Schall, Verbiest, and Western methods were vindicated. The committee reported the results of their investigation on 26 February and concluded that calendar making should again be entrusted to the Jesuits.

That might have ended the controversy, but apparently K'ang-hsi was dissatisfied and wanted to get to the bottom of this matter. Why, he demanded to know, had the Deliberative Council decided four years earlier that Schall's methods were inaccurate and was now declaring them to be accurate? Had the committee not thought to question Yang, Wu, Verbiest, and officials of the Board of Astronomy about this reversal, or were they hiding something? K'ang-hsi put them to work again.[47]

The committee reported back on 8 March with the same decision as before but spelled out in greater detail. In addition, they recommended punishment for Yang and Wu, thinking perhaps that this was what K'ang-hsi was hinting at in his response to their first report. I think he was hinting at something more—something that might implicate Oboi and weaken his grip on government, but he did not get it. So, for the time being, K'ang-hsi settled for the cashiering of Yang Kuang-hsien and Wu Ming-hsüan.[48] On 17 April Verbiest was named vice-director (*chien-fu*) of the Board of Astronomy, and calendars were to be constructed by Western methods once again. The intercalary month after K'ang-hsi 8/12 was dropped and inserted instead after K'ang-hsi 9/2, as Verbiest had suggested. In this way, "the day of the rains" would come in the first month of the lunar calendar as it always had. On one matter, though, there would be no return to earlier practice: the phrase *i hsi-yang hsin-fa* would not be printed on the face of calendars.[49]

The calendar controversy of 1668–69 has given us the first glimpse of K'ang-hsi as a ruler. The trait for which he became justly famous—his insistence on thoroughness combined with a personal attention to detail—was exhibited here for the first time and very clearly. We get a preview, so to speak, of his style of decision making in such later crises as the revolt of the three feudatories or the famous examination hall case of 1711.[50] It seems he did not get the exact results he wanted from the calendar controversy, if we can ascribe to him a desire to link Oboi to the case; but it was, after all, his first attempt at government, and he was only fifteen years old.

Oboi was eventually implicated but only after K'ang-hsi had found other means to destroy him. Still, a review of the case was useful to the Jesuits if not to K'ang-hsi. On 5 September 1669, Father Verbiest charged that Yang Kuang-hsien had had the favor of Oboi in 1664–65 and had put it to good advantage to slander Schall and Christianity and eliminate his rivals in the Board of Astronomy. Then Yang had blundered along as director of the board, constantly showing his ignorance of astronomy. The Deliberative Council used these charges to bring Yang to justice and exonerate his victims. For Yang, they recommended decapitation, but K'ang-hsi spared his life. Schall, who had died in 1666, recovered his honorific titles and ranks and was given an official burial. The confiscated land on which Schall had built a church (known as Nan-t'ang) was given back to the Jesuit fathers. The families of the five executed astronomers were recalled from exile, and all officials who had lost their ranks now had them restored (some posthumously). Christianity, though, remained proscribed, and the missionaries were still confined to Canton and Macao. Only Verbiest and two other Jesuits then in Peking were free of these restrictions.[51] Thereafter, and on into the nineteenth century, Jesuits remained in charge of the Board of Astronomy.[52]

From this episode, K'ang-hsi developed a strong admiration for the Jesuits, particularly Verbiest, and the new techniques of Western science in which they were skilled. His interest in Western learning grew over the years and led to increasingly intimate relations with Western missionaries. I will return to discuss this fully later.

The Assumption of Personal Rule

Oboi and his party effectively stifled opposition for about seven years. It may be recalled that Sunahai, Suksaha, and others paid with their lives for opposing Oboi over the transfer of banner lands. But they were not the only victims. Much earlier, in 1664, Fiyanggu and his son Wehe were executed for some real or imagined slight to Oboi in the imperial presence.[53] When Ilibu, lieutenant-general of the Mongol plain white banner, crossed him, Oboi had him barred from court deliberations.[54] Chinese officials, such as Grand Secretary Li Wei, discovered that the only way to avoid trouble was to keep silent at court and not openly oppose Oboi, regardless of one's true feelings.[55]

Those who loyally supported Oboi were rewarded. Marsai, of the same banner as Oboi, was raised to the position of president of the Board of Revenue in 1668 even though another Manchu had already been appointed. To get around this difficulty, Oboi claimed that a precedent had been set in earlier reigns to have two Manchu presidents of the board simultaneously. Then, when Marsai died in 1669, Oboi granted him a posthumous honorific without imperial approval.[56] At the height of its power, the Oboi faction had placed thirty-nine men in high civil and military positions, including grand secretary Bambursan, a grandson of Nurhaci; Manchu board presidents A-ssu-ha, Chi-shih, and Ko-ch'u-ha; Manchu board vice-presidents Taibitu, Mai-yin-ta, and Loto; governor-general Molo; and governors Becingge and Ata.[57]

Once K'ang-hsi's personal rule began, a few officials dared to oppose Oboi. A censor in 1666 urged that K'ang-hsi take up the reins of government the following year when he would be fourteen *sui*, as this would follow the precedent set by Shun-chih.[58] No action was taken in response to this memorial, and K'ang-hsi reached fourteen *sui* (on New Year's day 1667) without making any preparations to limit the authority of the regents or to abolish the regency altogether. In the third month of his sixth year, the senior regent, Soni, again requested the assumption of personal rule by K'ang-hsi, and again nothing came of it. In fact, it was K'ang-hsi's intention, or so it was recorded, to wait several more years until he felt competent enough to handle the exacting job of being emperor. In this decision he was supported by his grandmother, the grand empress dowager Hsiao-chuang. But the regents—deftly balancing ideology and politics—insisted that K'ang-hsi at least formally take over while they continued to assist him. Thus the regents could honor the precedent of Shun-chih without loosening their grip on power. This plan proved satisfactory to the grand empress dowager, who set the Board of Rites to work on selecting an auspicious day for the ceremony. The twenty-fifth of August was chosen and on that day K'ang-hsi announced his assumption of rule and repaired to the Ch'ien-ch'ing palace to attend to government. Thereafter it became his regular practice.[59]

For their past and continuing assistance, K'ang-hsi bestowed honors upon the regents. Soni, being the senior member, was the first to be honored. In 1667 the emperor made him a first class duke and allowed him also to keep his earldom, with both titles hereditary.[60] Shortly after Soni's death (August 1667), K'ang-hsi announced his intention to reward the remaining three regents in a similar fashion, but by the time ranks were actually bestowed, Suksaha had been executed. Oboi and Ebilun each was given a first class ducal title, and their former titles (each already was a duke, Ebilun first class and Oboi second class) were passed on to their sons.[61]

Though policy was still dictated by Oboi and the other regents, somehow K'ang-hsi's assumption of rule emboldened critics of the Manchu regency. Perhaps now the emperor was more available and he could be appealed to. At first the expression of opposition to Oboi remained in a low key and dealt with small matters. Once Mishan, a minister of the Imperial Household, denied Oboi temporary use of imperial equipment. On another occasion, Feng P'u as president of the Censorate reported to K'ang-hsi an attempt by Oboi to alter the wording of an endorsement to a memorial after it had been issued. Feng was commended on his sense of propriety and Oboi received a stern rebuke from the emperor.[62]

The first man to broaden the range of criticism and launch a general attack on Oboi and the regency was Hsiung Tz'u-li. Hsiung (1635–1709) was a young Hupei provincial whose fame was made with these daring attacks on Oboi in 1667 and 1668. He spoke out from a position of no particular consequence or rank, being only an assistant reader (rank 6A) in the Three Inner Courts at the time. He had received his *chin-shih* a decade earlier, in the metropolitan examination of 1658, and was appointed a corrector in the Hanlin Academy. In 1663 he was transferred to the Imperial Academy, where he served as a tutor (*ssu-yeh*) until taking up his assistant readership post in 1665.[63]

Hsiung first came to notice in July 1667, at a time when the regents and the grand empress dowager were still debating what course to take with regard to the young emperor's assumption of rule. Hsiung submitted a long (1,636 characters) memorial in response to imperial concern over the shortcomings of government and the sufferings of the people. He offered recommendations for improvement in four areas, prefacing and concluding his recommendations with a general description of the essential prerequisites of reform.[64]

Hsiung's prologue presented a view of reform often expressed by Chinese memorialists: reform spreads through the body politic in the same fashion as increasingly larger concentric circles form in water around an impact point. Here is the argument: "Capital officials act as a model for provincial officials; the capital is a guide for the provinces. [Likewise], is not the court the source [of all guidance]?" Carry this one step further and you are back at the emperor as the pivot of the empire, but Hsiung left this step to his concluding remarks. Here, before getting into his specifics, he also noted that the masses were weighted down with two burdens: extra taxes and rapacious officials. To provide relief, Hsiung would look to the official rating and advancement procedures. Let local officials (*shou-ling*) be evaluated according to the happiness or suffering of the people they served, while provincial leaders (*tu-fu*) should be judged by the corruption or probity of their subordinates. This, he argued, was the way to eliminate corruption and alleviate suffering.

Hsiung first discussed the administrative codes of the empire. It was an urgent order of business for the present dynasty to compile its *hui-tien*, for otherwise men would continue to change the laws to suit their purposes. Such men can see only the visible gains of the moment and are blind to the pandora's box of abuses they create. A *hui-tien* based on ancient systems and present conditions would limit the manipulations of ambitious men and would also provide principles of action for the superior man and laws to follow for the inferior man.

Demoralization of officialdom was a second shortcoming. Hsiung recognized the essential Sino-Manchu duality in government and also the superior-inferior syndrome, but this was no excuse for Chinese officials to become no more than yes-men to their Manchu counterparts, nor any reason for inferiors to flatter superiors and superiors to protect inferiors. Every official—Manchu and Chinese, superior and inferior—must act on his own conscience and speak out against evil without any consideration or fear of the consequences.

Education and schools were also suffering, thought Hsiung, and needed imperial stimulation. Being a strict follower of the orthodox Ch'eng-Chu school of Neo-Confucianism, Hsiung was worried that students were not learning the true precepts of the classics but were being led astray by doctrines of the Lu-Wang school and other heterodox ideas.[65] The emperor must see to it that the curriculum throughout the nation's schools stick to the orthodox: the Six Classics, the Four Books, and the Ch'eng-Chu glosses. Hsiung also proposed a system of national scholarships whereby offspring of high officials and promising youngsters from every district would be sent to the Imperial Academy[66] for a three-year program of study.

The fourth and final aspect of national life that struck Hsiung as needing reform was the area of customs and rites. He railed against the current extravagance in dress and entertainment such that even lowly servants and courtesans had taken to wearing the garments and jewelry of gentlemen and ladies. He recommended that sumptuary laws be written and strictly enforced and that the emperor set an example by practicing frugality.

In concluding his memorial, Hsiung returned to the theme expressed in his opening remarks: that reform in the empire should begin at home. And he no longer hesitated, as he did in the introduction, to lay the burden of reform on the emperor. Now was the time, he urged, for K'ang-hsi while still young to cultivate virtue and broaden his knowledge. Tutors and attendants should be chosen with care to guide the young emperor in thought and deed. For his studies, Hsiung singled out the *Ta-hsüeh yen-i,* a Sung work on the precepts of the Great Learning,[67] as an excellent guide to the principles and practices of sagelike rule. In addition, the emperor should study the classics and histories.

There was no reaction to Hsiung's memorial—either favorable or unfavorable—but some of his comments must have put Oboi on guard. Ambitious men who manipulated institutions and laws for private ends; Manchus with sycophantic Chinese as yes-men; officials who protect members of their clique; inferiors who assume the airs of superiors—these types could easily be interpreted as caricatures of Oboi and his supporters. Charging the court with responsibility for the ills of the empire was still more pointed. But this time, for some reason, Oboi chose not to make an issue of it. The next time Hsiung spoke out he was not so fortunate.

Over a year passed between Hsiung's first and second memorials urging sweeping reform. In the interval he was promoted to a reader in the Three Inner Courts[68] and had a hand in stopping a proposed imperial tour into Manchuria. With regard to the latter, Hsiung suggested a postponement until a body of diarists were appointed to record what the emperor said and did,[69] while another memorialist urged the emperor to wait for better and more auspicious weather conditions: it was a cold October and there had been floods and earthquakes. K'ang-hsi accepted their objections and canceled the tour.[70] On the day the cancelation was announced (22 October 1668), Hsiung Tz'u-li submitted his second and equally outspoken memorial on the shortcomings of the present regime.[71]

This time Hsiung was unrelenting in his criticism of the emperor's failure to begin his studies and take over the direction of government. K'ang-hsi had the intellectual and leadership potentials of a true sage, and he had the people "standing on tiptoe with eyes wide open looking for the results of his virtuous rule." But so far, Hsiung noted sadly, the people's expectations had not been rewarded. He listed a few disappointments:

> You [the emperor] are up early and attend to government business with diligence, but administrative regulations are still unsettled; you have remitted taxes and relieved distress, but the people are still suffering; you have called for the repair of the Imperial Academy, but the bell of Pi-yung hall [where the classics are elucidated] has not yet pealed; you have been repeatedly urged to begin your studies, and yet no desk has been moved into the Wen-hua hall [for the emperor's use].

There were others, but they all boiled down to one indictment: performance had not matched promise. Hsiung's solution, as can be expected, rested on the education of the emperor. The same suggestions were presented here as before: appoint learned and upright men as tutors; design a daily program of reading and interpretation of the classics; and, above all, put into practice the principles he had learned.

As K'ang-hsi was reading this memorial, several phrases caught his eye: "The accumulated evils of the court have not yet been eliminated"; "There are hidden causes for concern about the nation's well-being"; "The expectations of the masses have not yet been satisfied." These phrases seemed pregnant with meaning to K'ang-hsi, and he demanded clarification. Hsiung's reply only heightened the emperor's anxiety. The memorialist took recent natural disasters as an expression of heaven's displeasure with the affairs of men, and it was to this belief that his words about "hidden causes for concern" alluded. As for "the expectations of the masses," he only meant that K'ang-hsi's subjects were expecting him to govern as well as the sage-emperors Yao and Shun. Hsiung justified his words of warning on the grounds that the time to be concerned about good government and security was before rebellion or danger arose.

K'ang-hsi could hardly be satisfied with Hsiung's answer. Indeed, Hsiung's parting words seemed even more ominous than the phrases he was called upon to explain. The emperor accused him of making reckless charges and turned his case over to the Board of Punishment. When the board decided to degrade and demote Hsiung, however, K'ang-hsi pardoned him.[72]

What can we make of this incident? Hsiung Tz'u-li's biography states that the edicts reprimanding him for vagueness were the work not of K'ang-hsi but of Oboi, who suspected that the criticism was aimed at himself, but this is not indicated by the phraseology of the preserved document.[73] Still, in 1669, one of the crimes with which Oboi was charged was that of oppressing Hsiung for his outspoken memorials.[74] I think that K'ang-hsi was probably acting on his own and censured Hsiung to forestall any demand by Oboi for a stiffer punishment. K'ang-hsi had failed a year earlier to save Suksaha's life in a direct confrontation with Oboi; so here he was testing the efficacy of a more indirect and subtle approach.

Hsiung Tz'u-li's second memorial and censure came right on the heels of K'ang-hsi's intervention in the calendar controversy, and together these two developments seemed to portend a political change. This impression is bolstered by an incident that had occurred earlier, in the spring of 1668. On the seventh anniversary of Shun-chih's death,[75] a gravestone was erected at his mausoleum that carried a eulogy composed by K'ang-hsi. There was nothing strange about this, but in the eulogy K'ang-hsi went out of his way to praise his father for, among other things, perpetuating the administrative practices of his predecessors, showing no discrimination between Manchus and Chinese, and keeping tight control over eunuchs.[76] Accurately or not, K'ang-hsi chose to commend Shun-chih in those areas of governing in which the Manchu regents had found the former emperor deficient. K'ang-hsi in this eulogy was undoubtedly trying to make amends for the posthumous humiliation his father had suffered at the hands of the regents. Perhaps K'ang-hsi was also issuing a challenge to the regents.

The shifting balance of power in court politics was also revealed in the appointment of compilers of the "veritable records" (*shih-lu*) of the Shun-chih reign. In October 1667, one of Oboi's leading associates, Bambursan, was named chief compiler. Precisely a year later, however, he was replaced by Duikana, K'ang-hsi's first appointment of a grand secretary.[77]

The end for Oboi and his clique came swiftly and without warning. On 14 June 1669, Oboi was seized at court by youths trained in the martial arts.[78] In this daring act K'ang-hsi received the counsel and support of Songgotu, son of Soni and vice-president of the Board of Civil Appointments. Songgotu had reason to dislike Oboi, because the latter had tried unsuccessfully to prevent the emperor from marrying the daughter of Songgotu's elder brother Gabuli.[79] Songgotu became one of the most prominent officials of K'ang-hsi's reign, and a good part of his success can be explained by the merit he earned in this affair. Also supporting the emperor in his move against Oboi were the grand empress dowager Hsiao-chuang and future Manchu notables such as Prince Giyesu and Mingju.[80]

The crimes of Oboi were briefly stated by K'ang-hsi on the day of his arrest, but he left it to Prince Giyesu, then presiding over the Deliberative Council, to present the government's case against Oboi and his followers in great detail. Giyesu, who less than two years earlier had been commanded by Oboi to draw up a list of twenty-four crimes attributed to Suksaha, now came up with an even lengthier bill of particulars (thirty in all) against Oboi.[81]

Some of the charges against Oboi dealt with matters already discussed: his usurpation of authority (such as issuing edicts without the emperor's approval and against his wishes); packing the government with men who supported him and blackballing those who did not; the execution of Suksaha and others for opposing the exchange of banner lands; his opposition to K'ang-hsi's marriage to Soni's granddaughter; his appointment of Marsai to a second Manchu presidency in the Board of Revenue; his oppression of Hsiung Tz'u-li and censors who criticized his rule; and his barring of lieutenants-general of Mongol banners from court deliberations.

In addition, Prince Giyesu and the Deliberative Council brought up such matters as Oboi's use of men who had been barred from office in Abahai's and Shun-chih's time, his purchase of personal slaves, his reversing the order of precedence established by Shun-chih so that he came before Ebilun, and his intimidation of K'ang-hsi and high officials with violent language and threats of physical abuse. K'ang-hsi himself recalled how on many occasions

Oboi had terrified into submission anyone at court who opposed him.[82]

After Oboi's crimes had been detailed, the Deliberative Council trained its sights on his supporters. When the carnage was over, K'ang-hsi had almost a clean slate to work with. Regents, grand secretaries, board presidents, banner officials, and on down the ranks—they all fell with Oboi. Ebilun, the only other regent still alive, was charged with twelve crimes, most of them stemming from his acquiescence in the acts of Oboi. Bambursan, a grand secretary who acted as Oboi's man in the imperial secretariat, was found guilty of twenty-one crimes. Again, many of them were due to his association with Oboi, but still others seemed to be of his own making, such as the numerous times he had altered the wording of edicts without imperial approval.[83]

The list of officials purged for being followers of Oboi was almost endless, and it is pointless to detail all the charges against them. Just identifying them by name and position alone will indicate the scope and numbers of men involved. They included board presidents A-ssu-ha, Marsai (who had already died and whose special position as a second Manchu president was now abolished),[84] K'o-ch'u-ha, and Chi-shih; board vice-presidents Taibitu, Cokto, and Mai-yin-ta; subchancellor (*hsüeh-shih*) Wu Kesai; governor-general Molo; governors Becingge and Ata; provincial commander-in-chief (*t'i-tu*) Liu Pang-chu; lieutenants-general (*tu-t'ung*) Liu Chih-yüan and his son Liu Kuang; and deputy lieutenant-general (*fu-tu-t'ung*) Hife. Among Oboi's adult male relatives, three brothers, a son, four nephews, a son-in-law, and a grandson-in-law were punished. Ten of those purged, including many already listed, were high officials in the Eight Banners, where Oboi had built his clique.[85]

The Deliberative Council was very liberal in passing out death sentences to Oboi and his supporters, but K'ang-hsi lessened most of them. In the end, only nine men were actually executed: Bambursan, Sai-pen-t'e and No-mo (two of Oboi's nephews), A-ssu-ha, K'o-ch'u-ha, Murma (Oboi's younger brother), Taibitu, Chi-shih, and Wu Ke-sai. K'ang-hsi said he singled out these men for execution because they had held high positions of trust as court officials or attendants, but this does not explain why other high officials like Cokto and Mai-yin-te were pardoned.[86]

Oboi was spared the death penalty but was thrown into prison, where he soon died, and all his possessions were confiscated.[87] Ebilun was pardoned and only lost his ducal rank, but even this was restored to him seven months later. He lived out his days in the inner court and died early in 1674.[88] Another man receiving special consideration was Ananda, an imperial guardsman from the Mongol plain yellow banner. It grieved K'ang-hsi to recall that Ananda, who had his trust, had constantly spoken of Oboi as a virtuous man, but the emperor refused to allow Ananda to be executed or even exiled.[89] Various physical, political, and economic punishments were inflicted on the other men implicated with Oboi. In one instance, however (a case of bribery involving several high officials), K'ang-hsi decided to forego any investigation for fear that it would implicate too many men. Many minor officials who had supported Oboi were also set free for the same reason.[90]

The purge of Oboi men from government was accompanied by the rehabilitation of officials who had opposed Oboi and suffered for it. The reputation and ranks of Sunahai, Wang Teng-lien, Chu Ch'ang-tso, and others who fought unsuccessfully against the transfer of banner lands in 1666 were now restored, and their sons were given *yin* privileges.[91] The fall of Oboi seemed like an opportune time for many men, including the Jesuits in Peking, to seek redress of earlier injustices, but in some cases the petitioners were found to have been degraded for legitimate reasons and not because of any arbitrary action on Oboi's part.[92]

With the regency abolished and Oboi's supporters all rooted out of government in this massive purge, K'ang-hsi began to rule in his own right. He could now apply to governing the empire the techniques he had used so well in deciding the calendar controversy and in breaking the regency. On 3 July 1669, while the purge was still in full swing, he issued a call to all his officials to pledge themselves anew to helping him solve the problems he faced. There was still corruption to be eradicated, rebels and bandits to be pacified, and, above all, the people's suffering to be relieved—yes, he particularly needed their cooperation to bring peace and prosperity to the long-suffering people. It was their job to recommend good men and beneficial policies and to denounce whomever and whatever was bad, evil, or harmful.[93] On this good Confucian note, K'ang-hsi inaugurated a long, productive reign.

Four

WAR AND THE FRUITS OF VICTORY

K'ANG-HSI BARELY HAD TIME TO GATHER HIS FORCES AND GET USED to governing when a military crisis of the first order broke upon him and the dynasty. What seemed to be a pacified empire—on land if not yet at sea—suddenly changed into a land of unrest and warfare. From the moment rebellion broke out in 1673 until the end of K'ang-hsi's early reign in 1684, and even beyond that to the Treaty of Nerchinsk in 1689, the youthful emperor gave priority to his role as commander-in-chief of the people and preserver of the dynasty in face of several military threats. Victory in these struggles was, of course, essential to the Manchus as military conquerors and overlords—essential to preserving their dynasty and their military control over China. But military victory also brought great political and psychological gains. The Manchu will to govern as well as its strength to conquer had been tested, and the sure way K'ang-hsi handled the several crises contributed to the final acceptance of Manchu authority by a Chinese nation weary of interdynastic civil war and chaos.

Brief accounts of three campaigns—the suppression of the three feudatories, the conquest of Taiwan, and the Albazin campaigns of 1684–86—will reveal the essence of K'ang-hsi's military leadership. The first two posed internal threats to the Manchu dynasty, while the third represented an external threat to the Chinese empire, but K'ang-hsi made no distinction between them in terms of the energy and planning invested. In the course of these struggles, the army systems of China underwent change, both in wartime and in peacetime, in response to new conditions.

Abolishing the Feudatories

Probably the most courageous step ever taken by K'ang-hsi was his decision in 1673 to abolish the three feudatories (*San-fan*)[1] and disband their armies. This decision precipitated the revolt of Wu San-kuei, as the emperor was forewarned, and threw China into an eight-year civil war that spread to ten provinces and threatened the very existence of the Ch'ing dynasty then still in its infancy. But K'ang-hsi had more in mind than the danger to himself and the dynasty; he also was acting as many another emperor had throughout Chinese history, fighting for the integrity of the empire against the centrifugal forces of regional warlords. The struggle against the feudatories could not be avoided without sacrificing the unity of China—without doing violence to the notion of one world, one China, one emperor.

The three feudatories were the result of a deliberate decision of the invading Manchus to "use Chinese to control Chinese"—turning the old Chinese maxim around to meet the times. This meant, as the Manchus carried the campaigns of conquest to south China, that Chinese troops led by Chinese generals would bear the brunt of the fighting and the responsibility for keeping the area pacified. There could be numerous reasons for sending Chinese rather than Manchu generals to the south: to get them out of the capital region where the Manchus were; to reduce the likelihood of social friction with native populations; the insufficient number of banner troops; and the fact that Chinese troops were better equipped to fight in the rugged terrain of the south.[2]

In 1649 three Chinese generals who had played key roles in the Manchu conquest of North China were sent southward with armies totaling forty thousand. K'ung Yu-te led twenty thousand into Kwangsi, while Shang K'o-hsi and Keng Chung-ming together headed another twenty thousand into Kwangtung. Each was given broad military and political discretionary powers and princely titles—K'ung as *Ting-nan wang*, Shang as *P'ing-nan wang*, and Keng as *Ching-nan wang*.[3] Two years later a fourth Chinese, Wu San-kuei, who was made a prince (*P'ing-hsi wang*) in 1644, was also put in command of an army and sent to Szechwan.[4]

These princes were shifted around throughout South China in the 1650s according to military exigencies.[5] By 1660 three of them had established semiautonomous feudatories in the south. Shang K'o-hsi ruled Kwangtung from his headquarters at Canton, while Keng Chi-mao (who had succeeded to the title of *Ching-nan wang* after his father's death in 1649) was shifted to Fukien.[6] Wu San-kuei campaigned successfully in Shensi, Szechwan, Kweichow, and Yunnan before receiving control of the latter province in 1659 at the suggestion of Hung Ch'eng-ch'ou.[7] K'ung Yu-te, the fourth prince, committed suicide in 1652 when surrounded by Ming loyalist forces. Since no male heir survived to inherit his rank or command, the Kwangsi feudatory was temporarily abolished.[8]

To keep a measure of control over the feudatory princes, the court kept one son of each prince in Peking as a hostage—in fact if not in name. Wu Ying-hsiung remained in the capital when his father went south, and he became the consort of a princess (*ho-she e-fu*) in 1653 by marrying Abahai's youngest daughter, Princess K'o-ch'un. He stayed in the capital until his execution in 1674 except for a brief visit with his father in 1670.[9] Shang K'o-hsi sent his second son and heir, Chih-hsin, to Peking in 1654 to be in attendance on the emperor. Some time later, however, the younger Shang went back to Kwangtung, because in 1668 it is recorded again that he was sent to serve the emperor. Shang Chih-hsin left Peking for good in 1671 to relieve his ailing father of the burdens of military command.[10] Keng Chi-mao's son, Ching-chung, was also sent to Peking in 1654 to wait upon the Shun-chih emperor, and he too married a Manchu princess. The father requested his son's return to Fukien in 1664 so that he might "learn the ropes" and prepare eventually to take over command of the feudatory. Keng Ching-chung held temporary military command in 1671 and then inherited complete control of the feudatory and his father's title (*Ching-nan wang*) upon the latter's death in June 1671.[11] So when the rebellion broke out in 1673, only Wu San-kuei's son was still a hostage in Peking, and the father's revolt cost the son his life.

The threat the feudatories posed for the imperial government is best seen in the career of Wu San-kuei, the strongest of the three princes. Shang K'o-hsi probably controlled an army of about ten thousand men, and Keng Ching-chung about twice that number.[12] Wu, in comparison, had over sixty-five thousand troops under him in Yunnan at the time of his revolt.[13] Wu's position was further bolstered by special honors and privileges not accorded the other feudatory princes. First of all, he was elevated in 1662 to the highest rank of nobility, and one normally reserved for members of the Manchu imperial family—prince of blood of the first degree (*ch'in-wang*), for his successful campaign against Chu Yu-lang, the last of the Ming pretenders.[14]

The military and civilian authority given Wu San-kuei when he was stationed in Yunnan in 1659 was enormous. He could decide on all administrative, military, and financial matters in the province with no interference from either provincial or capital officials. This power (known as *tsung-kuan*) was, however, only temporary and would end when Yunnan was completely pacified.[15] Wu managed to justify his continuing presence and unchallenged authority in Yunnan many years after the Ming pretender had been eliminated and the area stabilized by submitting exaggerated reports of trouble with non-Han ethnic minorities. The governor-general of neighboring Kweichow, where some of the minorities lived, did not see any particular military threat from these people.[16] Wu San-kuei, nevertheless, maintained his power and in fact had extended it on this pretext. On 30 January 1663, the throne gave Wu the same authority in Kweichow that he already had in Yunnan, and the only specific reason cited for the move was that the Miao and Man problems of the two provinces were inseparable. Thereafter, at Wu's request, the phrase "accept control of the Prince [of Pacifying the West, Wu San-kuei]" (*t'ing-wang chieh-chih*) was added to the patents (*ch'ih-shu*) of Yunnan and Kweichow governors-general and governors.[17] Then, when in 1665 several governor-general posts were either abolished or combined, the court sought and accepted Wu's advice to station the Yun-kuei governor-general at Kweiyang, Kweichow. The presence of a high-ranking official in Yunnan's and Wu's capital would have acted as a restraint on his ambitions. The Board of War also deferred to Wu in picking the location of the Kweichow *t'i-tu*'s headquarters.[18]

Finally, Wu San-kuei had the power of appointment (*hsi-hsüan*, "selected by [the Prince of Pacifying] the West"), and he used it to place his associates and subordinates in key posts, not only in Yunnan and Kweichow but in other areas as well.[19] Many appointments of regional commanders (*tsung-ping*) were made at Wu's request.[20] At times, two appointments to the same post were made—one by the central board in question (War, or Civil Appointments), and one by Wu. Since the latter's candidate always took precedence, the board officials gave up. In 1666 they refused to make any more appointments to vacant posts in Yunnan or Kweichow unless Wu San-kuei specifically requested them to do so.[21]

Obviously Peking was paying a high price politically by maintaining Wu's feudatory. It was also paying a high price financially, for the central government spent millions yearly to support the armies of Wu and the other feudatory princes. By the end of the Shun-chih period, Wu's army expenses totaled nine million taels, which was about two-fifths of the nation's cash revenues. Yunnan itself could not provide the necessary revenue, which had to be obtained from other provinces, such as Kiangnan, Hukuang, and Honan.[22] The favorite solution of memorialists was the establishment of military colonies (*t'un-t'ien*) in Yunnan and Kweichow.[23] However many military supplies the *t'un-t'ien* program might have provided, a memorialist was still complaining in 1667 that one-half of the empire's yearly revenue was spent for the three feudatories' military provisions. Yunnan and Kweichow alone required four million taels, about ten tiimes the provinces' tax revenues.[24] By 1672, *San-fan* military expenses had dropped to five million taels: Yunnan, 1,700,000; Kweichow, 500,000; Fukien, 1,600,000; Kwangtung, 1,200,000.[25]

The above expenses were only the ones borne by the imperial treasury and, through it, the wealthier provinces. In addition, the people within the feudatories paid special taxes levied by the three princes.[26] They also faced extortion and unfair competition in commercial activity from client-merchants of the princes and regular officials as well.[27]

Warnings on the feudatories reached the court continuously from their inception, but it was not until the late 1660s that any serious thought was given to abolishing them. The first known warning came from a Szechwan regional inspector, Hao Yü, who in 1652 spoke of Wu San-kuei's ambitions. Wu in turn accused Hao of untruthfulness in his memorials and caused him to go into exile for twenty years before being used again in government.[28] Another Szechwan censor, Yang Su-yün, was similarly maligned by Wu in 1660 for daring to question his *hsi-hsüan* privilege. In his own defense, Yang denied having any personal animosity toward Wu, whom he had never met, but was moved to speak on general principles. He felt that it was unwise and an encroachment upon the state's authority to permit anyone other than the emperor to appoint and transfer officials at will. That, he claimed, was all that lay behind the "nipping the matter in the bud" comment in his original memorial. He was not predicting a rebellion on Wu's part.[29]

In the 1660s, two highly placed Chinese officials cautioned the court on the feudatories. Wei I-chieh, president of the Censorate, suggested in 1662 that the regime station trusted Manchu troops in the Ching-chou and Hsiang-yang areas of Hupeh to be prepared for emergencies. His proposal was rejected, but the Hukuang governor-general was transferred from Wuchang to Ching-chou as a precaution. Another president of the Censorate, Wang Hsi, urged the court to reduce the number of troops under Wu's command and hence his strength.[30] Even an imperial family member, Jirgalang, tried without success to have the throne withdraw the three feudatory leaders' princely titles.[31]

The court missed an opportunity to regain control of Yunnan and Kweichow in 1667 when Wu San-kuei tested the political winds by requesting the right to retire because of failing eyesight and generally poor health. The throne and the Board of Civil Appointments were inclined to accept Wu's offer and were preparing to bring Yunnan and Kweichow into the normal administrative structure, but they changed their minds. The decisive factor in this reversal was a joint memorial from the Yun-kuei governor-general and the commander-in-chief of each province stating that the military situation demanded the retention of Wu's special position. Expressing concern about Wu's health and not wishing it to deteriorate further, the throne suggested that he reserve his strength for military matters.[32] This implied giving up civil authority, but there is no evidence that Wu ever did, and the relationship between the central government and the feudatory was not affected in any way.

The court, however, was confronting the issue, and within the next few years its suspicions about Wu's intentions grew. For instance, one man was passed over for the Yunnan governor's post in 1668 because he was a subordinate of Wu San-kuei.[33] Wu Ying-hsiung in Peking knew of the court's suspicions and kept his father informed.[34] So both sides were prepared for an imminent showdown. Much later K'ang-hsi recalled that he was fully aware of Wu's power and realized the tenuousness of imperial rule as long as independent authority existed outside the normal framework of government. He also appreciated the task he faced in challenging Wu, but he felt that sooner or later the challenge had to be made, and it might as well be sooner, before his opponent grew any stronger.[35]

An opportunity to alter the situation came again in 1673 when Shang K'o-hsi, the most trusted of the feudatory princes, sought permission to retire because of old age and leave control of Kwangtung to his son, Chih-hsin. Fifteen days later, on 13 May, the Deliberative Council approved of Shang's retirement but not of his son's assumption of either princely rank or command in Kwangtung. They reasoned that it was unprecedented for a son to inherit his father's title while the latter was still alive, unnecessary to maintain a feudatory in Kwangtung because it was already pacified, and improper to separate father and son.[36] In effect, Shang K'o-hsi had given K'ang-hsi the wedge he needed to disband the feudatories, and perhaps that was Shang's intention.

The other two princes really had no choice but to follow Shang and go through the motions, as it turned out, of voluntarily retiring and relinquishing their authority. Wu San-kuei did so on 14 August, Keng Ching-chung on 20 August.[37] Since the decision had already been made to abolish one feudatory, there should have been no delay in responding to these latest "trial balloons," and in Keng's case there was none. On 8 September the emperor ordered the transfer of Keng and his men back to Liaotung.[38]

Wu's memorial, though, was handled more carefully, and it touched off a great debate. The Deliberative Council, when it reported its decision thirty-three days later (compared with fifteen days in Shang's case and nineteen in Keng's case), was divided on the question. One group recommended abolishing the feudatory but keeping Yunnan heavily defended with Manchu banner troops. A dissenting opinion in the council opposed the shift on the grounds that it would needlessly burden the people of Yunnan as well as the families being moved.[39] That could hardly have been the dissenters' true reason, because it would have applied as well to the Kwangtung and Fukien feudatories, whose transfer the council had just approved. It is clear that what they really feared was Wu San-kuei's response, which many officials predicted would be open revolt.

The two alternative proposals coming out of the Deliberative Council left the decision squarely up to K'ang-hsi. The young emperor (then only nineteen) sought the opinion of his advisers. In the end he acted on his own, because the majority of men consulted opposed the abolition of the feudatories. The only named opponents of the move K'ang-hsi was about to take were Songgotu, Tuhai, and Hsiung Tz'u-li, but every high-ranking official save four was said to have opposed the decision.[40] Not a single grand secretary agreed with K'ang-hsi. His four supporters were all board presidents—three of them Manchus and one a Chinese. They were Mingju, Mishan, Molo, and Wang Hsi. Mishan's support was coupled with the assurance that the national treasury, which he supervised as president of the Board of Revenue, could support a ten-year war, if necessary, without recourse to extra taxation.[41] Opponents reasoned that Wu San-kuei was getting old, and that his feudatory could be abolished after his death with no risk, but to do it now would surely precipitate a revolt. K'ang-hsi dismissed this as wishful thinking. "Wu San-kuei," he argued, "has long nurtured evil ambitions. If we disband [the feudatories now] he might revolt, but if we do not disband them he is likely to revolt anyway. It is better to force the issue now." On 16 September he forced the issue by recalling Wu San-kuei and his troops from Yunnan.[42]

The San-fan Rebellion

To carry out his decision to disband the feudatories, K'ang-hsi sent special commissioners to Yunnan, Kweichow, Kwangtung, and Fukien with instructions to make the move as quick and as easy as possible for the men involved. In addition, the vice-president of the Board of Revenue was sent to Sheng-ching (Mukden) to confer with his counterpart in the Manchurian government on locating land for resettling the soldiers and their families transferred from the south.[43]

K'ang-hsi also took special pains to win Wu San-kuei's acceptance of the move. He sent the prince a letter in his own hand explaining the reasons for his course of action. He cited the precedent of disbanding troops after a military threat had passed and also his concern for Wu's health. Thanking Wu profusely for his loyal service to the dynasty, K'ang-hsi assured him that every effort would be made to care for his needs and those of his people.[44] Wu's first response seemed to indicate a willingness to go through with the move: on 11 December he requested additional land in

Manchuria for his men, and K'ang-hsi readily assented.[45] But before the year was out Wu had unfurled the banner of revolt.

The man who first invited the Manchus into China was now very confident of his ability to drive them out again. Wu had a large army under his command, which he believed could easily overcome the weak Manchu forces. He reputedly warned the imperial commissioners that "I will return to Peking, if they insist, but it will be at the head of eighty thousand men."[46] Many of his former subordinates were strategically placed in the southwest as *t'i-tu* or *tsung-ping*. His son in Peking was in a position to cause trouble and did. And Wu must have imagined himself as a rallying point for the still lingering anti-Manchu racial hatred of Ming loyalists.[47]

The rebellion began on 28 December 1673, when Wu imprisoned the two imperial commissioners sent to arrange the transfer of his feudatory; executed the governor of Yunnan, Chu Kuo-chih; and proclaimed a new dynasty, Chou. It started three days earlier than planned because the governor was moving up troops to guard the route to be used in transferring the feudatory northward. The rebellion was an instant success in Yunnan and Kweichow. Most of the civil and military provincial leaders, including the governor of Kweichow and the *t'i-tu* of each province, joined Wu's rebellion. The governor of Yunnan refused to join and was killed; the governor-general of Yun-kuei, Kan Wen-k'un, also resisted and committed suicide when surrounded by former imperial troops who had defected to Wu; the Yunnan provincial judge and Yunnan-fu's prefect and sub-prefect refused to submit, and they were either imprisoned or exiled.[48]

The first reports of Wu San-kuei's revolt reached Peking by the end of January 1674, as two of the imperial commissioners drove their horses day and night along the post road system to inform K'ang-hsi of the awful events in the south. Near panic gripped the capital and scapegoats were sought. Those, like Songgotu, who had earlier opposed the decision to disband the feudatories, now wagged their fingers and their tongues, suggesting that Mingju and his crowd be executed for precipitating the revolt.[49] Rumors were circulating that the Manchus would abandon Peking and return to their homeland. Ferdinand Verbiest, the Flemish Jesuit, made preparations for the journey in the expectation that K'ang-hsi would take him along.[50] Many Chinese officials, preparing for the worst, sent their families home, and some even felt that troops should not be sent out to meet the rebels. Commoners were fleeing the city and became highly agitated when the city gates were temporarily closed while the leader of an abortive revolt was hunted down.[51]

Obviously, many people felt that Wu San-kuei could not be successfully challenged and that the Manchus had no stomach for a fight. Father Domingo Navarrete, who had worked in China until 1670, hinted at the magnitude of the task facing the Manchus when he commented on the news of the rebellion as it reached him at Madrid: "The letters from Manila of 1674 inform me that a governor of four provinces in China has revolted, and has many followers; the letters of 1673 from China made no mention of it, which makes me doubt it; nor do I know of any governor of four provinces there is, unless it be Wu San-kuei; and if he has revolted, the Tartar is in danger."[52]

But K'ang-hsi was up to the challenge. He took full responsibility for the turn of events and refused to put the blame on his advisers. He quelled unrest in Peking by executing Wu Ying-hsiung and breaking up the "revolt of the slaves" associated with him. The uprising was planned by a certain Yang Ch'i-lung, who called himself Chu San-t'ai-tzu, or "the third Crown Prince Chu [of the Ming dynasty]."[53] Yang was apparently recruiting household servants of bannermen to prepare for a general insurrection on 29 January. They planned to burn down the imperial palace and put to the knife any official they came across. Two days before the chosen date, some of the servants revealed the plot to their masters, who immediately swung into action. Troops led by Tuhai of the plain yellow banner rounded up several hundred of the men implicated, but Yang Ch'i-lung himself escaped.[54] Scores were executed, and an intensive search for Yang was made, but apparently he was never found.[55]

Wu Ying-hsiung's relation to Yang Ch'i-lung's planned insurrection is not clear. Most Western accounts pictured Wu as the instigator of the uprising, planning it to coincide with his father's revolt.[56] But the Chinese record is ambiguous. A few days after the plot was uncovered, the Deliberative Council made known its suspicions about Wu Ying-hsiung, who was consequently held for questioning.[57] Nothing, however, was found to implicate him directly, and K'ang-hsi was reluctant to approve the many requests to execute Wu San-kuei's son. When the emperor finally relented and ordered him to commit suicide—instead of death by mutilation as a gesture towards his past service—it was not for any specific crime but because K'ang-hsi was infuriated with his father's request that the Manchus leave China and because, as Wang Hsi reasoned, the son's execution would dishearten the rebels and let the people know of the Manchu's will to fight.[58]

As immediate as the Peking unrest was, the greater danger came from the father's open rebellion and not from the son's secret machinations. K'ang-hsi moved rapidly to meet the military challenge. He first canceled the orders to disband the other two feudatories, hoping no doubt to keep Shang K'o-hsi and Keng Ching-chung loyal despite Wu's blandishments and to use their troops against him.[59] Wu was stripped of his princely title and declared an outlaw, but from the outset the government announced its intention to deal more liberally with the mass of people in the rebel movement. It was the time-honored stratagem of driving a wedge between leaders and followers and encouraging the latter to defect to the imperial side with promises of amnesty and even rewards if they should kill or capture any of their leaders or surrender troops and cities.[60] This kind of general amnesty offer was renewed periodically throughout the war until 1680–81, when victory was within the grasp of the imperial forces. Then K'ang-hsi felt safe in narrowing the scope of his amnesty policy, figuring that the rebels had had plenty of opportunities to submit.[61]

Militarily, the emperor from first to last personally directed the campaigns of suppression—from Peking, to be sure, but with good strategic moves. His initial response to news of the rebellion was to secure Ching-chou and Ch'ang-te, and later Wuchang, to prevent Wu's forces from sweeping through Hunan toward the Yangtze River.[62] But K'ang-hsi realized that there were other options open to the rebels and he moved to close them off. Szechwan and Shensi were occupied to prevent an invasion of Peking from the northwest, and Kwangsi generals were alerted to stop any rebel drive aimed at linking up with wavering elements in Kwangtung.[63] Finally, the rich tax-producing area of Kiangsu-Anhwei-Kiangsi was heavily fortified, not because of any immediate military threat but because it was absolutely essential to control this area then and in the future to assure a strong financial base for the imperial government.[64]

Behind this outer perimeter of defenses, K'ang-hsi constructed his supply and reinforcement lines. He selected Taiyuan in Shansi and Yenchow in Shantung as the transfer points on the western and eastern routes to the south. Men and material from the north would gather at each place before advancing to trouble spots, at which time they would be replaced by reinforcements, and so on. Advance bases were located at such places as Sian in Shensi, Wuchang in Hupei, Nanchang in Kiangsi, and Anking in Anhwei.[65] Governors and governors-general were usually responsible for supplying the armies operating in their provinces, but often jurisdictional disputes hampered their efforts. To correct this situation, K'ang-hsi would send out special commissioners to collect supplies and coordinate their distribution without regard to normal jurisdictional boundaries. This policy, for instance, was followed in supplying the army at Yüeh-chou in northern Hunan, which relied on the neighboring provinces of Hupei for most of its supplies.[66] K'ang-hsi also improved the military intelligence system by adding more translators to the Board of War and intelligence officers to the various armies in the field. He also established new army remount stations along the major routes from Peking to the fronts.[67]

K'ang-hsi's strategy and planning did not immediately pay off, for which he later blamed his generals for not responding quickly enough to his commands. What really undermined the emperor's plans was the defection to Wu's side of several key military leaders. By the end of 1674, Keng Ching-chung in Fukien, Sun Yen-ling in Kwangsi, and Wang Fu-ch'en in Shensi had rebelled.[68] Fortunately, Shang K'o-hsi in Kwangtung remained loyal; if he had not, the whole imperial position in the south would have been hopeless. As it was, the first year of fighting left the rebels in control of Yunnan, Kweichow, Szechwan, Shensi, Hunan, and Kwangsi, and threatening Kansu and Kiangsi. Later, in 1676, Shang Chih-hsin in Kwangtung allied himself with Wu.[69]

Despite Wu's military success, he was never able to attract an equally significant number of anti-Manchu Ming loyalist scholars to his cause, as he might have expected. When he proclaimed himself emperor of the Chou dynasty in 1678 at Heng-yang, Hunan, he failed even to get the support of Wang Fu-chih, who was a native of that place.[70] Wang was a prominent Neo-Confucian scholar and historian who in 1648 had raised a local army to fight the Manchus, so his rebuff to Wu San-kuei thirty years later was symptomatic of the erosion of the Ming cause and of the feeling of Ming loyalists toward Wu. After all, it was Wu who had welcomed the Manchus into China, and it was he who had hunted down and murdered the last Ming prince in Burma for the Manchus, so any appeal to their anti-Manchu racial feelings would be suspect. Furthermore, Wu was not now attempting to restore the Ming dynasty but establish a new one in his own name. Ku Yen-wu, another leading scholar and Ming loyalist, was cautiously hopeful at the outset of Wu's rebellion, but he later scornfully called it "the wiggling of worms."[71] Only two relatively well-known Ming scholars joined the rebellion—Ch'ü Ta-chün, a Kwangtung poet, and Ku Tsu-yü, a geographer from Kiangsi.[72]

I do not intend to describe in detail the eight years of military campaigning against the *San-fan* rebels,[73] but will note some special problems and how K'ang-hsi handled them. Wu San-kuei's early successes brought about half the empire under his control, and this gave rise to talk of cutting China in half at the Yangtze, with the Manchus in the north and Wu San-kuei's Chou dynasty in the south. The rebel chief's rapid advancement into Hunan and then his reluctance to cross the river into Hupei suggests that he wanted to solidify his claims in the south. The first of Wu's territorial demands reached K'ang-hsi in May 1674 in the form of a memorial that Wu sent with the two imperial commissioners he had released. Wu at that time was making very few concessions: he promised the Manchus only their homeland and Korea. No direct reply was issued, but K'ang-hsi's response was firm and personally crushing to Wu San-kuei: the execution of his son in Peking.[74] This act ended all hope of reconciliation and all direct corespondence between the two protagonists. Wu's next offer came through an intermediary—the Dalai Lama of Tibet.

After the conquest of China, the Manchus continued to patronize Lamaism as part of a policy to hold the allegiance of Mongols and Tibetans.[75] The Dalai Lama had visited Peking in 1652 at the invitation of Shun-chih, and early Ch'ing rulers (particularly K'ang-hsi) made many personal visits to Wu-t'ai-shan, the holy mountain of Lamaism, to manifest their support.[76] When the rebellion broke out, K'ang-hsi sent two commissioners to the Tibetan leader to ask for his support, which Wu San-kuei was seeking also. Even before he rebelled, Wu had established ties of friendship and trade with the Dalai Lama by ceding to him parts of

Yunnan's far west. The Dalai Lama, however, protested to K'ang-hsi in 1675 that he was not friendly with Wu, that Wu had taken the territory back upon revolting, and that he (the Dalai Lama) in turn had recovered it by force.[77] It seems more likely that Wu willingly gave the territory to the Dalai Lama a second time in 1674 or 1675 in exchange for the latter's intercession with Peking on splitting the empire in half.[78]

Whatever his reasons, the Dalai Lama did make this proposal to K'ang-hsi sometime before May 1675 (when the emperor referred to it). K'ang-hsi indignantly refused to compromise the integrity of his empire and lectured the Dalai Lama on his troops' plundering in Kansu. The Tibetan leader had been warned late in 1674 by K'ang-hsi that he should not use China's request for help as a pretext to plunder the northwestern border areas. If he needed supplies for an expedition, the emperor insisted, he should get them from the Szechwan-Yunnan area—that is, from territory already occupied by Wu's forces, which would be a difficult task.[79] This edict may have been a public relations effort by K'ang-hsi to hide the fact that he was inviting Mongol troops into Chinese territory, which he surely knew would result in some plundering, to help fight Wu San-kuei. The emperor later regretted this move—a move made when the situation in the south was bleak and he was not sure of the government's ability to suppress the rebels unaided.

K'ang-hsi remained suspicious of the Dalai Lama, and, when the imperial forces were closing in on Yunnan in 1680, he ordered his generals to search for any correspondence between the rebels and the Dalai Lama. At the same time, troops were sent to the border to keep a watchful eye on the Dalai Lama's activities.[80] As they were advancing on Yunnan-fu in 1681, imperial generals did find correspondence between the Tibetan leader and Wu Shih-fan, who succeeded to leadership of the rebels after his grandfather's death in 1678. Convinced anew of the Dalai Lama's duplicity, the emperor called for a comprehensive interrogation of all captured rebels for further information on this matter.[81]

K'ang-hsi was more fortunate in his relations with the Chahar Mongols as allies during the campaigns of suppression. As soon as they heard of Wu's revolt, several Chahar princes came to court to offer men and horses for the campaign. The emperor appreciated this gesture and promised tax remission to all who provided pack animals, but he told them to wait until late spring to see if Mongol troops were needed. The first sign of Mongol assistance was the sending of men in February 1674 to help defend Yenchow in Shantung, one of the two supply transfer points. Later, Chahar Mongols were fighting in campaigns as far south as Fukien.[82] After the rebellion had been crushed, K'ang-hsi sent delegates to all Mongol tribes to thank and reward them for their aid.[83]

The emperor was never very satisfied with the quality of military leadership exhibited by his generals during the rebellion. Throughout 1674 he had appointed a number of Manchu princes as commanders-in-chief (*ta-chiang-chün*): Lergiyen, Dongge, Giyesu, Labu, Shang-shan, and Yolo. To this group were added Tuhai in 1676, Cani in 1678, Jangtai in 1679, and Laita in 1680.[84] Trying to rationalize what appeared to be a case of rampant nepotism, K'ang-hsi pointed out that as imperial relatives their prestige and authority facilitated on-the-spot decision making. But the princes did not live up to K'ang-hsi's expectations, and in 1675, when Wang Fu-ch'en revolted, and again in 1678, when the campaign to recover Yüeh-chou was bogged down, K'ang-hsi was so furious as to threaten to take field command himself. In each case, he was dissuaded by his ministers, who argued that the safety of the emperor and the security of the capital were much more important than the success of a field operation.[85] Besides incompetency, K'ang-hsi was also unhappy over the failure of his commanders to maintain strict discipline among their men.[86]

As long as the war was on, the emperor tolerated his generals' incompetency, procrastination, and lack of discipline, but the approach of victory brought a day of reckoning. By that time K'ang-hsi was depending more on Chinese than Manchu generals in the final operations against the remaining rebel strongholds in Yunnan and Kweichow. From the end of 1680 until he grew tired of it in the summer of 1683, K'ang-hsi received a steady stream of reports on his generals' failings in the campaigns just ended, and he handed out appropriate punishments—loss of title, loss of rank, whippings, and the confiscation of property. Only Laita among his Manchu commanders-in-chief was spared, and even two of the three Chinese generals in the final pacification campaign were reprimanded.[87]

The tide of war turned in 1676–77. One by one, Wu San-kuei's major allies deserted him and submitted to the imperial side—Wang Fu-ch'en in July 1676, Keng Ching-chung in November, and

Shang Chih-hsin in January 1677.[88] Sun Yen-ling was murdered in 1677 by Wu's own men when he appeared to be wavering in his support of the rebellion.[89] When Wu himself died on 2 October 1678, the rebel cause was lost. Wu Shih-fan, his grandson, ruled as the second emperor of the Chou dynasty for another three years, but imperial forces slowly—too slowly for K'ang-hsi—and methodically encircled him and drove him back to Yunnan-fu, where he committed suicide on 7 December 1681. Thus the rebellion ended.[90]

K'ang-hsi prepared for peace as carefully as he did for war. In the spring of 1679, just after Yüeh-chou and Changsha had been recovered from the rebels, he ordered the boards of War and of Civil Appointments to ready a list of candidates for appointment to leadership posts in Yunnan and Kweichow. These men were to follow the army into the conquered territories and bring them back into the normal administrative framework of government.[91] Someone had suggested that another prince be stationed in the southwest, but the idea was dropped: it would have negated eight years of war to get rid of one feudatory prince only to establish another.

Even before the rebels' capital fell, K'ang-hsi held a feast for his high officials. It was not yet a victory celebration, but with his goal in sight he wanted to thank all of them for their loyal, untiring efforts on behalf of the dynasty during the crisis.[92] The real victory celebration came on 20 February 1682, when the emperor again feted his officials and composed a poem with ninety-three of them to welcome the peace.[93] To the populace he extended a general amnesty and a promise of peace and good government.[94] To the people formerly under the rule of the feudatory princes, he announced (in late 1680) an end to all illegal exactions and a return of all land seized from them by feudatory officials over the past three decades.[95]

For himself, however, K'ang-hsi refused any laurels. He made a major point of this, and its propaganda value was obvious. It would not be right, he said, for him to add honorifics to his title for restoring peace, because it was his decision alone in 1673 that brought on eight years of suffering. It was the efforts of his generals and officials that were responsible for winning the war. Besides, he added, winning the war would be a hollow victory until he could point to some achievements in the area of providing good government and security for the people. When that happened he could indulge in self-glorification. The hard working, selfless, benevolent emperor was a good image to project, but K'ang-hsi was sincere enough about his position to refuse persistently the requests of officials and princes (including his elder brother Fu-ch'üan) that he accept honors. He bestowed honorifics instead on the grand empress dowager and the empress dowager (the latter posthumously).[96] Again, in 1682, when the decision was made to compile a record of the *San-fan* campaigns (*P'ing-ting San-ni fang-lüeh*, edited by Ledehun), K'ang-hsi insisted that the standard ceremonies attending any imperial compilation be foregone in this instance.[97] Finally, K'ang-hsi brought to a close the first, highly successful phase of his military leadership by personally announcing the victory before the tombs of his ancestors.[98] I am tempted to believe that they smiled with silent satisfaction and pride over their descendant's accomplishment even as they were disconcerted with the mistakes of Manchu generals in the field.

The Subjugation of Taiwan

After the suppression of the revolt of the three feudatories, the emperor turned to a less pressing but still necessary military matter—the Cheng rebels based on Taiwan. Throughout the 1660s and 1670s, the evacuation of the coastal populations and the trade ban remained the chief strategic concepts in the imperial government's campaigns against this group of Ming loyalists. These policies were not very effective because the enemy's possession of Taiwan gave them a firm economic and military base, but on the other hand the rebels were kept off the mainland and were generally quiescent during this period.

The spread of Wu San-kuei's rebellion to Fukien in 1674, however, changed the picture drastically. With the coastal province opposite Taiwan in the hands of another anti-Manchu group, Cheng Ching (son and successor to Koxinga in 1662 after a bitter intrafamily struggle) had an opportunity again to expand his operations to the mainland. The renewed pressure of Cheng on the mainland reminded the Manchu court of its old antagonist and of the need to devise a new strategy to deprive him of his island stronghold. It was not that Taiwan was irredenta to be recovered for the sake of unity, but rather that the rebels could periodically harass the mainland and cause trouble for the dynasty as long as the island remained outside Manchu control.[99] Gradually, then, imperial policy changed from a defensive to an offensive phase, and ultimately, after the *San-fan* rebellion was over, imperial forces invaded Taiwan.

Keng Ching-chung rebelled and became an ally of Wu San-kuei in April 1674.[100] Even while contemplating this move, Keng had sent an envoy to Taiwan to seek Cheng Ching's aid. The price of his aid, which apparently Keng was willing to pay at first, was that Cheng be given control of Ch'üan-chou and Chang-chou prefectures. Liu Kuo-hsüan and other commanders of Cheng Ching preceded him at Amoy, and, by May, Cheng had arrived with a flotilla of about one hundred ships.[101] Cheng's presence along the southeast coastline made the Manchus nervous about the security of Ch'ung-ming island off the Kiangsu coast, which they promptly reinforced.[102]

The grand alliance of Keng and Cheng did not prove as threatening as the government feared because it was riven with mistrust and jealousy. Keng reneged on his promise of territory; so Cheng attacked and took a number of Fukien coastal towns for himself. Furthermore, Cheng considered himself equal or superior to the feudatory prince because he was an independent ruler on Taiwan and was fighting for the restoration of the Ming dynasty. Wu San-kuei tried to patch up the quarrel of his two allies but without notable success. Eventually the two went their own ways without establishing any effective cooperation.[103]

The imperial side profited by this dissension in the enemy ranks, and K'ang-hsi tried to widen the rift by making conciliatory gestures toward Cheng Ching.[104] But it was Keng Ching-chung who changed allegiance back to the imperial side (in November 1676), while Cheng Ching continued his raids along the Fukien coast until March 1680, when he was driven from Quemoy and Amoy back to Taiwan.[105] For over a year Dutch aid was sought for this campaign before the Chinese decided to go ahead on their own.[106] The successful attack on the offshore islands was not as glorious an episode as its participants claimed: it was later discovered that the rebel defenders had secretly agreed to surrender the territory as it was attacked.[107]

Victory at its approaches was not immediately followed up with an invasion of Taiwan itself. At the time, K'ang-hsi was directing the final drive into Yunnan and was unwilling to divert manpower and energy elsewhere. In the fall of 1680 he took Mingju's advice and decided that the invasion could wait. In the meantime, Fukien officials should try again to induce Cheng's surrender.[108] Cheng Ching died early in 1681 and was succeeded by his second son, Cheng K'o-shuang, after the eldest son had been forced to commit suicide. With this evidence of internal dissension among the rebels and with the favorable winds of spring coming, K'ang-hsi thought the time ripe for an invasion.[109]

Up to this point Wan Cheng-se was chiefly responsible, as naval *t'i-tu* of Fukien, for the campaigns against the Cheng rebels. He was ably supported by Wu Hsing-tso and Yao Ch'i-sheng as governor and governor-general of the province. Wan had achieved notable success against the *San-fan* rebels in naval engagements on T'ung-t'ing Lake. When he was no longer needed in Hunan, K'ang-hsi transferred him to Fukien, his native province. But when the emperor in 1681 turned in earnest to the task of subjugating Taiwan, he replaced Wan as naval *t'i-tu* with Shih Lang.[110] No explanation was immediately given, but earlier Wan had been accused of unjustly claiming credit for a victory, and later K'ang-hsi recalled Wan's having stated that Taiwan could not be taken, exhibiting a lack of confidence that angered the emperor.[111]

Shih Lang was one of the earliest supporters of Cheng Chih-lung and his son, Ch'eng-kung (Koxinga), but he defected to the Manchus in 1646. Because of his naval skills and his knowledge of the Cheng rebels' strategy, he was appointed to a number of military posts in Fukien. He bore the title of *Ching-hai* (Pacifier of the Sea)—first as a general in 1664 and later as a marquis. He submitted a plan for conquering Taiwan as early as 1668 and even went to Peking to explain his ideas in person, but the plan was shelved at that time. In 1681, at the urging of Li Kuang-ti and Yao Ch'i-sheng, K'ang-hsi recalled Shih Lang and sent him south to coordinate the Taiwan campaign.[112]

K'ang-hsi instructed Shih Lang before he left Peking to cooperate with local officials and to move as quickly as possible to destroy the sea rebels.[113] Shih Lang did neither. Friction developed between him and the Fukien *tu-fu*, Wu Hsing-tso and Yao Ch'i-sheng, over questions of command responsibility. Shih Lang several times complained that they and other officials were interfering with his planning. He wanted to have sole responsibility—and sole credit afterward—for the invasion, with the others eliminated or downgraded to various supporting roles. The emperor decided in favor of Shih, whose ability he respected and trusted, and gave him the freedom of action he sought.[114] As for speed, Shih Lang asked for several postponments—citing unfavorable winds—before he was ready to launch the invasion in July 1683, almost two years after he was appointed. By then he had trained a force of twenty thousand and had gathered about three hundred ships.[115] His nominal superior, Governor-general Yao, still wanted to delay the invasion while the peace feelers he received from Cheng K'o-shuang were followed up. The rebels were willing to send tribute as the Ryukyu Islands did, but they refused to wear the Manchu queue or return to the mainland. K'ang-hsi considered these terms unacceptable and ordered Shih Lang to attack the island.[116]

Shih's fleet moved out and wrested the Pescadores away from Cheng K'o-shuang's best general, Liu Kuo-hsüan, in a week-long battle in July 1683, which really decided the issue. Liu fled back to Taiwan and there he convinced his master that the cause was hopeless. On 5 September Cheng K'o-shuang sent a letter of submission to Shih Lang. The latter set sail for Taiwan on 1 October, arrived two days later, and formerly received Cheng's submission on the eighth of the month.[117] The island—and with it the Cheng empire—had fallen without a shot being fired. Cheng K'o-shuang and his generals shaved their heads in the Manchu style and went to Peking, where they handed over all the Ming seals and titles received by the Cheng family since 1644. In return, Cheng was made a duke in the Chinese plain yellow banner, two of his generals were made earls, and their men were either incorporated into banner armies or sent home.[118]

On the imperial side, K'ang-hsi amply rewarded Shih Lang for his part in ending forty years and four generations of Cheng family opposition to Manchu rule. Shih was given the hereditary rank of marquis, which was handed down to the end of the dynasty, and his troops were given bonuses and not disbanded (as was the custom) so that they could have a continuing means of support. Shih Lang's exploits helped two of his sons off to illustrious careers, one as a high civilian official with a reputation of incorruptibility and the other as an admiral who in 1721 put down a serious revolt on Taiwan.[119] Again, as after the *San-fan* rebellion, K'ang-hsi personally announced this latest victory over enemies of the dynasty at his ancestor's mausoleum.[120] This time, however, he visited only the tomb of Shun-chih northeast of Peking; the first two emperors of the dynasty, Nurhaci and Abahai, were never involved with the Cheng family as they were with the feudatory princes.

The emperor was still left with one piece of unfinished business: what to do with the regime's latest acquisition. Should Taiwan be defended and incorporated into the empire, or should it be abandoned now that it was no longer a rebel haven? On several occasions in the 1660s and 1670s, the Dutch had been told that Taiwan would be given back to them after it was pacified. K'ang-hsi at first had a very ambivalent attitude toward Taiwan and its value to the empire. Great effort, of course, went into the pacification of the island, and thus there were significant personal and emotional commitments there. Also, when Cheng Ching offered to submit if he were given tributary status similar to the Ryukyus, K'ang-hsi reminded him that he was Chinese and that many of the islanders were Fukienese and could hardly be considered foreign tributaries. But when Taiwan had submitted and the court as in 1683 urged K'ang-hsi to add honorifics to his title, his response was: "Taiwan is outside the empire and of no great consequence."[121]

Others apparently agreed with this latter sentiment and favored abandoning the island. This group remained faceless but was frequently mentioned by those arguing for retention of Taiwan. Shih Lang brought the whole matter up in the first place while making his report on Cheng K'o-shuang's submission, and he asked for an imperial decision. K'ang-hsi turned the matter back to Shih Lang, asking for his opinion as well as those of the Fukien *tu-fu* (Yao Ch'i-sheng and Tung Kuo-hsing, who had replaced Wu Hsing-tso as governor in 1682) and Subai, a vice-president of the Board of War who had been sent to Fukien to oversee the supply operation for the Taiwan campaign and had then stayed on to help resettle the disbanded rebel troops.[122] There is no record of Tung's opinion, but both Shih Lang and Subai urged retention of the island, and for the same reason. If we do not defend it, they argued, the Dutch will come back to seize it and cause trouble in the future. Yao Ch'i-sheng later subscribed to this view. The emperor then put the question to a court conference, which on 5 March 1684 supported the proposals of Shih Lang and Subai.[123] Taiwan was incorporated into the empire as a prefecture of Fukien, with a garrison of eight thousand men under a regional commander to defend it.[124]

With all threats of coastal raids eliminated for the first time since the late Ming period, K'ang-hsi quickly moved to end the trade ban and the evacuation of coastal populations to the interior. Both these policies had been under attack for some years. One of the results of the maritime ban was to restrict the activity of Fukien officials seeking to buy rice and transport it by sea from neighboring provinces to offset the high prices in their own province. The depopulation of coastal areas, on the other hand, meant a loss in tax revenue and great hardship for the people.[125]

Now that the empire was at peace, these policies were no longer relevant. Wu Hsing-tso, then governor-general of Kwangtung, memorialized the throne for permission to return the coastal populations around Canton to their native areas. In response to this request, the emperor on 6 December 1683, decreed the end of the policy of removal: "Let high officials be sent to extend the boundary; let them also carefully inspect and correctly decide on where the boundary should start and end, and in what areas to station soldiers for defense. Do not let the coming of spring and the time of tilling the fields pass without acting."[126] Subsequently, several officials were appointed to make an investigation of the coastal boundaries and supervise the resettlement project. Tu Chen, vice-president of the Board of Civil Appointments, and Hsi-chu, subchancellor of the Nei-ko, were ordered to go to Fukien and Kwangtung, while Chin Shih-chien, vice-president of the Board of Works, and Ya-ssu-ha, vice-president of the Censorate, were sent to Chekiang and Kiangnan.[127] When these officials had completed their mission, agriculture, sericulture, fishing, and salt production in the area began to revive. In Kwangtung, 28,192 *ch'ing* (one *ch'ing* equals 100 *mou*) were reapportioned to 31,300 resettled peasants; in Fukien, 31,108 *ch'ing* were divided among a returning population of 40,800; in Chekiang, 9,000 *mou* of farm land and 74,000 *mou* of salt lands were restored to the people.[128]

The commissioners also recommended the reopening of trade along the coast, as had been urged by Shih Lang, Wu Hsing-tso, and others ever since the submission of Taiwan.[129] Imperial commissioner Chin Shih-chien's report in May 1684, urged that the people be allowed to go out to sea to fish and trade. He proposed several precautionary measures: (1) their boats should be limited in capacity; (2) their names should be registered with the local officials, who would issue them a sailing passport which could be checked by defense officials of the various seaports; (3) a number of ships should be distributed along the seacoast to guard and patrol the waters.[130]

Hsi-chu reported in person to the emperor and briefed him on some opposition among Kwangtung and Fukien officials to the opening of trade.[131] K'ang-hsi, however, went ahead with plans for resuming trade and bringing this trade more firmly under imperial control. According to Father Verbiest, the emperor's intention in opening trade was primarily to conduct a financial experiment. If the emperor found after two years that his treasury had been augmented, he would stand firm in his intentions; if the trade proved to have no advantage, then he would close the ports as before.[132] In ordering a resumption of trade in 1684, K'ang-hsi himself reasoned that customs revenue could help offset military expenses in Kwangtung and Fukien and that in turn would lighten the burden on the interior provinces that had provided grain and financial aid to the coastal areas.[133] K'ang-hsi's pragmatic attitude toward foreign trade reflected an early Manchu experimentation and openness that ran counter to traditional Sino-Confucian views of commerce and foreign relations that later emperors (notably Ch'ien-lung) accepted and defended.[134]

Trade and customs collection fell within the jurisdiction of the Board of Revenue. In the summer months of 1684 the board was busy deliberating on regulations and choosing officials to go to the coastal areas. The board made its initial recommendation on 4 October. The emperor, however, in an edict to the Grand Secretariat, objected to the suggestion of levying customs at inland roads, ferries, and bridges. The board met K'ang-hsi's objection in its final report of 18 October, which contained the following suggestions: (1) customs should be levied only on the trading cargo of ocean-going vessels; (2) the people who go out to sea to trade should be registered and granted permits by the local supervisors as a means of control; (3) the special commissioners should decide on customs regulations in accordance with precedent and on where to locate customs houses; (4) the special commissioners should be permitted to send in their accounts only twice a year (in place of the usual quarterly reports), and each should be allotted an extra clerk to manage affairs. The emperor sanctioned the board's proposals on 22 October.[135] On 1 December, he reconfirmed the abrogation of the maritime trading ban while reminding provincial officials to enforce the normal prohibition on contraband trade.[136]

Customs houses for handling the prospective foreign trade were established at Macao and Canton in Kwangtung, Chang-chou and Amoy in Fukien, Ningpo in Chekiang, and Yün-t'ai-shan (at the mouth of the Shu River) in Kiangsu. Western merchants could now come privately to trade at these ports without being associated with a tribute mission.[137] To the Chinese coastal population the abrogation of the maritime ban and the evacuation policy meant a great deal more. They could once again earn their living by fishing and trading. As a contemporary exclaimed, with hyperbole that perhaps was not entirely unwarranted, "imperial bounty was unlimited, the old and young were all happy over the peace—it was indeed a great age."[138]

Northern Campaigns

The successful campaigns against internal rebellions in the 1670s and 1680s "lubricated the military machinery" which K'ang-hsi and his successors used to expand the external frontiers of China.[139] After the pacification of Taiwan, the emperor was free to pursue an aggressive policy to the north against the Russians and the Mongols, who now had more reason than ever to respect Manchu military and political capabilities. The final victories did not come by 1684, but a precedent had been set in K'ang-hsi's early reign for the later, more glorious campaigns of expansion into Central Asia.

Russian Cossacks in Eastern Siberia had been encroaching upon Chinese territory in the Amur River region since the 1650s, but the wars of conquest and then internal rebellion foreclosed any vigorous Manchu resistance. Minor campaigns, propaganda, and diplomacy, however, were employed to keep the situation fluid until a more active policy could be effected. At the same time, but in unrelated action, the Russian court in Moscow was sending diplomatic and commercial missions to Peking that met with little response.[140] At first, neither Peking nor Moscow linked their diplomatic efforts to the confrontation along the Amur, because they were largely confused about the identity of the antagonists there. Moscow may have perceived that the Amur Cossacks had fought with a subject people of China, but Peking did not identify the Cossacks as Russians, and the Eastern Siberian *voevodas* did not realize they were corresponding with Chinese emperors, until Milovanov's mission of 1670.[141]

K'ang-hsi's first encounter with the Russians came in 1669, when a commercial mission from Moscow arrived in Peking. Although the court recorded this visit as a tributary mission, trade was its primary purpose and the Russians traded freely in the capital under the watchful and interested eyes of the emperor.[142] A short while later, K'ang-hsi was making contact with the *voevoda* of Nerchinsk over the question of Ghantimur's status. Ghantimur was a Tungus chieftain in the Amur region who first fought the Cossack encroachment but later shifted his allegiance and tribute payments to the Russians. The Manchus considered him a fugitive and, to effect his return, K'ang-hsi dispatched a letter in April 1670 to the Nerchinsk *voevoda,* Arshinskii. The latter forwarded a translation of this letter to Moscow and sent back to Peking an illiterate cossack, Ignatii Milovanov, with the emperor's envoy. Not knowing exactly where or to whom he was sending Milovanov, Arshinskii's instructions included a call for the recipient to submit to the Russian tsar. The *voevoda* had apparently taken old patents from the tsar that contained speeches to be used in dealing with native chieftains and incorporated their language in his letter to the emperor of China. Fortunately for the safety of the Russian delegation, the text was incomprehensible to the Chinese officials, and Milovanov and the translator of the document had a chance to soften its tone and put it into a properly submissive form.[143]

When Milovanov returned to Nerchinsk with a letter to the tsar, Arshinskii realized his mistake—he had sent a delegation to Peking, to the Chinese emperor. K'ang-hsi, too, now made the connection between Cossack raids in the Amur area, the Nerchinsk *voevoda,* and the Russian state headed by the tsar. In his letter to the tsar, K'ang-hsi requested that the Russian leader make an effort to control his subjects in the Amur region in order to avoid further conflict and as a precondition for any commercial privileges. The emperor also demanded the return of Ghantimur, but the translation Arshinskii forwarded to Moscow omitted this portion of the letter.[144]

The receipt of K'ang-hsi's official letter in Moscow prompted the tsar to send another mission to Peking to seek trade and diplomatic relations. Nicolai Milescu (usually known as Spathari),[145] the leader of this delegation, reached the Chinese capital on 15 May 1676, after a four-month delay at the border. In Peking he spent another four months chafing under the traditional Chinese rules of diplomatic intercourse. Actually, at one point he was excused from the most odious (to a foreigner) of these procedures—the kowtow—when he protested vigorously. Milescu's generally refractory behavior annoyed the court so much that he was dismissed from Peking in September without any promise of improved Sino-Russian relations and without so much as a letter from K'ang-hsi to the tsar. Instead the emperor insisted that mutual friendship was possible only if Ghantimur and other fugitives were returned and a new, more reasonable envoy was chosen.[146] To offset his failures, Milescu obtained a testimonial letter from Father Verbiest (who aided him in many ways) on the way the envoy had carried out his mission in Peking.[147]

K'ang-hsi supplemented diplomatic probing with military watchfulness. After Milovanov's curious 1670 mission, the emperor instructed Bahai, the military governor of Ninguta, to be on the alert for any Russian activity and to inform Peking immediately.[148] In 1676, Bahai's headquarters were shifted from Ninguta to Kirin on the Sungari river where a naval force was amassed. At the same time, various Mongol tribes living along the Amur were moved to new settlements in the interior, to afford them better protection and also prevent their defection to the Russians. Most of the indigenous population of the Amur region also were organized into "New Manchu" banners as a ready pool for military mobilization.[149]

When the war of the three feudatories was over, K'ang-hsi prepared a well-coordinated, multistaged diplomatic and military campaign to halt the Russian penetration and delineate the northern boundary of the empire. He considered the campaign to be something of a model, judging from his remarks at the time of victory.[150] Even though his claim about planning to deal with the Russians ever since he formally took over government in 1667 was standard rhetoric, still, he had over a number of years thoroughly studied the terrain, transportation and communication facilities, the supply situation, and the talents of men involved. In the *San-fan* crisis, he acted under pressure. In the subjugation of Taiwan, he relied more on the advice of Shih Lang and other men skilled in naval warfare than on his own ideas. But in the Russian campaign he had time to prepare and devise his own strategy.

First came the intelligence missions. In 1682 K'ang-hsi commissioned two Manchu generals, Langtan and Pengcun, to go under the guise of a deer hunt to the vicinity of Albazin, the city founded by Russian fugitives in 1669 and a center of Russian colonizing efforts,[151] to study the situation. The emperor cautioned them against exhibiting any hostility to the Russians there, even to the point of falling back if attacked, because, he added, "I have other plans for defeating them." The only task the two "hunters" had was to determine the distance of roads leading to Nerchinsk, the course of waterways into the area, and the strategic points of their defenses.[152]

Langtan and Pengcun returned and reported in January 1683. In their judgment it would be an easy task to defeat the Russians—a task requiring only three thousand men. K'ang-hsi, although he professed to agree with them, was still wary about striking a quick blow. He did not like to go to war lightly or unprepared. He hoped peaceful negotiations would avert a war, but if fighting was necessary then he wanted to be ready for it. So throughout 1683 K'ang-hsi devised his basic strategy and began to translate plans into reality. He appointed Lin Hsing-chu, a Fukien man formerly serving Wu San-kuei, to supervise a naval construction program at Kirin, giving him fifteen hundred men for the project.[153] He also ordered the movement of Dutch cannon—and men who knew how to fire them—to the front, the construction of two outposts at Aigun and Kumarsk on the lower Amur River, the laying-in of an initial three year supply of military provisions, and the establishment of additional post stations. After government soldiers arrived at the outpost, they were to cultivate the land for their continuing food supply.[154]

Bahai, as the Ninguta military governor, had overall charge of this military buildup, but he objected to some of its details. He opposed the establishment of bases at Aigun and Kumarsk as being too distant from the Russian command center at Albazin. He was impatient for an immediate attack on Albazin before the Russians had time to bring in reinforcements. The emperor disagreed with Bahai and suspected him of jealousy, since Sabsu and Walihu were sent out as field commanders rather than he. There was also friction between Bahai (and Sabsu as well) in the field and the emperor's advisers in Peking. In such a situation, K'ang-hsi himself had to make most strategic and logistic decisions. At this point, he decided to wait until the two commanders had time to size up the situation and train their men well before starting an attack.[155]

Sabsu, who earlier had been in the Langtan-Pengcun spy mission, was elevated later in 1683 to the newly created post of military governor at Aigun, which now became the Ch'ing command center for the Russian campaign, thus further undermining Bahai's position.[156] Throughout the fall and winter of 1683–84, Sabsu and K'ang-hsi discussed the state of preparations and the problems still facing them. Cold weather and snow were holding up the transportation of men, supplies and ammunition—to say nothing of growing food—at E-su-li, a point between Aigun and Kumarsk originally proposed as the base of Ch'ing operations. E-su-li was finally abandoned in favor of Aigun as the permanent base, with Kumarsk as an advance intelligence base. Between Aigun and Kirin, a series of ten post stations was established for efficient communication. Sabsu complained that manpower at Aigun was insufficient to cultivate the land as well as build the fortified outposts. In reply, K'ang-hsi promised to send Sabsu six hundred soldiers from Sheng-ching in the spring but refused his requests for thirty-five hundred soldiers from Kirin and Ninguta. A force of twelve hundred men and eighty ships was gathered to transport a two-year supply of grain to Aigun.[157]

K'ang-hsi's careful and personal planning for the coming struggle with the Russians is evident from the brief description above of the intelligence and logistical phases of the campaign in 1682–84. At the same time, he did not forget diplomatic efforts. As he more than once said, "Going to war is a terrible thing,"[158] and he hoped his military preparedness would convince the enemy to settle their dispute without recourse to fighting. Two captured Russians were sent back with an imperial statement that threatened an attack unless the Russians returned Ghantimur and withdrew from Albazin and Nerchinsk. Any Russian settlers wishing to stay, however, could do so if they accepted Chinese suzerainty and comported themselves well.[159] There was no official answer to K'ang-hsi's letter, but some settlers did decide to remain in Manchuria on the terms offered. These Russians and others captured in border raids were organized in 1683 into a company (*tso-ling*) of the bordered yellow banner.[160]

The final stage of the campaign—the attack and capture of Albazin—was to begin as a raiding operation. Sabsu and Mala, an imperial commissioner sent to the front as an inspector, both recommended destroying the crops around Nerchinsk and Albazin in order to starve out the Russians. K'ang-hsi, while readily approving the idea, suggested the harvest not be destroyed but be transported back to Aigun to supplement Ch'ing supplies. But when it was time in the summer of 1684 to send the expeditionary force out, Sabsu held back, raising a number of objections to the project. The emperor was furious over this missed opportunity and determined to make others responsible for a direct attack on Albazin the following summer. If the capture of the Russian stronghold should prove too difficult then, K'ang-hsi was prepared to fall back to his initial plan of just destroying their harvest.[161]

Pengcun, assisted by Langtan and others, had command of the Albazin campaign of 1685. The defenders of the fort refused a last offer of peace based on a Russian pullback to Yakutsk, the exchange of fugitives (Ghantimur was not specifically mentioned), and the promise of border trade.[162] The attack began on 24 June and ended three days later when the Russians surrendered. The majority were escorted back into Russian territory, but about fifty stayed behind and accepted Chinese suzerainty. The fort at Albazin was razed but, contrary to imperial orders, the crops were not destroyed.[163]

One of the interesting aspects of this short battle was the participation of the so-called cane-shield brigade. This was a group of five hundred Fukien men formerly serving the Cheng family who were skilled in fighting with long knives and cane shields. Their unique skills had come to K'ang-hsi's attention in the winter of 1684 when he had a conversation with Lin Hsing-chu on the techniques of firepower and how to withstand it. Lin described the use of the shields made of cane (rattan) and wadded-up cotton, and he demonstrated their effectiveness. To the emperor's delight, six of his best archers could not penetrate them. Since K'ang-hsi was at that time planning the attack on Albazin, he inquired about the availability of shields and men trained in their use. Fearing it would take too long to bring Fukien men north, the emperor sent banner officials to Shantung, Shansi, and Honan, where many ex-rebels captured in the Taiwan campaign were settled, to find shields and five hundred Fukienese to be put under the care of Lin and Ho Yu, a former commander of Cheng forces. The emperor also ordered Shih Lang to send more shields and daggers to the capital from Fukien.[164] In the Albazin battle the cane-shield brigade was used to prevent Russian reinforcements brought on rafts from reaching the city. The men jumped into the water, protected their heads with the shields, and used their daggers to slash the ankles of the Russians on the rafts and to force them into the river.[165]

A second campaign was fought in 1686 because Russians returned to Albazin, which the Chinese had left undefended, to rebuild its fort and harvest the crops.[166] Sabsu and Langtan led another expedition to Albazin and laid siege to it from July until November when K'ang-hsi ordered the siege lifted to facilitate a peace conference as proposed by the tsar.[167] The emperor's eagerness to conclude a treaty rather than pursuing what appeared to be a successful campaign was inspired by his determination to prevent an alliance between Russia and the Mongol prince Galdan, who was rapidly expanding his power in the north. K'ang-hsi wanted to keep the Russians neutral and Galdan isolated for the coming showdown with the latter.[168]

The peace conference, when it finally came in 1689 after some delay, led to the famous Treaty of Nerchinsk,[169] China's first with a Western power and the first to accord dipomatic equality to the other side. Up to this point, the Manchus had remained cautious in their international relations, adhering to traditional Chinese concepts and practices as part of their effort to be accepted as legitimate rulers by the Chinese elite. Earlier Sino-Russian contacts had all been viewed and conducted within the framework of the tribute system, including the missions of Ablin in 1669 and Milescu in 1676.[170] But with the consolidation of Ch'ing rule completed by the mid-1680s, K'ang-hsi could and did take bold, imaginative steps outside the tribute system to settle the empire's outstanding differences with Russia. For the official record, however, the Treaty of Nerchinsk (negotiated for China primarily by imperial relatives and two Jesuits) was portrayed as another triumph of China's civilizational virtue.[171]

Trouble in the north during K'ang-hsi's early reign was not confined to the Russians. Two Mongol princes, Burni and Galdan, also challenged Manchu authority. Burni revolted in April 1675, when the dynasty had its hands full with rebellion in the south. Burni's aim was to free his father, a Chahar prince who had been imprisoned at Mukden for disrespectful behavior. The emperor dispatched Oja and Tuhai to meet Burni's force, which was marching on Mukden. It was on this expedition that Tuhai delivered the well-known exhortation to his men, a rag-tag band of banner servants and slaves—the well trained bannermen were in the south fighting the *San-fan* rebels. On the march through Shan-hai-kuan and on toward Mukden, Tuhai's army had been stealing and plundering at will, but when they were about to meet Burni their commander told them: "The Chahars are descendants of the Yüan dynasty and very wealthy; if you defeat them you can gain spoils many times more valuable [than what you have been nabbing now]."[172] His words did the trick: this undisciplined mob fell upon Burni's men with great abandon and defeated them on 16 May 1675. Burni fled but was seized and killed a few days later, thus ending the short-lived revolt of the Chahars.[173]

Galdan's open defiance did not come until the 1690s, but he, like Burni, took advantage of the rebellion of the three feudatories to stir up trouble in China's far northwest. K'ang-hsi first became suspicious of the Sungar leader's activity in 1678 and sent a scouting party to Liang-chou, Kansu. They reported back on Galdan's rise to power in recent months as he killed the Ochirtu Khan of the Khoshates and brought more and more Mongol tribes under his control. For the time being K'ang-hsi did not want to interfere in Galdan's affairs, but he instructed General Chang Yung in Kansu to watch the borders carefully.[174] In 1679 Galdan completed his conquest of Eastern Turkestan and was invested by the emperor with the title of Bushktu Khan of the Eleuths. Galdan and the Eleuths remained quiet for about a decade before beginning another phase of expansion, this time into Mongolia at the expense of the Khalkas. Eventually, Galdan's activities led to a confrontation with K'ang-hsi, who carefully planned and personally led three military campaigns against him in 1696–97 until Galdan committed suicide.[175]

In the campaigns just described, common elements in K'ang-hsi's military leadership emerge: the skillful use of former adversaries or their supporters (e.g., Shih Lang, the Fukien brigade at Albazin); the careful attention to detail—he would reject a memorial that was too sketchy on a military situation;[176] an unwillingness to accept his advisers' judgments at face value; the constant concern with his image as a leader; the eager and confident exercise of power. That kind of leadership served K'ang-hsi well in the fifteen years of his early reign, from 1669 to 1684, as he broke Oboi and overturned the regency, defeated a major enemy on land and another at sea, and defended the northern frontiers. All effective military opposition had been crushed. What remained of Ming loyalism went underground, into secret societies, not to surface again for another century. The new dynasty had proved itself and most Chinese patriots gave their grudging, at times admiring, support. Consolidation of Ch'ing rule was complete.

Military Systems

The strength of the banner forces increased steadily and significantly throughout the early years of K'ang-hsi's reign. In the years from 1662 to 1684, the number of banner companies jumped from 618 to 1,047. If each company consisted of 300 men of service age (and their families), then there were about 185,000 men enrolled in the eight banners at the beginning of K'ang-hsi's reign and about 315,000 in 1684. In this period, sudden increases in the number of companies occurred twice: 54 in 1674 in response to Wu San-kuei's rebellion, and 188 in 1684 to absorb former feudatory troops and in preparation for campaigns against the Russians and Galdan of the Eleuth Mongols.[177]

After the suppression of the rebellion of the three feudatories, most banner forces were recalled north and stationed either in the capital, its environs, or in Manchuria. But over 27,000 remained in the south, garrisoning seven strategic cities that formed two lines of defense against future challenges to the dynasty. A central line (troop figures in parenthesis) consisted of Chenkiang (2,740), Nanking (4,700), and Ching-chou (4,700) on the Yangtze, plus Sian (6,700) in Shensi. A coastal line connected Hangchow (3,700), Foochow (2,000), and Canton (3,000).[178] These forces, like the *ordos* of previous alien dynasties, acted as concentrated, mobile shock troops whose very presence was meant to deter rebellious activity. They were not intended to provide local security, which was left to the more numerous but scattered Green Standard forces.

Problems of discipline and training in the banners became more acute under peacetime conditions. K'ang-hsi in 1682 tried to offset the lack of actual fighting by instituting thrice-yearly hunting trips beyond the Wall, to be held in every fourth, tenth, and twelfth month. As many as seventy thousand men, all on horseback, were included in the emperor's retinue on these occasions. All necessary supplies were brought from Peking so as not to trouble the people in the areas they passed through, but special roads for the emperor's passage were constructed and maintained at great expense.[179]

The hunt was a Manchu custom dating from predynastic times that originally served two purposes. It could be a pleasurable event used either to celebrate a victorious campaign or to dispel the gloom and sadness surrounding a sickness or death in one's circle of family and friends. It also had an important military purpose: to practice archery and riding, and to learn to obey commands and maintain formation.[180] Consider this eyewitness report by Father Verbiest of a hunt beyond the Wall in 1682:

> The emperor then selected three thousand soldiers from those who formed his body guard, and who were all armed with bows and arrows. These spread themselves out on either side round the mountain in a wide circle, the diameter of which was at least three Italian miles. They were then arranged in a certain order and distance from each other on the circumference. In order to obviate any inequality or break in the circle by some moving quickly and others slowly, careful order was kept by officers, and among them even some of the great men, who were distributed in the circle. After the positions of all were arranged, each one moved straight forward, whether the ground before him were valley or thick underwood, or whether he had to climb the most rugged heights, and none was allowed to diverge to the right or the left. And thus traversing hill and dale they surrounded all the beasts within their circle as in a net.[181]

Clearly, the chase and encirclement of prey demanded the same kind of discipline as military formation and movement. In fact, the organization of the military machine used by Manchu leaders to expand their empire—the Eight Banner System—was patterned after older tribal hunting arrangements. A clear indication of this relationship survived linguistically in the name of the commanding officer of the basic banner unit of 300 men—the *niru ejen* (known as *tso-ling* in Chinese). It was an old Manchu custom to hunt in units of ten, with each man carrying arrows (*niru*) and one among them chosen as a leader (*ejen*) to maintain proper formation and direction of movement. Anyone breaking discipline would be relieved of his arrows in the field and then punished after the exercises were over. Once in 1637, Daisan (elder brother of the reigning Ch'ing emperor, Abahai) personally whipped one of his sons for errant behavior on a hunt.[182]

In K'ang-hsi's time, hunts also served to restore the emperor's health, if we can believe Father Verbiest's observation. He believed that K'ang-hsi went north to escape the summer heat of Peking and the tiring necessity of continual intercourse with his concubines.[183] It is unlikely that the emperor "tired" of this "necessity," but the good fathers in Peking worried often about this imperial habit. Another Jesuit, Louis Le Comte, saw still another purpose to the imperial hunt. Stating that K'ang-hsi sometimes received Mongol chieftains while he was north of the Wall, Father Le Comte noted that "while this crowd of petty sovereigns is in the camp, the Court is most sumptuous; and in order to impress these barbarians with an idea of the power of China, the train, the attire, and the tents of the mandarins, are rich to profusion and excess."[184] Finally, it is clear that K'ang-hsi personally enjoyed these hunting trips back in the Manchu homeland. Even in and around Peking, K'ang-hsi pursued his interest in the hunt. He had several small parks created and stocked with "wild beasts and fowl," particularly tigers, which he most liked to hunt.[185]

Garrison troops in the south were ordered to conduct similar hunts on a semiannual basis. K'ang-hsi warned their commanders, however, to take care to inform the residents of the area in advance and to prohibit any plundering by the men. He did not want to revive old fears in areas that not long ago knew Manchu atrocities. At the same time, in 1684, K'ang-hsi dealt with another problem unique to these southern garrisons—the possibility that the bannermen, living in centers of Chinese urban culture, might become too sinicized. The solution was to replace them continuously with fresh men from Peking.[186]

Besides the hunting games, K'ang-hsi also conducted archery and equestrian reviews. For instance, between 21 April and 9 May 1684, he watched the civil and military officials and soldiers of each of the eight banners in turn display their talents in shooting from horseback. When the review was finished, K'ang-hsi expressed his displeasure with their mediocrity. Oftentimes the emperor himself participated in these archery contests. He did so when in Nanking on his first Southern Tour, and the onlookers applauded wildly as their emperor hit the target on nine out of ten attempts.[187] At least that is what the official record said, but it is somewhat suspect. At an earlier exhibition of his skill in 1673, K'ang-hsi was officially reported to have hit the target on each of five tries while dismounted and on his only shot from horseback, but the draft entry of the daily diarist recorded it otherwise: the emperor missed twice from the ground.[188]

One organizational change in the banner system was made in

1683 when K'ang-hsi created a musketry battalion (*huo-ch'i ying*) in each banner composed of men from each company within the banner. He suggested that Chinese bannermen unskilled in the equestrian arts be chosen for the new units. The eight battalions were trained and commanded by two Chinese banner officials, T'ung Kuo-kang (an uncle of the emperor) and Chang So-chih.[189]

The Chinese Green Standard (*lu-ying*) forces, which may have totaled as many as 900,000 during the *San-fan* campaigns,[190] were reduced to less than 600,000 by 1685.[191] The excess Green Standard troops were disbanded in an orderly fashion—not filling vacancies due to sickness, old age, or death over a period of two years—and given help in adjusting to their new life as civilians.[192] The strength of the Green Standards, however, was still two or three times that of banner forces, which were variously estimated at 200,000 to 350,000.[193] Unlike the banner forces, *lu-ying* units were scattered throughout the provinces as local security and police forces and were under the command of a great number of governors-general, governors, provincial commanders-in-chief, brigade-generals, colonels, and lower officers (see table 1). The number of men under a governor-general varied widely from the standard of 5,000 set in 1683, but the governor's troops were very often either 1,000 or 1,500 as stipulated in a 1682 regulation.[194]

To insure against any personal buildup of power among Green Standard commanders, particulary *t'i-tu* and *tsung-ping*, K'ang-hsi in April 1683 required periodic audiences to instill a healthy fear in them and to keep them under surveillance. The spectacle of a military officer kneeling to a higher authority (the emperor) would serve to destroy some of the awe and respect accorded the officer by his men.[195] K'ang-hsi did not want the repetition of a Wu San-kuei, a Keng Ching-chung, or a Shang Chih-hsin. Provincial commanders and brigade-generals also were shifted about the empire to prevent them from establishing roots in any one locality, and they were denied direct access to the throne.[196]

The most important change to emerge through the war years of the 1670s and 1680s had to do not with the organization or disposition of either of the two army systems but with the relative value of each as a fighting force. It is well known that the banners decreased and the *lu-ying* increased in importance during the *San-fan* campaigns. I will add nothing new to this general conclusion, but I can show how the shift was perceived. At the outset of the

TABLE 1
Disposition and Strength of Green Standard Forces in 1685

		Command[a]					
Location	Total	Tsung-tu	Hsün-fu	Chiang-chün	T'i-tu	Tsung-ping[b]	Fu-chiang[b]
Capital	3300	. .	. .	. .	. .	. .	. .
Chihli	30700[c]	. .	1000	. .	. .	(3)29000	(1) 600
Shansi	25000	. .	1000	. .	. .	(2)24000	. .
Shensi	38587	7000	1500	. .	12123	(2)17964	. .
Kansu	47391	. .	1500	. .	5000	(3)40891	. .
Szechwan	30000	. .	1500	. .	2600	(4)15554	(4)10346
Yunnan	42000	5000	1800	. .	12200	(6)23000	. .
Kweichow	20000	. .	1500	. .	12440	(3) 6060	. .
Kwangsi	20000	. .	1500	. .	14900	(1) 3600	. .
Hukuang	40000	2000	1300	. .	26290	(4) 9110	. .
Hunan	. .	. .	1300	. .	. .	. .	. .
Kwangtung	73200	5918	1500	4000	16499	(8)45283	. .
Kiangnan	49850	4820	1000	2000	20474	(3)13691	. .
Anhwei	. .	6415[d]	1450	. .	. .	. .	. .
Chekiang	43450	. .	1500	. .	13275	(4)28675	. .
Kiangsi	15000	. .	1500	. .	. .	(2)11180	(2) 2320
Fukien	69726	2500	1476	. .	65750[e]	. .	. .
Shantung	20000	2874[f]	1000	. .	. .	(1)16126	. .
Honan	10000	. .	1000	. .	. .	(2) 9000	. .
Totals	578204[c]	36527	24326	6000	201551[e]	293134	13266

Source: *K'ang-hsi hui-tien, chüan* 94.
[a]For translations of command titles, see Brunnert and Hagelstrom, *Political Organization of China*, nos. 820–21, 744, and 750–52.
[b]Number of such commands in each province is given in parenthesis.
[c]Includes one hundred men under the command of a *shou-pei*.
[d]Under command of the director-general of grain transportation.
[e]Includes troops of seven *tsung-ping* and twenty thousand men under command of Fukien naval *t'i-tu*.
[f]Under command of the director-general of river conservancy.

war, K'ang-hsi relied on Manchus—and most of them members of the imperial family—to command the government forces. Even the use of Manchu troops was favored over Green Standard forces on the grounds that they were more loyal and trustworthy.[197] But as the war progressed the emperor, and some generals as well, began to commend the Green Standard units for their valorous efforts on behalf of the dynasty and began to rely more heavily on them.[198]

This is not to say that all doubts about the Chinese forces

dissolved. Manggitu in 1678 called the Green Standard troops' reputation groundless, and this view was echoed once by K'ang-hsi himself a few years later in an audience with a Shensi regional commander.[199] But circumstances led the emperor to use the Green Standards as the main force in suppressing the rebellion. Banner forces were not large, and their leadership suffered as talented bannermen were pressed more into bureaucratic service (as *tu-fu*, for instance). Manchu generals and their men were not distinguishing themselves in battle, and the southern terrain was unsuitable for Manchu cavalry.[200] So the final campaigns of 1679–81 in the southwest were largely fought by Green Standard troops led by Chinese generals.

K'ang-hsi set the stage in November 1679, when he ordered Chang Yung, Wang Chin-pao, Chao Liang-tung, and Sun Ssu-k'o to lead their Green Standard forces into southern Shensi and Szechwan. Chinese troops, he noted, were accustomed to fighting in this terrain and should form the vanguard, while Manchu cavalry followed in their wake. Furthermore, this would conform to the old practice of "using Chinese to pacify Chinese."[201] These four generals had gained prominence in 1674–76 in containing the rebellion of Wang Fu-ch'en in Kansu—Chang as *t'i-tu* and the others as *tsung-ping*. Chang in the end did not participate in the recovery of the southwest but remained in Kansu, where he kept the Khoshote Mongols at bay, and he was heavily decorated by K'ang-hsi and later emperors for his service.[202] Wang, Chao, and Sun each led an army through southern Shensi in 1679, into Szechwan in 1680, and finally into Yunnan, the original stronghold of Wu San-kuei, in 1681.[203]

Sun Ssu-k'o did not perform as well as his two colleagues and was severely reprimanded by K'ang-hsi for his reluctance to advance into Shensi, but Sun came back to win merit and honor for his role in defeating Galdan in 1695.[204] Chao and Wang, on the other hand, had a rapid succession of victories, which earned them not only the emperor's praise but also military and political leadership—Chao was appointed governor-general of Yunnan and Kweichow—of the campaign to recover the southwest.[205] Both men were rewarded after the war with the rank of viscount, although Chao was victimized by his jealous rivals (Wang and two Manchu generals) and had to wait over a decade to be so honored.[206]

A third, independent type of military organization—the local army—briefly made an appearance during the *San-fan* war. The first instances of locally raised and led armies in the Ch'ing period were those associated with such famous Ming loyalist scholars as Huang Tsung-hsi, Ku Yen-wu, Wang Fu-chih, Sun Ch'i-feng, Ch'en Tzu-chuang, and Chin Pao.[207] During the *San-fan* rebellion, however, the few local armies that were reported were all fighting with, not against, the imperial government. Yao Ch'i-sheng, a prominent figure in the recovery of Taiwan and governor-general of Fukien, got his start this way. In 1674 he organized a local force of about a thousand in his native district of K'uai-chi, Chekiang, and offered its services to Prince Giyesu for use against Keng Ching-chung. Yao was rewarded with a district magistrate's post. Two years later, Giyesu reported the aid of another local militia (*min-ping*), this one led by a commoner of the Ch'ing-yüan district of Chekiang.[208] A *t'uan-lien* local defense unit was created in Kiangsi in 1674 to protect Hsing-kuo district from former Cheng rebels who had revolted again. Its leader, a man named Ts'ai Chang, was later made naval *tsung-ping* at Nanching.[209] Local armies reportedly also existed in Kwangsi,[210] and a careful search of local gazetteers from other southern provinces would undoubtedly uncover still more.

There is no record of official concern or action after the war on such locally recruited armies, but it is unlikely that the Ch'ing court allowed them to become a permanent feature of its military establishment. Irregular units of the Green Standard forces were disbanded, and the same fate, or perhaps incorporation into a Green Standard unit, must have awaited local armies.

Five

MASTERING THE BUREAUCRACY

With military supremacy assured through the successful campaigns just described, K'ang-hsi turned his attention to the consolidation of bureaucratic control. Immediately after the fall of Oboi, the emperor began to surround himself with a new breed of men. His key advisers were still Manchus. But it is important to note that these Manchus were not the old warriors who had made their mark in military campaigns. They were instead a younger generation of Manchus who had risen to prominence through the government and palace administrations and had not participated in the wars of conquest.[1] It was a changing of the guard. Furthermore, K'ang-hsi was mindful of the still sensitive issue of ethno-political balance in government. The Chinese elite wanted to be reassured of the new dynasty's intention to share bureaucratic power with them. Increasingly throughout the *San-fan* period, Chinese civil as well as military officials of nonbanner backgrounds were advancing to the inner circles of power and trust. This development was not without problems, notably the growth of factionalism based on ethnic grounds. But K'ang-hsi could tolerate a moderate amount of factionalism and the other bane of Chinese bureaucratic politics—corruption—as long as Chinese regional power had been destroyed and channels of decision making were bent to serve the emperor.

Key Officials

The elder statesman of K'ang-hsi's new group of advisers was Songgotu, the third son of Soni. His early career is shrouded in mystery, and his rise to high rank can only be attributed to the support he gave K'ang-hsi in breaking Oboi in 1669. Before that crisis, Songgotu had served merely as an imperial guard and, for a brief period, as vice-president of the Board of Civil Appointments, but within three months after the fall of Oboi, Songgotu had been appointed a grand secretary.[2] This was K'ang-hsi's first major appointment, which was made to fill the opening created by the execution of Bambursan for his participation in Oboi's clique. In the next decade, Songgotu became the most influential official in government, even though K'ang-hsi had to call him to task on several occasions. Once it was for his advocacy of punishing advisers whom he felt had precipitated the rebellion of the three feudatories, and on other occasions it was for his unbridled haughtiness. It was an expression of the latter—failure to keep his brothers in check—that cost Songgotu his titles and posts in 1683.[3] He came back later to perform valuable service for the dynasty in negotiating the Treaty of Nerchinsk in 1689, but other Manchus replaced him after 1683 as the emperor's chief advisers.

Perhaps too much should not be made of Songgotu's opposition to Oboi as a determinant of future influence and high rank. Of the seven Manchu grand secretaries that served K'ang-hsi in the period 1669–84, only Songgotu and Batai had a record of opposition to the regent.[4] Information on four others (Tuhai, Duikana, Mingju, and Ledehun) is lacking, but the seventh grand secretary, Molo, was known as an Oboi supporter. Molo in fact had a remarkable career and was advancing rapidly into a position of power and influence when he met an untimely death in 1674.[5] His first recorded service to the state came in 1650 when he was appointed to middle-ranking posts in several capital ministries. More than a decade passed before Molo was mentioned again, this time (in 1667) as a vice-presidential appointee to the Censorate. Within a year he held the vital governor-generalship of the Shansi-Shensi-Kansu area. He held this post for three years and in the process rode out the storm following Oboi's fall in the summer of 1669.

The favor of Oboi can perhaps explain Molo's meteoric rise before 1669, but after K'ang-hsi assumed control his relationship with the disgraced regent was a distinct liability. Yet Molo overcame this liability to retain his high post and even went on to become a trusted official of K'ang-hsi. The retention of his governor-general post was due to the testimony on his behalf submitted not only by his fellow officials but also by the commoners of Shensi and Kansu.[6] Molo served in the capital as president of the Board of Punishments from 1670 to 1674, at which time he returned to Shensi as supreme commander (*ching-lüeh*) in charge of defending the northwestern provinces against the rebellious forces of Wu San-kuei. Molo had the distinction of being one of only four men (the others were Hung Ch'eng-ch'ou, O-er-t'ai, and Chang Kuang-ssu) to hold this position in the early Ch'ing period and the only one in the entire K'ang-hsi period.[7] Molo's authority in Shensi extended over both military and civilian officials and was strengthened by concurrent titles of grand secretary, president of the Board of War and of the Board of Punishments, and president of the Censorate.

Thus, five years after narrowly escaping disgrace and removal from office for being a supporter of Oboi, Molo was shouldering the highest possible wartime responsibility for K'ang-hsi. There seems only one ready explanation for this: Molo (and others soon to be noted) had been on the right side in the second critical decision of K'ang-hsi's early reign (the breaking of Oboi was the first)—the decision to disband the feudatories in 1673. This decision precipitated the eight-year civil war in which the very existence of the newly established Manchu dynasty was threatened, and K'ang-hsi gave the matter serious consideration. In the end the young emperor ruled against the majority of his advisers. Three Manchu board presidents, however, stood on K'ang-hsi's side—Molo, Mingju, and Mishan.[8]

Like Molo, Mingju and Mishan also profited by their stand on the feudatories. Mishan, unlike the other two, was known as an opponent of Oboi. K'ang-hsi's gratitude for Mishan's early support was deepened during the latter's tenure as president of the Board of Revenue, to which the emperor had appointed him immediately after the fall of Oboi. Mishan improved the fiscal system by getting surplus provincial funds shifted to the capital and built up the national treasury to the point where he could assure K'ang-hsi in 1673 that it would finance, if need be, a ten-year war with the rebellious feudatories.[9] Mishan died in 1675, at the age of forty-four and in the midst of a promising career. What he failed to achieve because of an early death was realized by his descendants, who through many generations held a number of hereditary titles and high posts and even produced an empress. The family founded by Mishan has been called "the most illustrious family of the dynasty."[10]

Mingju, the third of the board presidents supporting K'ang-hsi's decision to disband the feudatories, came in time to be the most powerful court official, overshadowing Songgotu in the 1680s. From extant Diaries of the Emperor's Movements for the eighth and ninth months of K'ang-hsi's nineteenth year (1680),[11] it is evident that the emperor was relying mostly on Mingju's advice (and occasionally that of Ledehun, one of the other Manchu grand secretaries) on appointments and personnel evaluation.

Two Manchu grand secretaries urged K'ang-hsi not to disband the feudatories: Songgotu, whose career has already been outlined, and Tuhai. The latter emerged in the civil war as the leading Manchu field commander and strategist. After his exploits in the north against Burni in 1675, Tuhai was sent to Kansu as commander-in-chief (*ta-chiang-chün*) in 1676. The area had been without an overall commander since 1674 after the death of Molo. Tuhai recovered Kansu for the imperial side, then worked closely with four Chinese generals to move into Shensi and Szechwan to complete the suppression of the revolt of the three feudatories.[12]

From this brief review of the careers of the Manchu grand secretaries in the period 1669–84,[13] it is evident that an official's previous stands and political loyalties were not the only determinants of imperial favor. K'ang-hsi promoted to the highest rank and put his trust in men who stood on both sides of what obviously were the two most important issues of his early reign. Songgotu and Batai served imperial interests against Oboi, but Molo had been in the regent's party; Molo and Mingju (along with Mishan, who was not a grand secretary) saw the wisdom of K'ang-hsi's position on the feudatories, but Songgotu and Tuhai had opposed the emperor's course of action.

Other considerations, therefore, must have weighed equally heavily in the emperor's decision to select these men as his chief advisers. Although the Imperial Household was a recruiting ground for such responsible and lucrative provincial posts as textile commissioner, salt commissioner, and customs house director, it was not necessarily the avenue to high metropolitan rank and power.[14] In the small sample of seven grand secretaries, only Mingju and Batai were known to have served in the Nei-wu-fu. In the final analysis, perhaps we can credit K'ang-hsi with choosing his inner circle of officials on the basis of proven or potential talent.

Of the ten Chinese grand secretaries who served in the period 1669–84, only one (Chiang He-te) was a bannerman, and he was a holdover from the Shun-chih and regency periods.[15] Chiang died in 1670 and thereafter all the Chinese grand secretaries were non-bannermen. The meaning and importance of the ethno-political affiliation of high officials will be discussed later. K'ang-hsi's closest advisers among Chinese grand secretaries were Li Wei, Tu Li-te, and Feng P'u.

Li Wei (1625–84) was the dean of this group, serving as grand secretary continuously from 1658 to 1684. Li was only thirty-four and a subchancellor of the Grand Secretariat when chosen by Shun-chih as a grand secretary—an unusually young age to be tapped for such high honor and responsibility. He survived the regency period by remaining silent, or "standing aloof" in the judgment of one biographer,[16] whenever his opinion differed from that of Oboi or the other regents. Li came into his own under K'ang-hsi, and particularly during the rebellion of the three feudatories. He received oral communications from the emperor dealing with military strategy and orders from which he drafted imperial edicts. At this task he worked long and hard and never once betrayed the emperor's confidence.[17] With Feng P'u (1609–92) and Tu Li-te (1611–91), Li Wei formed a triad of Chinese grand secretaries who were among K'ang-hsi's closest advisors during the *San-fan* crisis.

In addition to these three men, one other Chinese official gained K'ang-hsi's confidence during this period. Wang Hsi, who was instrumental in drafting Shun-chih's will in 1661, was one of the earliest officials to warn the emperor of the growing power of the three feudatories. As president of the Censorate in 1667, he memorialized on the excessive claims on imperial revenues made by Wu San-kuei to support his forces in the southwest, and he suggested that Green Standard forces in the area be drastically reduced.[18] Shortly after Wang became president of the Board of War in the spring of 1673, the question of disbanding the feudatories arose, and Wang joined with three Manchu board presidents (Mingju, Mishan, and Molo) in support of K'ang-hsi.[19]

Immediately after the rebellion broke out, a wave of unrest spread through Peking as officials and people waited to learn of the government's response. Part of the anxiety was caused by the presence in the capital of Wu Ying-hsiung, son of Wu San-kuei and the consort of a princess. It was at the urging of Wang Hsi that K'ang-hsi executed Wu Ying-hsiung early in 1674, and this act had the salutary effect that Wang intended: restoring the people's confidence in the ability of the Manchus to meet this crisis. Later in the same year K'ang-hsi began to entrust Wang with the reading of secret military documents.[20] Wang continued as president of the Board of War until retiring in 1678 to mourn the death of his father. By then, Wu San-kuei was dead and the defeat of the rebellious forces was only a matter of time. After the final pacification, Wang returned to service as president of the Board of Rites and then in 1682 as a grand secretary. By the late 1680s, he had replaced Mingju as perhaps the most influential man at court.

A Manchu-Chinese Dyarchy?

We have long been accustomed to attributing Manchu success, at least in part, to the Manchus' willingness to share power with Chinese in high central and provincial posts. This administrative practice of the Ch'ing dynasty is often described in terms of a Manchu-Chinese duality or "dyarchy."[21] While dyarchy adequately describes the situation in the nineteenth century, it makes no sense at all in the early Ch'ing period, because it ignores a third, intermediate group: Chinese bannermen. While a system of dual appointments of Manchus and Chinese operated in the capital and Chinese dominated local officialdom,[22] Chinese bannermen held a pivotal place in the provincial administration as governors-general and governors (*tsung-tu* and *hsün-fu* respectively, or *tu-fu* collectively). As the chief agents of imperial authority outside the capital, *tu-fu* were vital instruments of Manchu control over the Chinese empire.[23]

Appointments of *tu-fu* were generally made without regard to the ethno-political affiliation of the candidate. The Shun-chih emperor, as we have noted before, embraced the ideal of impartiality and propagated it as basic dynastic policy. K'ang-hsi was equally concerned about maintaining an impartial attitude toward all his subjects. An example of his concern would be his appointment of Mingju to head a delegation to offer the emperor's condolences to Board of War president Wang Hsi on the death of his father in 1679. Since this was done in the case of Manchu high officials, K'ang-hsi reasoned that equal consideration ought to be given to Chinese high officials.[24] Likewise, K'ang-hsi in 1682 decided to fete Chinese officials in the same hall used for Manchus.[25] The emperor could look back in 1712 on his already long reign and say with evident satisfaction that never had he made any distinctions between Manchus, Mongols, or Chinese. What prompted his review was the mutual impeachment case of Gali and Chang Po-hsing which K'ang-hsi mediated and decided essentially in favor of the Chinese official.[26]

K'ang-hsi, however, did not shrink from criticizing Chinese on occasion. He once complained that too many Chinese officials were blaming their Manchu counterparts when things went wrong but were claiming the credit if all went well. Shortly after this incident, the emperor also challenged dissident Chinese officials to present evidence of their charges of imperial favoritism towards Manchus.[27] K'ang-hsi's grandson Ch'ien-lung once claimed: "All the emperors of this reigning dynasty from my grandfather, my father, and on down to me have held fast to the principle of impartiality without a trace of favoritism."[28]

Such was the image and the ideal of Manchu ethnic policy in government, as expounded by early Ch'ing emperors. But the validity of this image is open to question. For instance, a censor in 1651 pointed out that every governor-general and seventeen of the twenty-two governors were Chinese bannermen (the other five governors were nonbannermen Chinese).[29] While this did not represent strictly ethnic discrimination, it was an excessive reliance on those Chinese politically allied with and controlled by Manchus. Again, in 1667, a *chin-shih* candidate claimed that between twenty and thirty percent of current *tu-fu* were Chinese, and all the rest were Manchus.[30] In point of fact, Manchus were not considered for either post until late in 1667.[31] But the writer obviously included Chinese bannermen in the "Manchu" category, and as such he was more than justified to register his complaint. In fact, he understated his case, because at the time Chinese bannermen held twenty-eight of the twenty-nine *tu-fu* posts. Only the single post of Yunnan governor was occupied by a Chinese.

These examples of ethno-political imbalance in favor of Manchus and bannermen in the appointment of *tu-fu* certainly tarnish the imperially propagated image of impartiality. However, political more than ethnic considerations guided Manchu rulers in the selection of *tu-fu*. The Manchu court just once ordered the exclusive use of Manchus in *tu-fu* posts. An imperial decision in 1668 reserved *tu-fu* positions in the Shensi-Shansi area for Manchus only. Thereafter, and until the beginning of Yung-cheng's reign (1723) when this policy was abandoned, all appointments of *tu-fu* in the Shensi-Shansi region were Manchus.[32] With that single exception, ethnic affiliation was no bar to the holding of power in high provincial posts. Bannermen and nonbannermen alike could be chosen as *tu-fu* "according to their capabilities, the locality, the circumstances, and the time"[33]—in short, according to the dictates of dynastic policy.

A chronological listing of Ch'ing *tu-fu*, with their provincial or banner registration given, is available, but the information provided for the crucial early years of the dynasty is not trustworthy.[34] Officials listed as registrants of Fengtien have almost invariably turned out to be Chinese bannermen. Their banner affiliation, so scrupulously avoided in local and dynastic histories, becomes apparent after checking the official banner history.[35] Even a few men with registrations in central provinces have turned out to be bannermen.[36] But a careful collation of these sources and the standard biographical collections[37] will yield fairly accurate statistics on the ethno-political background of early Ch'ing *tu-fu*.

Over the life of the dynasty, *tu-fu* positions (when taken together) were shared fairly equally by bannermen (Manchu, Mongol, and Chinese) and by nonbannermen Chinese, as seen in table 2. When these totals are divided into separate figures for governors-general and governors, they show bannermen holding a clear majority of the former posts and Chinese holding a slight majority of the latter posts. These proportions, however, do not yet tell the whole story. A good percentage of the bannermen totals in each case consist of Chinese bannermen (36 percent of governors-general, 46 percent of governors, or 44 percent of *tu-fu* as a whole).

Early Manchu rulers appreciated the unique position of Chinese bannermen and appointed them with great frequency to top provincial posts (see tables 3 and 4). Unlike Manchus and ordinary Chinese, Chinese bannermen brought both political reliability and linguistic and administrative skills to their posts. But when K'ang-hsi began to rule personally, a major shift occurred, and thereafter there was a steadily declining use of Chinese bannermen as *tu-fu*. After Yung-cheng's reign (1723–35), they never accounted for more

TABLE 2
Composition of Ch'ing *Tu-fu* Personnel

Ethno-political Affiliation	*Tu-fu* Number	*Tu-fu* Percentage of Total	*Tsung-tu* Number	*Tsung-tu* Percentage of Total	*Hsün-fu* Number	*Hsün-fu* Percentage of Total
Chinese bannermen	287	22.0	115	20.8	252	22.4
Manchus	342	26.3	187	33.7	270	24.1
Mongols	26	2.0	14	2.5	21	1.9
Bannermen (total)	655	50.3	316	57.0	543	48.4
Chinese	646	49.7	238	43.0	579	51.6
Total[a]	1301	100.0	554	100.0	1122	100.0

[a]The total number of *tu-fu* (1301) does not match the added totals of *tsung-tu* (554) and *hsün-fu* (1122) because 375 (or two-thirds) of the *tsung-tu* had previously served as *hsün-fu*, and such officials were counted only once in calculating *tu-fu*.

than ten percent of new personnel and usually much less.[38] A comparison of *tu-fu* statistics for the Regency (1662–68) and K'ang-hsi's early rule (1669–83) reflects well the divergent policy goals of Oboi and the emperor. Oboi and the other regents continued to rely heavily on Chinese bannermen, but regular Chinese were replaced by Manchu appointees. K'ang-hsi, on the other hand, began to use both Chinese and Manchus. The regency's personnel policy confirms their basic commitment to Manchu nativism: to elevate Manchu institutions, values, and officials over

TABLE 3
Changing Composition of Early Ch'ing Governors-general

Period	Total New Personnel[a]	Chinese Number	Chinese Percentage of Total	Chinese Bannermen Number	Chinese Bannermen Percentage of Total	Manchus Number	Manchus Percentage of Total
1644–61	49	10	20.4	38	77.6	1	2.0
1662–68	9	--	--	7	77.8	2	22.2
1669–83	21	2	9.6	12	57.1	7	33.3
1684–1722	64	13	20.3	27	42.2	24	37.5
1723–35	39	17	43.6	12	30.8	10	26.6

[a]No Mongols were appointed governor-general in these periods.

their Chinese counterparts. The emperor was moving in a different direction: toward an accommodation with his Chinese subjects.

K'ang-hsi's decision to increasingly use both Chinese and Manchus was based on several factors. Intermarriage and other forms of sinicization were beginning to blunt Manchu-Chinese cultural differences.[39] Manchus now possessed the necessary language and administrative skills to be appointed *tu-fu*. An edict of 5 March 1671 abolished the post of interpreter (*t'ung-shih*) in capital boards and courts and in provincial and Tartar-general (*chiang-chün*) yamen on the grounds that Manchu officials now knew Chinese.[40] Within two years, K'ang-hsi in fact was expressing fears that Manchus were becoming too sinicized. He was afraid that future generations of Manchus would entirely forget their native tongue. To preclude this development, he ordered the compilation of a Manchu-Chinese dictionary.[41] Still, however, an occasional Manchu official would be found who did not know Chinese. This was true in the case of Dadu, who served for several months in 1674–75 as governor of Chekiang.[42]

Perhaps even more significant than the increasing competence and acculturation of Manchus was the decreasing political risk of using either Chinese or Manchus. By K'ang-hsi's time, the forging of imperial supremacy over Manchu clan interests was largely accomplished, through the work of Abahai, Dorgon, and K'ang-hsi himself. The early years of K'ang-hsi's personal rule also marked the end of any Chinese hope of military opposition to the Manchus. By 1683, the rebellion of the three Chinese feudatory princes had

TABLE 4
Changing Composition of Early Ch'ing Governors

		Chinese		Chinese Bannermen		Manchus	
Period	Total New Personnel	Number	Percentage of Total	Number	Percentage of Total	Number	Percentage of Total
1644–61	124	30	24.2	94	75.8	--	--
1662–68	13	1	7.7	10	76.9	2	15.4
1669–83	53	13	24.5	27	51.0	13	24.5
1684–1722	164	55	33.5	69	42.1	40	24.4
1723–35	81	36	44.4	19	23.5	26[a]	32.1[a]

[a]These figures include two Mongol appointees.

been crushed and Taiwan had been recovered from Ming loyalist forces. In these circumstances, the dynasty was firmly established and the emperor no longer feared sharing high governmental responsibility with nonbannermen Chinese.

If length of service of *tu-fu* personnel is also considered, a more complete picture of the Manchu government's sharing of power can be drawn. The average length of term and the average length of total service varied significantly according to ethno-political affiliation.[43] Chinese bannermen were the most favored group, and Chinese were the least favored (if the statistically insignificant Mongols are excluded). Considering dynastic averages, a Chinese bannerman would serve in a particular governor-general post for three and one-half years and have a total length of service as governor-general (in two or more posts) of six years and seven months. A Chinese official, on the other hand, would on the average serve for only two years and eight months in any single governor-general post or a total of four and one-half years in his career, more than two years less than the average career service of Chinese bannermen. Among governors, the same situation existed: Chinese bannermen served, on the average, nine months longer than ordinary Chinese in any single post and eight months longer in terms of overall career service. Manchus generally fell between the high and low averages of service in both governor-general and governor posts. Only in average length of term as governors did Manchus fare worse than Chinese.

It might be supposed that Chinese bannermen emerged with better average length of term in dynastic statistics because the bulk of their service came in the early years of the dynasty, when perhaps a lack of talent and the unsettled conditions resulted in longer terms of office for all *tu-fu*. Would not, then, Manchus and Chinese serve in *tu-fu* posts just as long as Chinese bannermen in the period of conquest and consolidation, 1644–83? The statistics for this period, given in table 5, provide an answer. Chinese served on the average a year less than Chinese bannermen in governor-general posts and eight months less in governor posts.[44] The averages of these two groups for 1644–83, then, are roughly comparable to the dynastic averages given above. Manchus, on the other hand, did serve significantly longer in this early period than they did over the whole dynastic span. In fact, Manchus outdistanced both Chinese groups. As noted previously, few Manchus in the beginning of the dynasty had the requisite skills to head the provincial administration. Those who did stayed in their posts longer. In contrast, Chinese talent—when the Manchus felt secure enough to tap it—was plentiful. Perhaps this helps explain their generally shorter terms of office throughout the Ch'ing dynasty. Frequent shifting would also prevent Chinese from establishing roots in any one area.

TABLE 5
Average Length of *Tu-fu* Appointments, 1644–83

Affiliation	Aggregate Service (Years/months)	Appointments (Number)	Average Length of Term (Years/months)
Tsung-tu			
Chinese bannermen	307/11	87	3/6
Manchus	49/3	12	4/1
Chinese	36/11	15	2/6
Hsün-fu			
Chinese bannermen	572/0	177	3/3
Manchus	56/10	16	3/7
Chinese	135/8	53	2/7

Ethno-political composition of *tu-fu* personnel, then, was not a static arrangement, but varied according to dynastic needs and the divergent goals of successive leaders. Shifting ground slightly, we can consider the question of Manchu sharing of power from another perspective: ranking of officials. Until Shun-chih's fifteenth year (1658), Manchu officials were ranked higher than their Chinese counterparts in capital posts. For example, Manchu grand secretaries and presidents of the boards and of the Censorate were all given rank 1, while Chinese holding the same posts were given rank 2. For a time, though, spanning the years from 1658 to 1667, Manchu and Chinese ranks were equalized.[45] Then in March 1667, shortly after Oboi had completed the banner land shift and had become in effect a dictator, a partial reversion to pre-1658 discriminatory rankings was instituted. This discrimination went out with Oboi; within a year after K'ang-hsi took over government, Manchu and Chinese ranks were once again equalized. This was accomplished by lowering Manchu ranks to the level of the Chinese ranks—but not immediately. Men already in office retained their current rank, but future appointees would fall under the new regulations.[46]

Emperor, Officials, and Cliques

In 1679 K'ang-hsi addressed court officials on the subject of personnel management. He was not interested, he professed, in closely examining every official for minor faults in order to dismiss him. In employing men, he argued, you must use them in areas for which they have talent; you cannot expect to find perfect men.[47] One of K'ang-hsi's officials had many years earlier said much the same thing in a memorial entitled "Toleration of shortcomings is the key to good personnel management."[48] Extending these ideas somewhat, the emperor once approvingly quoted the statement, "It is better to employ one who has erred [and redeemed himself] than one with merit."[49] On another occasion, he claimed he would "rather err in leniency than in harshness." He supported this last statement with the story of a banner official who was falsely accused and unjustly executed during the regency. To avoid a repetition of similar incidents, the emperor was determined to give condemned men a second chance, to reopen their cases for further examination until no doubt of their guilt remained.[50] The preceding statements indicate a certain laxity or indulgence on K'ang-hsi's part, but he could also be tough and sarcastic with officials. Overall, an ambivalence seems to inform his handling of men.

K'ang-hsi treated his favorites with great kindness, as in the well-known case of Hsiung Tz'u-li. Hsiung had helped educate the young emperor and had been one of the first officials to speak out against Oboi's regency, and he was not forgotten by the mature K'ang-hsi. He honored him twice on Southern Tours (in 1684 and again in 1707) and upon Hsiung's passing in 1709. After Hsiung's death the emperor was very solicitous about the welfare of his family. Financial assistance was provided by textile commissioners Li Hsü and Ts'ao Fu at K'ang-hsi's direction, and two of Hsiung's young sons were received in audience and encouraged to continue with their studies. Sons or nephews of other eminent officials, such as Chang Ying, Chang Yü-shu, Li Wei, Tu Li-te, Li Kuang-ti, and Wang Hsi, received equally fine treatment and were given capital posts via the *yin* privilege.[51] The emperor often went beyond kindness and overlooked, or perhaps tolerated, the shortcomings and malpractices of officials. He would halt investigations of official venality when it was on the verge of implicating too many highly placed men. For example, the investigation of Hukuang's governor, Chang Ch'ien, who was impeached for corruption in 1688, was halted when it implicated Hsü Ch'ien-hsüeh, Kao Shih-ch'i, and Ch'en T'ing-ching, all eminent scholars and officials who were close to the emperor.[52]

On the other hand, K'ang-hsi valued honesty very highly. The emperor was fond of reminding his tutors and advisers that the empire was governed by men, not laws, hence the emphasis he put on the search for virtuous ministers.[53] K'ang-hsi held up two men, both named Yü Ch'eng-lung, as paragons of virtue in his early reign.[54] During the elder Yü's tenure as governor of Chihli in 1680–82, K'ang-hsi called him the most honest official in the empire and without a peer.[55] The younger Yü was Nanking prefect at the time of K'ang-hsi's first Southern Tour. The emperor was pleased to note that the Yü he met in person was as honest as the Yü he knew in Peking only through reports. He urged the prefect, soon to be appointed provincial judge of Anhwei, to emulate his namesake, the elder Yü, and live up to the emperor's trust.[56]

The two Yü's were apparently talented as well as upright—a rare combination. Given a choice, though, K'ang-hsi gave priority to the latter attribute. He knew talent was not easy to come by, but honest officials were even scarcer. This attitude partially explains why K'ang-hsi carried Chang Po-hsing, an incorruptible provincial official, along so far despite his very serious personal and administrative failings. When Chang was impeached and condemned to death in 1712, the emperor refused to punish him and noted: "He is truly not a man fit to be a governor. Yet he can prevent bribery and has great integrity. Let him be put in charge of some financial post where there's not too much going on."[57]

Another official singled out as incorruptible was Sung Wen-lien, the prefect of Shuntien. Grand secretary Feng P'u, who recommended Sung, noted that he had the added burden of being poor. K'ang-hsi, however, denounced the idea that probity, or the lack of it, had anything to do with a man's material wealth.[58] But K'ang-hsi's son, Yung-cheng, was wiser in this regard, and the *yang-lien* ("cultivation of incorruptibility") stipend he established went far toward eliminating one of the basic causes of corruption—inadequate official salaries.

K'ang-hsi by the end of his early reign seemed satisfied that he had made great strides in rooting out corruption, particularly in the central government. He admitted, though, that evil practices still existed in the provinces—a situation that would be remedied only if governors and governors-general would set a personal example of incorruptibility on the one hand, and be quick to investigate corrupt subordinates on the other.[59] K'ang-hsi's concern with provincial corruption led him in 1682 to depute special officials to each province, starting with Chihli, for an inspection tour in cooperation with the governor.[60]

The emperor's optimism in this matter would seem unfounded in the light of later developments. In the late 1680s such trusted ministers of K'ang-hsi as Mingju, Kao Shih-ch'i, and Wang Hung-hsü were impeached for corruption—many of them by Kuo Hsiu, who built a reputation for being a fearless censor on these cases.[61] K'ang-hsi in the twilight years of his reign also witnessed a disastrous struggle for succession and the formation of cliques around the contenders. Although these developments lie outside the scope of this study, a few words need be said about the emergence of cliques in the period 1661–84 and K'ang-hsi's attitude toward them, which will reveal the toughness mentioned earlier.

Although K'ang-hsi did not publish a major essay on factions, as Yung-cheng did, still on occasion he discussed the topic with his ministers. In general, he stayed within the Confucian tradition that disparaged such formations. For example, in August 1677, he called in his grand secretaries and denounced officials who formed cliques. "One should work only for the common good," K'ang-hsi argued, "for if officials split up into factions and cliques, then it will harm the nation and ultimately visit ruin upon the individuals themselves." "It is intolerable," he continued, "to decide the rightness or wrongness of any stand on the basis of whether or not the person is a member of your clique," or, as Confucius phrased it, "because the speaker is what he is." The emperor concluded by warning his ministers to shun factionalism and to cooperate with others for the common weal.[62]

Not long after this discussion, K'ang-hsi was faced with his first crisis in factional politics. In the period 1661–84, three factions succeeded one another. At the outset of K'ang-hsi's reign, of course, a faction formed around Oboi, the leading regent. After K'ang-hsi's assumption of personal rule, two cliques headed by

Manchus were in power for a decade each: Songgotu's from 1669–79, followed by Mingju's in the period 1679–88.

Songgotu's preeminent position in the first decade of K'ang-hsi's personal rule was attributable to two factors: he played a decisive role in breaking Oboi, and he was uncle to K'ang-hsi's empress and a great-uncle to Yin-jeng, who was declared the heir apparent (for the first but not the last time) in 1675 at the age of two.[63] From this base, Songgotu soon became the most feared man at court, as K'ang-hsi himself once noted.[64] Songgotu's firm grip on political power was finally shaken by an earthquake! The natural calamity hit Peking on 2 September 1679, damaging or destroying about thirty thousand homes and killing nearly five hundred people, and it was immediately interpreted by K'ang-hsi as an inauspicious sign reflecting serious failings in the administration of the empire. He singled out factionalism as one of the worst evils of the day, denouncing those who would only praise their friends and discredit others.[65]

Taking a cue from the emperor, the president of the Censorate, Wei Hsiang-shu, submitted a memorial that was a not-so-veiled attack on Songgotu and then defended this view in an audience.[66] The day after that (4 September) K'ang-hsi called in all his leading officials and in strong language blamed them as well as himself for the bad political order. He spelled out six areas needing reform: (1) the growing disparity between the people's bitter lot and the wealth of officials which was aggravated by excessive local exactions, (2) factionalism in court discussion of personnel appointments, (3) undisciplined activity of generals in the field who are more interested in personal glory than in settling the people, (4) the failure of provincial leaders to report the people's suffering and of capital officials to take necessary steps to relieve their distress, (5) the slow and at times unfair administration of justice, (6) imperial relatives and officials of the Imperial Household Agency using their power and influence to engage in profitable enterprises at the expense of commoners. K'ang-hsi concluded that although the outlined abuses were all different, they were all manifestations of a single sickness—the corruptibility of high officials of the central government. They set the whole tone of government operations right down to the local level.[67]

The emperor admitted to an early awareness of these abuses in government, but he had held back because of the military situation and because he had hoped his ministers would reform of their own accord. With the *San-fan* campaigns about wrapped up and his faith in self-generating reform shattered, K'ang-hsi was ready to put his house in order. Songgotu, as the leading official of the day, was the prime target, and his fall from power came within a few years. He retired from court in 1680 with the emperor's praise in hand, but thereafter Songgotu's former benefactor turned on him with a steady line of criticism and abuse. In 1681 Songgotu's former advocacy of punishment for officials who precipitated the *San-fan* rebellion was recalled anew by K'ang-hsi for derision. In 1683 the behavior of his younger brothers led to another attack on Songgotu. For failing to curb their activity as well as his own haughtiness and acquisition of personal wealth, Songgotu lost his posts in the Deliberative Council and the Imperial Bodyguards and the honorary title of grand tutor of the heir apparent. In 1690 K'ang-hsi rebuked and degraded him for letting Galdan's army retreat and escape from a recent battle.[68]

Finally, in 1703, the emperor gave Songgotu one of the most severe tongue lashings ever given out by him. He accused him of extreme factionalism, of attracting all the discontended rabble-rousers, and of charging into the heir apparent's residence without dismounting. K'ang-hsi topped off this tirade by calling Songgotu an "ingrate less worthy of attention than a dog." Songgotu was thrown in jail, where he died, but five years later K'ang-hsi still felt it necessary to attack him personally, as if beating a dead horse. The occasion was the degrading of Yin-jeng, the heir apparent. Yin-jeng had been supervised by Songgotu, and now the latter was being blamed posthumously for the former's extravagance and immorality. In summing up Songgotu's career, the emperor designated him "the dynasty's number one criminal."[69]

K'ang-hsi's intemperate remarks were born perhaps of his own feelings of inadequacy as a father, but they also reflect the frustration and anger he felt at the prevalence of factionalism. He had not seen the last of it either, nor said his last word against cliques. Another inauspicious natural occurrence, this time (in 1682) the appearance of a comet,[70] brought K'ang-hsi's attention back to the causal relationship between natural and societal disorders. While most of his officials sought relief in demilitarization measures, such as troop reductions and cancelation of the Taiwan expedition, so as to give the people a much needed rest after a decade of warfare, the emperor himself pointed an accusing finger at cliques. For Manchus, he claimed, cliques were formed around friends or relatives, and for Chinese around classmates or scholarship.[71] A third focus of factional loyalties was provincial origin, as K'ang-hsi ruefully noted, also in 1682, upon the retirement of Feng P'u, a grand secretary from Shantung.[72]

Mingju's clique, which dominated court life after Songgotu's retirement in 1680, differed from its predecessors in one important respect: it consisted of both Manchus and Chinese. From the sketchy information available on Songgotu, it appears that all or most of his followers were Manchus.[73] Many of Mingju's supporters, on the other hand, were Chinese (both bannermen and nonbannermen). A list would include such notables as Chin Fu, Ts'ai Yü-jung, Yü Kuo-chu, Li Chih-fang, and Hsü Ch'ien-hsüeh. The first two were bannermen, but the other three were not.[74] This is further proof that by the end of the early K'ang-hsi period Chinese were back at the center of political life. Significantly, after the fall of Oboi, Songgotu, and Mingju, the most prominent official at court was not another Manchu but a Chinese, Wang Hsi.[75]

Mingju's influence in government in the period of 1679–88 was pervasive. He dominated the Grand Secretariat with the assistance of Yü Kuo-chu, who was considered the ringleader of the Chinese group in Mingju's party. The latter tried to impose his will in the selection of provincial officials and sought bribes from candidates for the offices. He even tried to gag the censors, whom he reportedly feared the most, by making prospective appointees agree to submit their memorials to him for prior approval. What made all of this possible was the fact the Mingju gained the emperor's confidence. It was noted earlier that K'ang-hsi turned to Mingju throughout the 1680s for advice and personnel evaluation. The grand secretary apparently betrayed the emperor's trust at will by daily divulging what went on in court discussions and even imperial remarks uttered in private. With access to the emperor's thoughts, Mingju also could and did peddle his influence. If K'ang-hsi praised someone. Mingju claimed it was due to his intercession; if K'ang-hsi spoke ill of anyone, then Mingju sought the man out and offered to promote his cause for a price.[76] In these various ways Mingju gathered around him a coterie of sycophants.

K'ang-hsi's experience with official corruption and factional politics was just a foretaste of things to come. The fruit of his early personnel practices was not sweet-tasting to the emperor in old age, but he lacked the energy and vision to do anything about it. He was by that time a caricature of senility, losing both physical and mental vitality.[77] His son and successor, Yung-cheng, fought in and lived through the intense factional politics of the day and as victor he took steps to see that there would be no repetition of that situation in his reign.[78]

Style of Decision Making

Recent scholarship has fully documented the institutionalization of the secret palace memorial system in the late K'ang-hsi reign,[79] but the emperor's concern for secrecy and steps taken by him to gather confidential information necessary for decision making were evident even in the early years of his rule. In August 1669, not long after Oboi's fall, K'ang-hsi complained of leaks from the Deliberative Council (*i-cheng wang ta-ch'en*). The council only took up matters of great importance and gravity, and K'ang-hsi was insisting on—but not getting—absolute secrecy.[80]

The Deliberative Council, with a few exceptions in personnel, was a Manchu institution that grew out of predynastic political organs, as described above. Originally small in number, its size grew during Abahai's reign as Abahai packed the council with his appointees from the eight banners. After the conquest of China, Manchu grand secretaries and board presidents were added. In time, the number and type of officials eligible for council membership were reduced. First to be relieved of this responsibility were the Manchu grand secretaries in 1656, followed by the special banner representatives in 1662.[81] Then K'ang-hsi, who was concerned about information leaks from the council, further reduced their number by excluding the banner lieutenant generals.

The expansion and contraction of council membership seems to have been linked to the tempo of military activity. From its inception until the conquest of China, military campaigning kept many council members out of Peking. A need was felt, therefore, for increased membership to insure a full complement of councillors in the capital for deliberation of major issues. With the pacification first of the mainland provinces by 1662 and then of Taiwan by 1684, the supernumeraries, particularly from the military, were dropped from the council. It still remained quite large (with eligibility extended again to a wider group of civilian officials toward the end of the century) and unwieldy. It should be recalled that one of the offenses of which Mingju and his clique were accused in 1689 was the divulgence of state deliberations.

Another step taken by K'ang-hsi to insure secrecy came in 1679 when he barred daily diarists (*ch'i-chü-chu kuan*) from court sessions dealing with confidential matters and private interviews with key officials.[82] It was the latter practice that K'ang-hsi was to use so effectively in gathering information, particularly about conditions in the southern provinces in the 1680s after the *San-fan* campaigns and before he began his Southern Tours or formally established the palace memorial system. In fact, there is reason to believe that the private interview technique, when extended, was one of the historical components of the palace memorial system.[83]

Only a few of these interviews with provincial officials and imperial commissioners are noted in the historical records of this period,[84] but one of them so well reflects K'ang-hsi's voracious appetite for and thoroughness in securing detailed information that it is worth quoting from liberally. The interview, actually consisting of two sessions, was with Hsi-chu, and it took place on 21 August and 1 September 1684. Hsi-chu was an imperial commissioner who was sent to Fukien and Kwangtung in 1684 to investigate the coastal situation and supervise the resettlement of people after the subjugation of Taiwan.[85] Upon his return to Peking he reported personally to K'ang-hsi on the situation in the two southeastern provinces:[86]

> I received an imperial commission to proceed to the sea and extend the boundaries. The coastal populations of Fukien and Kwangtung gathered together in great numbers to welcome me. They said: "We have been separated from our land for over twenty years and had already given up hope of ever returning to our villages. We rejoice in the emperor's virtue and majesty. He has crushed all the rebels and even the seas are calm." At present, the people have returned to their former lands. Their homes are protected and their livelihood is secured. They will respect and honor Your Majesty's benevolence for generations to come.

The emperor at this point observed that "the people are pleased with living along the coast because they [can support themselves] by trading and fishing. Realizing this, why has not anyone previously recommended approval of sea trade?" Hsi-chu cited precedent: "It is because coastal trade has been prohibited since the Ming dynasty that no one has suggested it." K'ang-hsi did not consider this argument convincing: "Previously it was because of pirates," he reasoned, "that a maritime ban was deemed proper. Now that pirates and rebels have all been defeated, why should we still hesitate [to open trade]?" Hsi-chu's response shifted the burden of responsibility to others:

> The governors-general and governors of the coastal provinces say that although Taiwan, Chin-men [Quemoy], and Hsia-men [Amoy] are now defended by government troops, still they are newly acquired regions [of the empire]. We ought to wait for a few years, they maintain, to study the situation before opening [up trade].

K'ang-hsi did not accept this interpretation of the provincial officials' position but saw hidden motives:

> Provincial officials ought to take state economy and the people's livelihood as their chief concern. Hitherto, despite severe maritime prohibitions, they consistently engaged in private, secret trade. The reason the *tu-fu* now say that coastal trading is not feasible is that they are selfishly thinking about their own profit.

With the argument taking this turn, Hsi-chu readily agreed that "the emperor's viewpoint is quite correct."

Having covered the official purpose of Hsi-chu's trip, K'ang-hsi then shifted the nature of his inquiries and asked for an opinion of the Kwangtung governor-general. Hsi-chu reported that "the local people say that Governor-general Wu Hsing-tso is a very good official. [Furthermore,] Governor Li Shih-chen is considered better than the previous governor, Chin Chun." K'ang-hsi commented:

> This kind of talk is natural. It is very hard to follow a good official and get a good name, but after a bad official it is very easy to be considered a good official by the populace for the slightest reason. Former Governor Liu Ping-ch'üan [1668–75] was not bad, but Lu Hsing-tsu [1661–65], Wang Lai-jen [1665–67], and Chin Chün [1678–82] were corrupt and caused the people nothing but grief. So when

> Li Shih-chen [1682–87] arrives and is a little better, he is immediately praised as a good official. The fact that these former corrupt officials have now all been rebuffed is proof that Heaven's retribution comes quickly.[87]

The emperor then inquired about other officials: "On your passage through Kiangnan, what have you learned about [former] Governor-general Yü Ch'eng-lung [the elder]?"[88] Hsi-chu replied that "the people say Yü is very honest but too trusting, so that he is often fooled by his subordinates." The emperor was surprised to hear this, but not completely so:

> Yü Ch'eng-lung did such a fine job [as governor, 1680–82] in Chihli that I appointed him governor-general of Kiangnan. Later I heard he was not his old self and [that his work there] was only average. It was only after his death [in May 1684] that I first learned of how his incorruptibility in public affairs won praise from the people. Perhaps Yü is just being maligned by men he formerly antagonized by his normally honest behavior. What you heard may not be true. Officials like Yü are rare.

Chin Fu, the director-general of river conservation from 1677 to 1688, was K'ang-hsi's next subject.[89] The emperor asked if Hsi-chu had seen him and how the waterways were functioning. The commissioner replied:

> I did see Chin Fu and he looked haggard from work and worry. The river work is fine; grain transport is unhindered. When I arrived [in Kiangnan, I went] to Su-ch'ien [33°55′ by 118°20′] to see the dikes that separate and channel the water [of the Grand Canal]. Of the five dikes, two are in perfect [working order] and the other three are now being repaired. When the water is high, the dam sluices are open to diminish the force and control the dispersal of water into four separate channels without bursting [the dikes].

K'ang-hsi was pleased:

> The canal system is essential for grain transport and hence of the utmost importance. The last time I called Chin Fu to Peking for an audience,[90] everyone urged me to replace him, but I felt it would do no good to change officials in the middle of a project. Instead, I kept Chin Fu at his

> post and gave him the work of repairing the dikes. Now the task is complete and the water is coursing through its old channels, bringing benefit to the merchant [users of the canal]. If I had so lightly changed officials, I would have regretted it.

At this point, a subchancellor of the Nei-ko, Tuna, spoke up. He had been to Kiangnan often and claimed expertise in hydraulic affairs. It was his contention that "to be successful in river work, you must work in harmony with water's nature and not against it," as dikes presumably would. K'ang-hsi snorted at the idea and dismissed it as "an outmoded approach to water conservation." "The Yellow River," he noted, "did not follow its old path but changed its course. To try and divert it back to its old course 180 *li* away is impossible. What difficulty we would face if we used this 'managing the river according to its nature' (*shun shui-hsing hsiu-chih*) approach!"

Continuing his interview with Hsi-chu, K'ang-hsi asked about the fields he passed and their productivity.[91] Hsi-chu's impressions were mixed:

> The Fukien fields are bountiful, and Kiangnan and Chekiang production are also good. In Shantung, rainfall has been moderate and the people are predicting a good harvest. But from Te-chou [37°27′ by 116°23′, on the northwestern border of Shantung] to Chen-ting [38°20′ by 114° 40′, in southwestern Chihli] rainfall has been insufficient and the fields are somewhat parched. From there to the capital, however, it again looks good.

The first session ended with the emperor discoursing on the basis of good government:

> Agriculture is the foundation of the state and frugality the way of managing a family [i.e., the empire, his "family"]. I have always given top priority to these two areas in governing. If the officials closest to the people carry out my wishes and work hard [on these matters], then what concern can there be for the well-being of the people?

No Confucian would quarrel with these words.

The second half of this interview was held eleven days later.[92] It was much shorter and the conversation covered only one topic: a comparison of the talents and character of Shih Lang and Wan

Cheng-se. Wan had preceded Shih as coordinator of the Taiwan campaign,[93] and K'ang-hsi wanted to learn more about the two men. Hsi-chu, talking about Wan first, said that "as a person he was very loyal and agreeable, and as an official he was excellent." K'ang-hsi then explained his objection to Wan: "When he was naval *t'i-tu* [in Fukien], he [once] memorialized that Taiwan could not be taken. Seeing that he was incapable of the task, I replaced him with Shih Lang [in 1681] and commanded the latter to attack. Consequently he did and in one battle subjugated [the island]."[94] To the emperor's inquiry about how the two men were getting along now, the commissioner stated that "outwardly they are friendly, but secretly they are jealous and vengeful." Then the conversation moved on to Shih Lang's qualities. Hsi-chu thought "he had great ability, [particularly] in commanding troops, but he was proud and boastful." K'ang-hsi agreed with this judgment and observed that "it was only natural for unlettered military men to become proud over their accomplishments."[95]

The interview with Hsi-chu shows well the give-and-take interplay between K'ang-hsi and his officials—although the emperor usually gave—and how the emperor used the interview technique as an essential information-gathering process. Still, the private audience had its limitations. Officials in the provinces could not be called away from their posts often enough to keep the emperor fully informed without great cost, inconvenience, and a neglect of their duties. Occasional interviews afforded K'ang-hsi personal and retrospective views on provincial matters, but to be fully and constantly apprised of problems as they arose and developed demanded a new method. The logical next step was the secret palace memorial system, which assured Ch'ing emperors a steady flow of information and independent judgments and gave them a chance to have a frank exchange of views with provincial informants.

Secrecy was not the only reason pushing K'ang-hsi to devise new systems of information gathering. He was also disgusted with the blandness, repetitiousness, triviality, and superfluity of memorials crossing his desk. His repeated commands to officials to speak out fearlessly on important matters and his plea for simplicity of style and brevity in memorial writing indicate his lack of success in getting them.[96]

With censoring officials specifically, K'ang-hsi faced another problem—the use of rumor (*feng-wen*) in their memorials. Under the regents it was forbidden to base impeachments on information taken from unsigned placards, and K'ang-hsi continued this policy.[97] In 1671 the use of rumor was specifically forbidden.[98] The whole issue, however, came under review in 1679. Metropolitan Censor Yao Ti-yü, in response to the same earthquake that prompted Wei Hsiang-shu's attack on Songgotu, urged K'ang-hsi to again allow rumor to be used if he wanted (as he did) censorial reporting to be fearless and forthright as in Shun-chih's reign. If not, Yao argued, unscrupulous officials will act in the knowledge that censors are too timid to censure them. A court conference did not support Yao's proposal, and neither did the emperor. He felt the practice would not affect upright censors, who would never make wild, unsubstantiated accusations anyway, but it would give morally dishonest ones an excellent opportunity to work off private grudges. This had happened at the end of the Ming dynasty, and he did not wish to follow their example.[99] While he wanted censors truly to be his "eyes and ears" on all matters, he was not willing to give them free rein to make charges based only on rumors.

K'ang-hsi's personnel management complemented his military leadership in securing Ch'ing control. Most notably, he broadened participation in government beyond the old Manchu warrior group and its allies to include Manchus and Chinese of varied backgrounds. Statistical evidence reveals a dramatic shift towards an increasing reliance on non-banner Chinese in the highest metropolitan and provincial government posts. The emergence of Chinese leaders such as Li Wei and Wang Hsi paralleled the increasing importance of Chinese military forces and commanders in the *San-fan* war years. That war and the struggle against Oboi earlier formed the crucible in which K'ang-hsi forged his team of key advisers and his policies of rule. Concerned with the quality of reports from his ministers, the emperor began to develop a system of communication that would provide him with complete, accurate and independent information for effective decision making. The emperor also sought to promote honesty, eliminate corruption and control cliques, but he had only limited success. Toward the end of his long reign, these problems remained to haunt him and his successor. But K'ang-hsi had achieved his primary objective of securing the services and loyal support of the Chinese as well as Manchu bureaucratic elite and utilizing their talents in the imperial cause.

Six

IMPERIAL SCHOLARSHIP AND CHINESE SCHOLARS

K'ANG-HSI WAS MORE THAN A HARD-RIDING MILITARY LEADER AND political strategist; he was also an examplar of the Confucian monarch, the grand patron of learning. As a Manchu ruler of China, he had two new fields of learning to master (in addition to his native Manchu)—classical Chinese studies and the new Western knowledge entering the Middle Kingdom with Jesuit missionaries. K'ang-hsi's intellectual achievements and leadership contributed greatly to the "unity of state and culture" forged by Ch'ing emperors. K'ang-hsi complemented his personal example of scholarship with a successful effort to recruit Chinese scholars for the Manchu government. Manipulation of the examination system and its auxiliaries hindered the campaign, but ultimate success came in 1679 with the holding of a special examination for "erudites" (*po-hsüeh*).

CHINESE STUDIES

K'ang-hsi's early education, as a prince and then as a ruler, remained informal until after the fall of Oboi in 1669, despite the many requests that he undertake a more formal tutoring program. With the Oboi crisis behind him, the emperor turned with characteristic energy to the matter of his own education in the classics. From that point on, the emperor devoted much of his time to acquiring the veneer of a Confucian education, one that would at least allow him to manipulate the symbols of China's orthodox ideology and maintain the tradition of imperial leadership in the realm of culture despite his alien origins. The outbreak of the

San-fan rebellion in 1673 made him forgo this project temporarily, but even in the war years the tutoring continued on a reduced scale. This was, no doubt, a calculated attempt to impress Chinese scholars at a time when they might be wavering in their support of the new regime, but it was also due to his increasing realization that a systematic knowledge of Chinese culture and institutions would be essential for an alien monarch to govern the Chinese. Oxnam has concluded that the regents' hatred of Chinese elite "blinded them to the possibility of using Chinese norms as a means of imperial control,"[1] but K'ang-hsi did not share their attitude.

The emperor formally participated in two tutorial programs, but one of them—the Lecture on the Classics (*ching-yen*)—was purely ceremonial and for propaganda purposes. These first began in 1657 and were held twice yearly, in the spring and the autumn. Two Manchu and two Chinese lecturers (*ching-yen chiang-kuan*) were chosen each time to direct the ceremony. They would choose a passage from the classics to elucidate and submit it to the emperor for further comment, which would then be included in the text of the lecture. On the appointed day, the lecturers would read the selection and their elucidations to the assembled court, after which the emperor would repeat his remarks.[2]

Obviously it was a sterile form as far as the emperor's education was concerned. The real learning process took place under different auspices—the Daily Tutoring (*jih-chiang*), a practice which began in 1655. The daily sessions started each year in the second month immediately after the spring Lecture on the Classics ceremony was concluded, and they continued until the "arrival of summer" (*hsia-chih*)—21 June or sometime in the fifth lunar month. They were resumed in the eighth month after the fall Lecture on the Classics and ended for the year when winter arrived on 21 December. Two or three tutors would see the emperor each day after he had attended to the day's memorials, and they discussed with him the lesson they had chosen for him a few days earlier.[3] The Daily Tutoring session, too, could have had a deadening effect on the emperor's intellectual growth, but he altered its format to make it a more meaningful educational experience.

K'ang-hsi in November 1670 set in motion the machinery to start his formal education. He ordered the Board of Rites to pick auspicious dates for beginning both the Lectures on the Classics and the Daily Tutoring, and to spell out the procedural details as to scheduling, curriculum, and the selection of tutors and lecturers. The board decided to follow the practices of the Shun-chih period and set 1 January and 27 March 1671 as the dates of the first Daily Tutoring session and the Lecture on the Classics ceremony, respectively. The lecturers and tutors were to be chosen by the recently revived Hanlin Academy.[4] The ceremonious Lecture on the Classics was held on 27 March as scheduled, a day after Grand Secretary Tu Li-te sacrificed in the emperor's name to China's greatest teacher, Confucius. For some reason, however, Daily Tutoring did not begin until 18 May, five months behind schedule.[5]

The identity of the 128 lecturers and tutors appointed in the early K'ang-hsi period (through 1684) is significant in several ways. First of all, there is a difference in the ethnic composition of the two groups. Manchus and Chinese were represented equally among the lecturers: twenty-five of the former and twenty-six of the latter. In contrast, only twenty of the seventy-seven tutors were Manchus.[6] These figures reflect the differing purposes of each activity. The semiannual Lecture on the Classics served the ceremonial and political purpose of portraying the Manchu rulers as good Confucian monarchs, and a rigorously balanced selection of Manchu and Chinese lecturers would strengthen that image. Daily Tutoring, being more for the emperor's education than the empire's edification, would require the appointment primarily of Chinese versed in the Confucian Classics.

A second difference between tutors and lecturers was their rank and position at the time of appointment. This data for the 128 appointees in the period 1671–84 is compiled in table 6. It is immediately clear that the majority of the lecturers were high officials of various administrative bodies and of the Hanlin Academy, while tutors were exclusively members of the Hanlin Academy and the Supervisorate of Imperial Instruction and generally low-ranking officials of those two educational bodies. Again, as in the case of ethnic composition, the difference can be attributed to the dissimilarity of their purposes: high administrative officials were appropriate for an important function of state, but middle- and low-ranking officials of literary bodies could better meet the demands of the Daily Tutoring program. The latter were the literary specialists of the court and were not burdened with administrative duties. Their low rank also gave the emperor a desirable flexibility not only in appointing them but also in his

TABLE 6
Rank and Position (at Time of Appointment) of Lecturers on the Classics and Daily Tutors, 1671–84

Position[a]	Rank[b]	Lecturers	Tutors
Administrative bodies			
President of a board or of the Censorate (207)	2A	7	
Vice-president of a board (279)	3A	10	
Subchancellor of the Nei-ko (133)	3A	14	
Hanlin Academy			
Chancellor (192)	3A	5	8
Reader (194)	5B	8	9
Expositor (195)	5B	2	18
Subreader (196)	6A		9
Subexpositor (197)	6A		6
Compiler 1st class (200A)	6A		4
Compiler 2nd class (200B)	7A		9
Corrector (200C)	7B		4
Imperial Academy			
Libationer (412A)	4B	2	
Supervisorate of Imperial Instruction			
Chief supervisor (929.1)	5B	2	
Supervisor (929.2)	5B	1	1
Deputy Supervisor (929.3)	6A		3
Secretary (929.4)	7A		2
Assistant secretary (929.5)	7B		4
Summaries			
	1–3	36	8
	4–6	15	50
	7–9		19
Total		51	77

Source: *Huang-ch'ao tz'u-lin tien-ku, chüan* 59–60, with exceptions as noted in n. 6 of this chapter.

[a]The numbers in parentheses refer to Brunnert and Hagelstrom, *Political Organization of China*.

[b]For ranks, see *HTSL*, pp. 17506–07(1044.1a–3a) for the Hanlin Academy, p. 17626(1057.3a) for the Supervisorate, and pp. 5300–02(18.31b–36b) for the others; ranks given in Brunnert and Hagelstrom reflect later changes and cannot be used here.

working relations with them. Many of the Chinese best known for their scholarly association with K'ang-hsi came from ranks 6 and 7. This was true of Chang Yü-shu, Kao Shih-ch'i, T'ang Pin, and Han

T'an (all 6A); Chang Ying, and Wang Hung-hsü (both 7A); Hsü Ch'ien-hsüeh, and Chu I-tsun (both 7B). Two other famous scholars of the day, Hsiung Tz'u-li and Li Kuang-ti, had a more prestigious position and rank when appointed, that of chancellor of the Hanlin Academy (3A).

A third important aspect of these two groups' identity was their philosophical affinity. Chinese historians have often noted that Ch'ing rulers from K'ang-hsi on championed the Ch'eng-Chu school of Sung Neo-Confucianism as orthodoxy and selected only scholars of that school as tutors and lecturers.[7] For example, K'ang-hsi in 1670 honored the Ch'eng brothers by choosing two descendants as Scholars in the Classics (*wu-ching po-shih*), and in 1713 he wrote a preface to an imperially sponsored compilation of Chu Hsi's complete works (*Chu-tzu ch'üan-shu*).[8] More importantly, for the point I am trying to make, the most famous men of the Ch'eng-Chu school in the early K'ang-hsi period were indeed serving as the emperor's tutors—scholars such as Li Kuang-ti, T'ang Pin, Hsiung Tz'u-li, and Chang Yü-shu. Other noted adherents of the Ch'eng-Chu school, such as Wei I-chieh, Wei Hsiang-shu, and Chang Po-hsing, held important posts in government. It was reported that K'ang-hsi made T'ang Pin governor of Kiangnan in 1684 because he was impressed with T'ang's understanding of orthodox Confucianism.[9] K'ang-hsi's support of these men's political and moral philosophies, with their largely passive theories of personal and political relationships, was just one step in a continuing campaign by Ch'ing rulers to enlist Confucianism as a servant to the increasingly authoritarian state.[10]

The emperor's alert mind and his inquisitiveness could not long be contained within the confines of the Daily Tutoring program. At the outset, apparently, tutors did not even come every day but only on alternate days. This changed in March 1673, when K'ang-hsi decided that there should be no interruptions in his education. He found that he was simply reading too much on his own and wanted to discuss daily what he had learned.[11] For the same reason, he frequently paid no attention to the passing of the seasons. Tutoring did not stop every 21 June and 21 December, as it had done in Shun-chih's time, but continued throughout the year.[12] On those occasions when K'ang-hsi did temporarily suspend his lessons because of the weather, it was for a shorter period of time than stipulated by the regulations.[13] To mitigate any hardship his year-round program might cause the tutors, K'ang-hsi saw to it that they were warmly clothed in the winter and provided with food and lodging at his summer residence when he continued his studies there.[14] K'ang-hsi neglected his studies for a while after the outbreak of the *San-fan* rebellion, but by October 1674 he was back on a daily schedule of tutoring.[15] Not even the celebration of his birthday was allowed to interrupt his studies.[16]

The emperor also changed the time of his Daily Tutoring in 1683. His lessons came before receiving memorials and attending to affairs of state rather than after. This meant that tutors had to enter court a little earlier in the day, and no matter how early they arrived, it was reported, K'ang-hsi was always dressed and waiting to barrage them with questions.[17] The tutors complained that they were working day and night just trying to keep up with the emperor's demand for more selections from the classics and histories to read and ponder over. Their Western counterparts, the Jesuits Bouvet, Gerbillon, and Thomas, had a similar problem.[18]

The tutoring format itself came in for imperial criticism almost from the beginning. K'ang-hsi objected to the notion that he should just sit and listen to tutors expound on the day's texts. To listen passively may be tradition, he noted, but it was no good for his intellectual growth and not a very good example to set. He wanted a chance to engage his teachers in a dialogue: to discuss the lesson at hand but also to ask them questions about passages he read on his own in the palace. So in 1675 he changed the script: thereafter, when the tutors had finished their lecture, he would give his own discourse.[19] At first K'ang-hsi apparently talked on whatever subjects came to mind, but in 1677 it was decided that he should confine his discussions to the Chu Hsi commentaries on the Four Books or to the General Mirror of History (*Tzu-chih t'ung-chien*). By this time also K'ang-hsi was discoursing before and not after his tutors.[20]

In these various ways, then, K'ang-hsi changed the Daily Tutoring structure to make it a more viable vehicle for imperial education. Sessions with his tutors were more frequent than before, and the emperor became an active participant. But no matter how it was altered and improved, the tutorial program was still formal and restricted, and K'ang-hsi was chafing under it. Unable to find the kind of personal, informal, and flexible educational program he desired within the framework of Daily Tutoring—to say nothing of the Lecture on the Classics—K'ang-hsi in 1677 created a new office, the Imperial Study (*Nan-shu-fang*).[21]

The first two men taken into the Imperial Study were Chang Ying and Kao Shih-ch'i—the latter expressly because of his fame as a calligrapher. It is known that the emperor was not very good with the brush, and he could find no one among his palace attendants who was.[22] Nor could he find anyone among them learned enough to discuss with him the books he had read. That is why he decided in November 1677 to choose two Hanlin Academy officials as scholars-in-residence at the palace. A vacant apartment (the Nan-shu-fang) in the Inner City was located for Chang and Kao by the Imperial Household Agency, and they were considered for all practical purposes members of the inner court. They were taken off the normal promotion and transfer lists and were also expressly forbidden to become involved in any way with court politics.[23]

Now K'ang-hsi had near him, on call at any time of the day or night, Chinese scholars who could coach him in calligraphy, help him draft edicts, compile numerous imperial works, and converse with him about the Confucian classics and histories he was sampling. These men, and their successors, were the constant companions of the emperor in Peking, on his Southern Tours, and on his hunting trips beyond the Wall.[24]

I have thus far traced only the form of K'ang-hsi's Chinese studies and said nothing about its content or the emperor's performance as a student. As to the content of his Daily Tutoring program, the emperor started off with the Classic of Filial Piety and the Four Books (Analects, Mencius, Doctrine of the Mean, and Great Learning).[25] An exposition of the Classic of Filial Piety (*Hsiao-ching yen-i*) was commissioned in 1671 and compiled by Hsiung Tz'u-li, Yeh Fang-ai, and other tutors.[26] Likewise, a Sung work elaborately elucidating the precepts of the Great Learning (*Ta-hsüeh yen-i*) was reissued in 1672 in a bilingual (Manchu-Chinese) edition for the emperor, and at the suggestion of his grand empress dowager, it was distributed to every official in the empire.[27] A complete text of the emperor's lessons on the Four Books was published in 1678 in book form (*Jih-chiang ssu-shu chieh-i*), with a preface by the emperor himself.[28]

After finishing these works so closely identified with Chu Hsi and so familiar to every Chinese schoolboy, the emperor and his tutors moved on to other classics—the Book of Documents (*Shu-*

ching), and Book of Changes (*I-ching*), and the Book of Odes (*Shih-ching*). After studying each of them to his satisfaction—and he reportedly reread them several times[29]—K'ang-hsi had compiled and disseminated the texts of his tutors' lectures on them (e.g., *Jih-chiang Shu-ching chieh-i*).[30] Concurrently with his reading in the classics, the emperor was studying the *Tzu-chih t'ung-chien.* He had been tutored in this work (using the *T'ung-chien kang-mu* arrangement of Chu Hsi) since 1676, but when his tutors decided in 1680 that it was time to take up the *I-ching,* K'ang-hsi continued his investigation of the *T'ung-chien* with Chang Ying in the palace at night.[31] The emperor's comments on the General Mirror of History were incorporated into a new edition of the work brought out by Sung Lao in 1708.[32]

The official records do not afford much of a glimpse into the imperial classroom to see how the student was doing. What comes across in print is just short imperial jabs at a topic followed by sycophantic platitudes from the tutors. Occasionally it goes beyond that into more substantial discussion, and I shall describe two of these instances as representative of K'ang-hsi's thought on traditional Chinese studies.

The first example is an exchange of views in 1673 with Hsiung Tz'u-li on heterodox ideas.[33] After a session with the three tutors of the day (Hsiung, La-sha-li, and Sun Tsai-feng), K'ang-hsi called Hsiung forward and said, "Since man's mind is very active and his imagination knows no bounds, then if he is not constantly in contact with his books, he is likely to go astray. That is why I study so hard in the palace." Hsiung responded with the observation that "the profound principles of the universe are contained in man's mind and recorded in books," and therefore the emperor through diligent study can seize the essence of things.

On the subject of heterodoxy, K'ang-hsi avowed that "I have always disliked Taoism and Buddhism, so when you urged me to reject heterodoxy and venerate orthodox Confucianism, I followed your advice without wavering once." The tutor seized this chance to warn the emperor not only of Buddhist and Taoist heresies but also of the confused and wayward teaching of the Hundred Schools. One must be careful, Hsiung said, to avoid their attractions and not "be led astray from some initial little mistake." K'ang-hsi again raised the subject with Hsiung a week later. He recalled that when he was nine, a lama visited the court to promote

Buddhism. The emperor—K'ang-hsi had just ascended the throne—had refuted his arguments then and had an aversion to the Buddhist heresy ever since. He noted, however, that people today frequently call on priests and monks to conduct funeral services and even to cremate the dead. He could not see how this conformed with the rites prescribed by Chu Hsi and considered orthodox. Hsiung assured him that they did not, but that "stupid commoners" and, amazingly, even some intelligent men do believe in the efficacy of the priests' and monks' rituals. These practices could be eliminated, however, if the emperor continued to take Yao and Shun as his models and strive to transform the people.

The emperor's denunciation of Buddhism and Taoism to his tutor is interesting because for reasons of state K'ang-hsi patronized Lamaism, made frequent visits to the holy mountain of Buddhism (Wu-t'ai-shan), and constructed numerous Buddhist temples.[34] With Chinese scholars, though, he took a strictly orthodox Confucian view—also for reasons of state. It was part of a many-faceted campaign to win the support of this critical social and political group and their recognition of the Manchu regime as a preserver, not a destroyer, of Chinese culture. The message here and elsewhere was that the Manchus were not to be taken as superstitious barbarians but upholders of enlightened Chinese values.

The second imperial discourse I want to relate was a short judgment rendered in 1675 on the Mencian view of human nature as good. Here is K'ang-hsi's statement in entirety:

> The goodness of human nature is not distinguished by intelligence or stupidity, but must be consciously cultivated through one's best effort. Tung Chung-shu said: "Everything depends on conscious cultivation." If scholarship is consciously cultivated, then one's knowledge will be more extensive and his understanding clearer. If behavior is consciously cultivated, then virtue will grow daily and become more efficacious. This really is the essence of study.[35]

K'ang-hsi, then, is agreeing with the Han philosopher Tung Chung-shu in his slight deviation from the Mencian position. Tung believed in the *potentiality* for good in man's nature, but held that it had to be fully developed through the teachings of the sage-kings.[36] This view exalted the role of the emperor in the educational process—certainly a position K'ang-hsi would want to support. The emperor was also saying that knowledge is virtue and should be actively sought.

Western Studies

K'ang-hsi's first acquaintance with Western knowledge came in the 1668–69 calendar controversy already described in chapter 3. From his personal examination of the case, the emperor began to realize the degenerate state of scientific knowledge in China and gained an admiration for Western methods of astronomy and mathematics, whose accuracy had just been demonstrated. For the next several years, K'ang-hsi studied mathematics, geometry, and astronomy with Father Verbiest and music with Father Thomas Pereira.[37]

Verbiest also translated Euclid's Elements of Geometry into Manchu for the emperor.[38] Matteo Ricci, the founder of the Jesuit mission in Peking, had translated the first six books of Euclid into Chinese in 1607 with the help of the famous convert Hsü Kuang-ch'i, who died in 1633 while holding the highest office, that of grand secretary. The *Chi-ho yüan-pen,* as it was called, was the first and most famous of the Western mathematical works introduced into China by the Jesuits, and it ran through numerous editions.[39]

The methodology of Euclidean geometry—how a theorem was stated and then logically proved—so fascinated the Chinese who read the Ricci-Hsü translation that they insisted on more translations of Western scientific works.[40] Chinese interest was reflected in the number of Jesuit translations into Chinese on astronomy and mathematics in the period 1582–1773 (from Ricci's arrival to the dissolution of the Society of Jesus). Out of a total of 352 translations, 71 were on astronomy and 20 on mathematics. Together, they constituted about 25 percent of the total, and this group of translations was exceeded only by those on theology (196, or about 56 percent of the total). If the number of translations on astronomy and mathematics is broken down by centuries, it becomes clear that the bulk of them were done in the seventeenth century: 65 of the former and 17 of the latter.[41] From another source, which lists the slightly higher number of 132 scientific translations (this includes works of geography) in the same period, 42 appeared in the

K'ang-hsi period. On all subjects, Verbiest alone is credited with 30 translations.[42] To cite a third source, which gives the most complete description of all translations of Western works into Chinese, 134 manuscripts or printed works were completed during the period 1666–88 when Verbiest headed the Jesuit mission.[43] These bibliographical figures indicate how much Western knowledge, and particularly mathematics and astronomy, was entering China through the active translation project of the Jesuits.

Verbiest's Manchu edition of Euclid's Elements was completed in 1673 on the eve of the *San-fan* rebellion that forced K'ang-hsi to temporarily cut back on his studies (both Chinese and Western). During the war, however, the emperor came to learn of and appreciate greatly another skill of Father Verbiest: the manufacturing of cannon. Foreign style cannon (*hung-i p'ao* ["red barbarian cannon"], so-called because the Dutch first introduced them to China) were constructed by the Jesuit missionary on command of the emperor, and imperial forces used them to great advantage in various campaigns. Verbiest was put to work making 132 heavy cannon in 1674 despite his protestations that he was a man of God and had no training in cannon making.[44] Throughout the *San-fan* war, Verbiest made over 300 cannon of a lighter weight than the first group. The emperor praised his work, was fond of having Verbiest test each model for him, and once even aimed a cannon himself—but he let a servant fire the frightening-sounding instrument.[45] These cannon, however, were more than imperial playthings (although K'ang-hsi had eight especially constructed and decorated with gold dragons for his personal use on hunting trips); they were effective weapons of war that were in great demand by K'ang-hsi's field commanders. Prince Yolo twice requested them for Hunan campaigns and contended that the battles could not have been won without them. Foreign cannon were also used in the recovery of Szechwan in 1681 and by Yao Ch'i-sheng in Fukien against the Cheng rebels in 1679.[46]

Verbiest's premium service to the dynasty, though, was still calendar making. After his 1669 triumph over Yang Kuang-hsien, he directed the work of the Board of Astronomy, but not without conservative opposition and attacks. In 1672 they charged the Jesuit with having miscalculated the intercalary month and the "arrivals" of spring and autumn (*li-ch'un, li-ch'iu*). A blue-ribbon committee of grand secretaries and court dignitaries investigated the charges and cleared Verbiest.[47] In 1676 an eclipse of the sun was the occasion for another test of the Western and traditional methods of astronomical calculations. Verbiest and An-t'ai, Manchu vice-director of the board, each using his own method, had reckoned the duration of the total eclipse differently. When the eclipse came on 11 June, An-t'ai's estimate was quite inaccurate, and Verbiest had to admit that his calculations were not exactly right either, although much closer. He explained, however, that the discrepancy was more apparent than real, because the eclipse had occurred as the sun was setting (between six and seven p.m.) and nearing the horizon, where atmospheric conditions distorted the size of the sun and the observed duration of the eclipse.[48]

K'ang-hsi took a keen interest in these scientific matters and in the knowledgeable Jesuits who were introducing him to Western ideas and methods. Verbiest was flattered by the attention and realized the opportunity it presented for proselytizing work, but the Jesuit mission was understaffed and in poor financial shape. This prompted him in 1678 to write a letter to his superiors in the order asking for more recruits and more money. The letter, translated into many languages and often republished, was read by Louis XIV's confessor, who showed it to Colbert, the king's chief minister. The latter was at that time engaged in promoting the arts and sciences and was interested in communicating with Chinese scholars. He obtained the king's approval to send Jesuits to China to gather geographical and astronomical information for the use of the royal Academy of Science.[49] It was several more years before the project actually got started. In 1685 six Jesuits were sent to China on the ship carrying France's first ambassador to Siam.[50]

The subsequent career of the first French mission to China goes well beyond the temporal scope of this study, but certain events surrounding it touch upon the subject of K'ang-hsi's acceptance of Western science and should be noted. When the Jesuits arrived at Ningpo in July 1687, the governor of Chekiang and the Board of Rites were disposed at first to send them back home, but the emperor, then on a hunt in Manchuria, overruled his officials upon his return to Peking. He imagined the Jesuits were skilled mathematicians and astronomers and he wanted to employ them in the court.[51] Verbiest influenced K'ang-hsi's decision and it was to be his last act for the Jesuit mission, for he died on 20 January 1688, just a few weeks before the new recruits reached the capital.

Although all the French Jesuits were trained mathematicians, K'ang-hsi eventually agreed to keep only two of them—Bouvet and Gerbillon—for his personal service and let the others undertake missionary work in the provinces.[52] A few years later, early in 1690, K'ang-hsi granted an audience to the four Jesuits then in Peking—Thomas Pereira and Antoine Thomas in addition to the two just mentioned—and ordered them to translate Western works into Manchu.[53] Father Bouvet in his portrait of the emperor gave a lengthy account of the scholarly work undertaken by the Jesuits and of K'ang-hsi's reception of Western science. A substantial portion of Bouvet's remarks follow:[54]

> He [K'ang-hsi] employed the four Jesuits then in Peking to explain [Western science] to him in both Chinese and Manchu. Father Gerbillon and myself found Manchu to be much easier and clearer than Chinese, and in seven or eight months we had made enough progress to converse reasonably well with the emperor in his native tongue. To improve our Manchu so that we could use it to explain our science to him, K'ang-hsi assigned to us tutors who for a month took us every day to the palace for lessons. At the same time, Father Thomas explained to the emperor in Chinese the uses of various mathematical instruments and the applications of geometry and arithmetic that Verbiest had already taught him. The emperor had us first explain Euclid's Elements, which he desired to know more thoroughly.
>
> For convenience, K'ang-hsi took one of his own apartments, where his father [Shun-chih] had resided and where he himself ate, and personally saw to furnishing it with whatever we needed. He provided a carriage to bring us to the palace early every day and carry us back every evening.[55] Two bilingual officials of his court were assigned to help us with our compositions, and some scribes were engaged to copy them. Every day the emperor called us to lecture to him. He listened attentively, repeated the explanations we gave him, made diagrams for himself, and told us of any doubts that arose in his mind. We then left our compositions with him to reread. He practiced calculus and the use of instruments and often went over the most important theorems of Euclid in order to remember their proofs. In five or six months he had mastered geometry and could instantly recall the theorem and proof

of any geometric figure he was shown. He once told us that he had read through Euclid's Elements at least a dozen times. We translated this book into Manchu[56] and included in it all the important theorems and their proofs found in the works of Euclid and Archimedes. K'ang-hsi also learned to use a proportional compass and other mathematical instruments.

The emperor studied very carefully and attentively. Neither the thorny problems of Euclidean geometry nor the poorness of our speech discouraged him. If he encountered a proof that he did not readily comprehend, because of its complexity or more often because of our inability to express our thoughts clearly in Manchu, he had no qualms about questioning either of us two or three times or returning to the matter another day until he had perfectly understood our explanation. He listened to us with patience and admirable attentiveness. He told us one day that he had no difficulty in applying himself to any inquiry; as a child he always carried out his prescribed tasks with diligence.

After learning Euclid's Elements, K'ang-hsi had us compose in Manchu a collection of practical geometry and its theories. We explained it to him as we had the Elements. Father Thomas composed in Chinese a collection of arithmetic and geometric calculations. It contained the most interesting problems found in both European and Chinese books.

K'ang-hsi took great pleasure in studying Western science. He regularly spent several hours each day with us and many more hours both night and day studying in private. Because he disliked indolence and idleness, he retired very late and arose early in the morning. Despite the care we took to get to the palace early, he often arrived before us in his eagerness to have us examine some calculations he had made or to ask us about some new problem. It is very surprising how the emperor on his own looked for problems similar to those we had already discussed, taking pleasure in the more curious aspects of geometry and the mathematical instruments.

The emperor gathered together a great number of instruments given to him or his father and had others made for him by fathers Pereira and Suarez. We also gave him all the instruments in our apartment. One of these instruments was a large and beautiful semi-circle with telescopes that the Duc de Maine had given us. K'ang-hsi used it frequently and took it with him on all his travels. It was carried on the back of one of his household officials, who felt honored to bear such precious cargo. The emperor used this instrument to measure the heights of mountains and the latitudes of important places. The court was astonished to see their emperor operate this instrument as well as had Father Gerbillon, who always accompanied K'ang-hsi on his travels.

Among the various mathematical instruments that we gave the emperor on our arrival in Peking were two devices which showed eclipses of the sun and moon and the positions of planets during various times of the year. We are indebted to the scholars of the Royal Academy for these machines.[57] We showed K'ang-hsi how to use them in terms of the Chinese calendar. He valued these machines highly and placed them on either side of his throne, where I saw them still on the day before my departure. . . .[58]

By the time he had finished studying practical and speculative geometry, K'ang-hsi to our deep satisfaction had become a good geometer. To express his pleasure with the results of our work, he had two books (Euclid's Elements and the work on practical geometry) translated from Manchu into Chinese. He revised them, wrote a preface for each, printed them in his palace, and circulated them throughout the empire in both languages.[59] This marked the beginning of K'ang-hsi's project to introduce European sciences into China.[60]

This account of K'ang-hsi's exposure to Western science reveals a point of great interest to Western scholars on China and to cultural historians in general—the difficulty of the Chinese language. Neither K'ang-hsi nor his Western tutors felt very comfortable with Chinese. The emperor, Bouvet implied, did not have too thorough a mastery of Chinese and was constantly calling for translations of Western works into his native tongue or, at the least, into bilingual Manchu-Chinese versions. As another Jesuit put it, "he knows Tartar and Chinese, but he likes the Tartar best."[61] The Jesuits, for their part, testified openly to the greater success they had with Manchu than with Chinese.

The emperor's interest in Western knowledge did not stop with mathematics and astronomy. Bouvet and Gerbillon gave him lessons as well in philosophy, medicine, chemistry, and anatomy.[62] Then, in 1693, K'ang-hsi sent Bouvet back to France as his personal envoy with instructions to recruit additional Jesuits, particularly those trained in the sciences, for the French mission in Peking. Bouvet returned to China in 1698 with ten colleagues and the Italian artist Gheradini.[63]

Bouvet's picture of K'ang-hsi's intellectual curiosity and skill was questioned by his contemporaries. His book was part of a campaign to generate support in France for the China mission, so the author was open to the charge of distortions for political and personal reasons. An optimistic report on the Chinese emperor's interest in Western science and religion and his close relations with Jesuits would justify mission work and strengthen the argument for royal backing. European reviewers of his book gave it such tags as a "panegyric," a "marvelous tale," and a "romance rather than history." Matteo Ripa, a missionary in China, wrote that "the emperor supposed himself to be an excellent musician and a still better mathematician, but though he had a taste for the sciences and other acquirements in general, he knew nothing of music and scarcely understood the first elements of mathematics."[64]

The available evidence, though, indicates that the emperor did indeed learn well and put his knowledge to practical use. For instance, he once explained to his courtiers that *pi* equaled 3.141+, not an even 3. He stressed the importance of using the more refined number by showing them how large an error would result from using the whole number only in calculating the circumference of a circle whose diameter measured one thousand Chinese feet.[65] The diaries of two of the emperor's personal secretaries in 1703 both testify to K'ang-hsi's knowledge of and interest in a wide variety of Western scientific subjects. Kao Shih-ch'i recorded that K'ang-hsi, upon returning from his fourth Southern Tour, guided him through the imperial summer villa (Ch'ang-ch'un-yüan) in the suburbs of Peking, where Kao saw Western musical instruments, paintings, and glassware. Several days later, Kao returned to hear the emperor talk about music and play a tune on a Western-style piano built by his engineers.[66] In the same year, on a hunting trip in Manchuria, K'ang-hsi fascinated his attendants with discourses and demonstrations on such diverse scientific and technical matters as trigonometry, iron mining, horticulture, surveying, telescopes, transmission of sound, and weather forecasting.[67] On earlier hunting trips, in 1682 and 1683, K'ang-hsi took Father Verbiest and his instruments along in his retinue so that the Jesuit could answer any questions on scientific matters that might arise.[68]

While often this scientific knowledge was used for the amusement of the emperor and his officials, it also had practical application. The new calendars and atlases compiled on the emperor's order are well known, but his working knowledge in medicine and agriculture are not. In 1710 and again in 1712, K'ang-hsi was giving Ts'ao Yin, his ailing confidant in Kiangsu, detailed clinical advice on medicine and herbs to take to restore his health.[69] The emperor was also a promoter of increased agricultural yields through the introduction of early-ripening rice strains. He himself grew some on the imperial grounds.[70] He also sent samples to Kiangsu for experimentation by the local farmers. When the experiment proved successful after several false starts, K'ang-hsi ordered dissemination of the new rice strains throughout Anhwei, Chekiang, and Kiangsi as well.[71]

K'ang-hsi placed a new emphasis on mathematical training during his reign. Feeling that astronomy and its related subjects were matters of great importance to the state, the emperor in 1670 decided to place students of the banner schools in the College of Mathematics in the Board of Astronomy to study alongside ninety-four Chinese students. Six Manchus and four Chinese were chosen from each of the eight banners and sent to the college.[72] Toward the end of his long reign, in 1713, the emperor established a second school for mathematical study in the Meng-yang-chai located in the summer palace. The special program was administered by high officials who were trained in mathematics and supervised by imperial princes. Sons of distinguished banner families were chosen to be students in the Meng-yang-chai.[73] The emperor also personally taught mathematics to his own children, of whom his third son Yin-chih had the most notable aptitude for science.[74]

K'ang-hsi's study of Western science encouraged a revival of Chinese mathematics. Of all the many mathematicians who lived and wrote during the K'ang-hsi period,[75] perhaps the most famous were members of the Mei family. Five generations of this family produced eight mathematicians, led by Mei Wen-ting and his grandson, Mei Ku-ch'eng. As a gesture of great honor to the former, K'ang-hsi brought the latter as a young man into the

Meng-yang-chai school to learn mathematics under imperial supervision.[76] Ironically, the importation of Western science and its incorporation into Chinese mathematical compilations led many native mathematicians to rediscover Chinese astronomy and mathematics, which had degenerated since the fourteenth century. Mei Wen-ting and Mei Ku-ch'eng were early leaders of this revival movement.[77]

After K'ang-hsi, the importation of Western science into China did not keep pace with the rapid scientific developments in Europe. The emperor's interest in Western science had gone beyond simple admiration of its refinements: he saw scientific and technical knowledge as the basis of a strong China that could resist the very countries which were the origins of that knowledge. The Jesuits' technical skills, but not their religion or cultural values, were accepted and utilized by K'ang-hsi for his own purposes. In the later stages of his reign, he refused to tolerate a papal challenge to his absolute power in China, forcing all missionaries to sign a certificate (*p'iao*) testifying to their intention to accept his and not the pope's ruling on the Rites Question if they wished to remain in the country.[78]

Recruitment and Employment of Scholars

One of the critical areas of friction between the Manchu ruling house and Chinese scholars was the openness or restrictiveness of the normal opportunities of employment and advancement in the great bureaucratic machine. Several complicating factors were at work during K'ang-hsi's early reign—reduced examination quotas, the possibility of purchasing degrees and posts, and the competition of bannermen.

As an alien dynasty seeking the support of the key social and political class among its subjects, the Manchus at the outset deliberately inflated the national examination quotas. During Shun-chih's reign, an average of 370 scholars passed each of the eight *chin-shih* examinations. This meant an average annual *chin-shih* production of about 185 for the period 1644–61. The K'ang-hsi period presented a stark contrast. The three subperiods of 1662–78, 1679–99, and 1700–22 show an average *chin-shih* per examination of 206, 159, and 216 respectively. The annual average had also drastically declined to 64, 56, and 88, respectively.[79] The number of *chin-shih* degrees conferred in the seven metropolitan examinations of the early K'ang-hsi period were as follows: 200 in 1664, 155 in 1667, 299 in 1670, 166 in 1673, 209 in 1676, 151 in 1679, and 179 in 1682—far off the 370 average of the Shun-chih period.[80]

At the other end of the examination system—the prefectural *sheng-yüan* examinations—there was also a tightening up of quotas. Student quotas at the end of the Ming dynasty had completely broken down so that *sheng-yüan* were glutting the academic market. No steps were taken to correct this situation in the early years of the Ch'ing dynasty, again because the Manchus were sensitive to the career expectations of the Chinese gentry class.[81] In 1658, however, entrance into this class through the prefectural examination was drastically curtailed, first by cutting the frequency of *sheng-yüan* examinations from twice to once every three years, and then by reducing the student quotas from each prefecture and district by more than half. Whereas quotas for large, middle, and small districts were originally 40, 30, and 20, they were now cut to 20, 15, and 4–5.[82] The two policies together reduced the *sheng-yüan* numbers by at least one-fourth. This prompted a censor in 1660 to count the narrowing of the path to officialdom as one of the eight serious problems of the day.[83]

In the K'ang-hsi reign, student quotas fluctuated. Taking the Shanghai district as an example, in 1673, *sheng-yüan* examinations were put back on a basis of twice every three years, but the number passing each examination was further reduced to 4 for a large *hsien*, 3 for an average one, and 2 for a small one. After the 1679 earthquake that shook Peking and provided a catalyst for political change, the student quotas were restored to their pre-1673 levels: 15, 10, and 7–8, according to the official status of the *hsien*.[84] Compared with the Ming period, however, the academic avenue to success was still constricted.

Despite the limited flow of new degree holders, their chances of success in the bureaucracy were diminishing, not increasing, in the early Ch'ing period. The first explanation of this seeming paradox lies in the alien nature of the dynasty. Political considerations required the extensive use of Manchus and Chinese bannermen in government posts to the evident disadvantage of Han Chinese. There was no problem at the top, in capital posts, because the dynasty simply created parallel positions for Manchus and Chinese. The crunch came at the provincial and local levels, where only one man filled each position. Wherever a bannerman was appointed, there was one less job available to Chinese scholars who had worked their way through the rigorous examination system.

As a result, holders of the *chin-shih* degree often found themselves in junior government posts or in none at all. For instance, in the Kiangnan area, a holder of the highest degree served less frequently as a governor, financial commissioner, or judicial commissioner than did men without that degree. In Soochow prefecture, only one of every four prefects and one of every five magistrates in the K'ang-hsi period were *chin-shih.* Even at this level, bannermen or Chinese of lower qualification were crowding out graduates of the metropolitan examination.[85] The plight of the Chinese scholar became so desperate that in 1664 some officials of the Board of Rites were urging the cancelation of upcoming metropolitan and provincial examinations to reduce the backlog of expectant officials.[86] There were simply too many candidates and not enough vacant positions.

Competition for office from bannermen was not the sole cause of the devaluation of the higher degrees. Equally as responsible, or even more so, was the government's policy to sell titles and offices. The Ming dynasty had resorted to the sale of *kung-sheng* and *chien-sheng* degrees (to the point of debasing the latter) since the mid-fifteenth century to offset military expenditures,[87] but it was the Ch'ing dynasty that turned the "unorthodox" route to office (i.e., on the strength of money rather than education) into an important means of socioacademic mobility. The early K'ang-hsi period reflected this development well.

Under K'ang-hsi, *sheng-yüan* could purchase both *kung-sheng* and *chien-sheng* degrees for varying amounts of cash or grain. For example, a 1668 regulation set 200 taels of silver or 600 piculs of rice as the price of a *chien-sheng* degree. As another example, studentships at the Imperial Academy were available in 1671 to Kiangnan *sheng-yüan* for 200 taels or 400 piculs and to *sheng-yüan* candidates for 300 taels or 600 piculs. The *kung-sheng* degree could also be purchased by several types of *sheng-yüan* for 200 taels after 1675.[88]

The real departure from Ming practice came in 1674 when the *sheng-yuan* title itself was sold at a price of 100 or 120 taels of silver.[89] Further yet, a man could buy himself a district magistrate's post. These practices first came to light in 1677 when Sung Te-i, then president of the Censorate, urged their abandonment. He reported that the government had raised about two million taels of silver from the sale of more than five hundred district magistrate positions over the previous three years.[90] Despite Sung's objections, the sale of degrees and offices reached a peak in the period 1678–82. This accounts for the abnormally high number of *sheng-yüan* at a time when student quotas were still low. The quotas, in fact, were deliberately kept low to encourage the sale of degrees. In several lower Yangtze valley counties, student numbers were up 200 to 400 percent in this period, with purchased degrees outnumbering those obtained by examination by five, ten, or more times.[91] As for the sale of offices, a critic of the purchase system claimed in 1679 that 60 percent of the district magistrates had bought their post.[92]

The raison d'être for the unprecedented selling of the *sheng-yüan* degree as well as the *kung-sheng* and *chien-sheng* degrees and district magistrates posts was to offset the extraordinary military expenses of the 1670s. Accordingly, provinces supporting an occupying army during the *San-fan* campaigns were most likely to resort to these practices. The selling of degrees and posts was introduced to Kiangsi, Fukien and Hukuang (Hupei and Hunan) in 1676, to Kwangsi in 1679, to Kweichow in 1680, and to Yunnan in 1681. Besides the purchase of posts and degrees, officials in these areas could also acquire merit ratings and higher rank with cash contributions.[93]

Most of the men proposing the use of *chüan-na* (purchase) looked on it as an expedient measure that should be eschewed as soon as the military crisis passed. Very few supported the practice on principle. So in the late 1670s and early 1680s, as the civil war drew to a close, critics began to press for an end to *chüan-na*. Sung Te-i, mentioned above, was probably the first and most prominent official to speak up. He was followed by others—Hsü Yüan-wen among them—who attacked *chüan-na* as corrosive of good government and scholarship.[94] They succeeded in stopping the sale of *sheng-yüan* after the *San-fan* and Taiwan rebels had been defeated, but the sale of offices continued and even spread throughout the country. The military need was gone, but the government still collected funds in this way for relief measures.[95]

The combined competition of bannermen and unorthodox degree holders made it harder than ever for Chinese scholars to climb the sociopolitical ladder in the early K'ang-hsi period. The whole K'ang-hsi reign was one of low mobility anyway, according to the study of Ping-ti Ho, and the commoners' share of *chin-shih* on the 1682 metropolitan examination was the lowest of the entire Ming-Ch'ing period—only 19.3 percent.[96] So the availability of degrees and posts for 100, 200, or 300 taels of silver just added insult to the already frustrated scholar class. To alleviate the situation, the emperor in 1684 ordered a decrease in the percentage of district magistrate vacancies that could be filled by purchase. The then current procedure followed by the Board of Civil Appointments was that of every 10 magistrate vacancies, 2 could be filled by promotion, 3 with men holding either a *chin-shih, chü-jen, kung-sheng,* or *chien-sheng* degree, and 5 by purchase. The new regulation stipulated the following division: 2 by promotion or transfer, 2 from *chin-shih* holders, 3 from *chü-jen, kung-sheng,* or *chien-sheng* holders, and only 3 by purchase. The stated reason behind this change was "to open up the *chin-shih*'s path to office."[97]

The government's policy, then, on the recruitment and employment of Chinese scholars did little to win their support. Their career goals were harder, not easier, to reach during the K'ang-hsi reign. But still K'ang-hsi was able in one masterful campaign to overcome the lingering alienation of the literary class. I am referring to the special *po-hsüeh hung-tz'u* examination given in 1679 and the subsequent employment of successful candidates on a history of the Ming dynasty. The two events broke the psychological resistance to Manchu rule as much as the *San-fan* campaigns broke the military resistance, and these successes came simultaneously.

The Po-hsüeh Examination of 1679

In the mid-seventeenth century many Chinese scholar-officials withheld their support and active participation from the Manchu government, awaiting (some of them hoped) the return of the native Ming rule. That never happened, and some Ming scholars never came out of retirement. Others, however, did return to their normal career patterns as a result of K'ang-hsi's blandishments. It was the 1679 *po-hsüeh hung-tz'u* examination, which Etienne Balazs has called a "booby-trap exam for literati,"[98] that capped the emperor's efforts.

The search for scholars to be personally tested and employed by K'ang-hsi began in the spring of 1678 and went on through 1679 as imperial armies were moving towards the stronghold of the rebels, leaderless since Wu San-kuei's death in the fall of 1678. The emperor requested that all capital officials of the third rank or above, all censors, and high provincial officials recommend worthy scholars for the *po-hsüeh* examination. Other officials wanting to submit names could do so through the *tu-fu* or the Board of Civil Appointments. Nominees could be either active officials or men in retirement. The grand secretaries immediately compiled a list of seventy-seven men, but K'ang-hsi set it aside until all capital and provincial officials had a chance to reply to his edict.[99] In response to K'ang-hsi's call, 202 scholars of wide repute were recommended. Not all of them took the examination: 14 declined the honor, hanging on to their principles to the last; another 14 took ill en route to Peking; and 22 of those reaching the capital did not take the examination because of illness or death.

Among the 14 officially recorded as refusing to participate were the noted Ming loyalists Ku Yen-wu and Wan Ssu-t'ung and the slightly lesser known Fei Mi and Li Ch'ing. Still other eminent scholars who resisted, among them Huang Tsung-hsi, Fu Shan, Li Yung, Ts'ao Jung, and Tu Yüeh, were officially listed as having accepted the honor of being recommended but prevented by illness from competing on the examination.[100] In truth, their illnesses were feigned. For instance, the philosopher Li Yung went on a hunger strike and almost committed suicide before being allowed to go home without competing.[101] Fu Shan, of literary and artistic fame, is another good example of resistance to serving the Manchus. He only relented under strong pressure to having his name submitted, but he had a change of heart when nearing the gate to the capital and would not proceed to the palace for the examination. He even refused to thank the emperor for the honorary title of secretary of the Nei-ko bestowed on him as a special favor.[102]

The pressure on these men, and others like them, to participate in the *po-hsüeh* examination was great and emanated from the emperor himself. When it was reported in September 1678, that 17 recommendees were declining to come to Peking for reasons of health or a death in the family, K'ang-hsi ordered their respective governors to escort them to the capital without further ado.[103] All 17 were sent off to Peking, but 8 of them (Li Yung was one of these) still managed to be relieved of this "honor" en route, and another 3 were excused from the examination after reaching the capital because of illness or a death of a relative. The remaining 6 of the 17, though, went through with it and were among the 50 successful candidates.

The sentiment of all those trying to avoid participating in the *po-hsüeh* examination and serving the Manchus was captured best by Chou Yung, one of the fourteen officially listed as declining the honor of being recommended. Chou was a Ming dynasty *chü-jen* who persistently refused to take the metropolitan examination under the Ch'ing. When told that he was to be recommended for the 1679 examination he replied: "Although I am called Chou Yung, I can really only tolerate the Shang."[104] In that terse statement based on a double pun, he proclaimed his allegiance to the former dynasty and at the same time reminded the Manchus of their alien origin by evoking the example of the Shang and Chou dynasties of antiquity.

In the end, 152 candidates took the examination in April 1679, after cold weather in Peking had delayed it for two weeks, and 50 passed.[105] The provincial registration of these 50 men was significant, because 40 of them (or 80 percent) came from the two southeastern provinces of Kiangnan and Chekiang. By this time, of course, these provinces were producing the bulk of scholars, as reflected in their share of *chin-shih* holders, but it was never in such a dominant fashion (see table 7). K'ang-hsi's preference for Kiang-

TABLE 7
Provincial Registration of 1679 *Po-hsüeh* and Early Ch'ing *Chin-shih*

Province	No. of *Po-hsüeh*	Percentage of *Chin-shih*[a]	
		1644–1661	1662–1722
Kiangnan[b]	26	(1) 19.4	(1) 20.4
Chekiang	14	(4) 10.4	(2) 14.3
Chihli	4	(2) 14.9	(3) 12.6
Kiangsi	3	(10) 2.9	(7) 5.0
Honan	1	(5) 10.2	(5) 7.8
Shansi	1	(6) 8.6	(6) 6.8
Shantung	1	(3) 14.4	(4) 10.8
Total	50		

Sources: Ch'in Ying, *Chi-wei tz'u-k'o lu, chüan* 2–3, for *po-hsüeh;* P'ing-ti Ho, *Ladder of Success*, p. 228 (table 28), for *chin-shih* (with bannermen figures subtracted from total).

[a] Rank of province as a producer of *chin-shih* in parenthesis.

[b] Includes natives of both Kiangsi and Anhwei.

nan and Chekiang scholars showed, first of all, a sensitive awareness of the north-south political rivalry mentioned earlier and the dynastic imperative of broadening its base of support. The Manchus had conquered and administered the Chinese empire at the outset solely with Chinese bannermen and other northern Chinese collaborators. K'ang-hsi, working hard to consolidate Manchu rule and "pacify" the country, could not restrict himself to the use of such early supporters; men from the southeast, where early resistance to the Manchus was strong, must also participate in governing. The selection of *po-hsüeh* was just dramatic evidence of what was occurring more slowly elsewhere in the bureaucracy: a shift toward the employment of noncollaborating Chinese in top metropolitan and provincial posts.[106]

K'ang-hsi had another, more specific motive in holding the *po-hsüeh* examination: he was trying to mollify the Kiangnan and Chekiang scholarly elite who had been alienated eighteen years earlier by policies of the Manchu regents. Four of the successful candidates, two who failed, two who declined, and a reader of the papers had all been involved in the Kiangnan tax case of 1661. Another *po-hsüeh* scholar had been personally touched by the 1661 literary inquisition concerning Chuang T'ing-lung's work. The involvement, willing or unwilling, of these ten men in the 1679 examination reflected the complete reversal of policy that had transpired between 1661, when the four Manchu regents came to power, and 1679, when K'ang-hsi was leading the effort to stabilize the new dynasty.

A few examples will illustrate what was happening. P'eng Sun-yü, from Hai-yen district in Chekiang, received his *chin-shih* degree in 1659 but was not appointed to the usual Hanlin post because of the tax arrears case. In 1679 he placed first on the *po-hsüeh* examination, for which he was recommended by Wu Cheng-chih, the same official who was instrumental in obtaining the release of several hundred licentiates held in the 1661 tax case.[107] A Kiangsu scholar, Ch'ing Sung-ling, had lost his *chin-shih* degree and Hanlin post in 1661 for a tax deficiency, but he recovered from this misfortune eighteen years later through K'ang-hsi's special examination. It was Sung-ling's great-great-grandson, Ch'in Ying, who compiled the basic account of the 1679 examination and its successful candidates.[108] Another Kiangsu *po-hsüeh*, Wang Wan, had been caught in the tax case, but his recovery of dignity and honor was complete in 1684 when the emperor presented him with an imperial scroll on the first Southern Tour.[109] The poet Wang Hao, a descendant of the famous Ming scholar and official, Wang Shih-chen, was hauled to Peking for questioning in 1661; in 1679, despite his refusal to take the examination, he was awarded an honorary post in the Grand Secretariat because of his age and reputation.[110] P'an Lei, whose elder brother was executed in 1663 for being a compiler of Chuang's seditious history, was one of the so-called Four Commoners (*ssu pu-i*) who passed the *po-hsüeh* examination and served in the Hanlin Academy.

Finally, consider Yeh Fang-ai, who was one of the four readers of the *po-hsüeh* papers as Hanlin chancellor.[111] He had gained a measure of notoriety in 1661 as the scholar who lost his *t'an-hua* (third-ranked *chin-shih*) degree for a minor tax deficiency. The fact that this man was officially involved with the *po-hsüeh* examination and later the *Ming-shih* (History of the Ming dynasty) project must have been particularly galling to one of the famous scholars refusing to associate himself with either event—Ku Yen-wu. Yeh Fang-ai recommended Ku Yen-wu for an official position on the Historiographical Board, but the latter refused and stated, in a letter to his recommender, that "if I should really be forced to go, nothing would be left to me than to escape by death."[112] This seemingly friendly relationship between Ku and Yeh hides the fact that the latter's elder brother, Yeh Fang-heng, held a mortgage on 800 *mou* of property belonging to the Ku household. The elder brother harassed Ku Yen-wu at every turn, leading to his imprisonment in 1655, an attempted assassination in 1656, and finally his flight from home to travel throughout North China.[113] Yeh Fang-ai's role in this affair is not known, nor is it known whether or not Ku Yen-wu held a grudge against him, but the difficulty between the two families, coupled with the Yeh family's acceptance of Ch'ing rule—both brothers took their *chin-shih* degree under the new dynasty—possibly reinforced Ku's own determination not to have any dealings with the Manchu government.

The emperor's campaign to dissipate the anti-Manchu energy of Chinese scholars did not end with the selection of fifty "scholars of broad learning." In another brilliant stroke, he put the successful candidates to work compiling a history of the Ming dynasty, the dynasty to which some of them still felt attached. Now their energies could be channeled into literary efforts and away from political or ideological warfare. K'ang-hsi also appointed the 50 men to the Hanlin Academy, overruling the Board of Civil Appointments' initial recommendation to keep everyone at essentially the same rank and post he held before the examination.[114] Six were capital officials, 3 were serving in the provinces, 7 each were awaiting appointment to capital and provincial posts, and 4 were on temporary leaves. There were also 2 *chin-shih*, 4 *chü-jen*, 13 holders of the first degree, and 4 commoners.

The new appointees to the Hanlin Academy were the object of much scorn by its regular membership. The latter disdainfully referred to the others as the *yeh-Hanlin* ("unofficial" or "wildcat" members) and criticized their scholarship before the emperor.[115] The honors accorded the "Four Commoners" passing the examination—Chu I-tsun, Yen Sheng-sun, Li Yin-tu, and P'an Lei—particularly excited the Hanlin regulars. Yen had not even finished the *po-hsüeh* examination but was passed (fiftieth and last) by K'ang-hsi personally.[116] Li returned home shortly after the examination to care for his mother, but the other three all served as diarists and tutors of the emperor and helped him draft edicts. Yen and P'an were included in the distinguished list of ninety-three officials who composed a poem jointly with K'ang-hsi in 1682 in celebration of the victory over the *San-fan* rebels.[117] By 1684 the three active members of the "Four Commoners" had been purged from the Academy. In that year, Chu I-tsun was impeached and degraded for copying Hanlin documents for private use, P'an Lei also lost his post on the charge of "petulance" (e.g., advocating the extension to lower officials of the privilege of direct access to the throne), and Yen Sheng-sun retired. Their departure was celebrated by the regular Hanlin membership as "sweeping the Academy clean" (*sao-i mu-t'ien*).[118] One result, then, of the examination—either intended or unintended—was to shift the focus of attention of the Chinese scholarly class away from racial attacks on the Manchus to attacks on each other's credentials as scholars.

So the examination served the Manchu rulers well in several respects, and Balazs' caustic description of it as a "booby-trap" was well-founded. But the examination was more than that as we have seen: it also signaled the beginning of a Manchu sharing of power and cooperation with noncollaborating Chinese. On a personal level, important Manchu and Chinese bannermen officials, such as Grand Secretary Mingju, his son Singde, and the emperor's confidant, Ts'ao Yin, befriended and supported a number of successful *po-hsüeh* candidates.[119] Even those who failed the examination could profit by their participation. For instance, Yen Jo-chü attracted the attention of Hsü Ch'ien-hsüeh, then in retirement but soon to be appointed a chief compiler of the *Ming-shih*, and the latter took on Yen as his personal literary aide.[120]

The most tangible result of the new working relationship was the Ming History project. Imperial interest in compiling a history of the Ming dynasty began early in Shun-chih's reign, but in 1648 the work was interrupted because of a lack of material for the years 1624 and 1627–44. All officials of the metropolitan and provincial governments were ordered to search their files for any memorandums or correspondence dealing with affairs of state in those years.[121] The search produced no results; so in 1665 the court again called for a concerted effort to uncover historical materials of the late Ming period. This time, punishment was threatened for those who did not undertake the task seriously. A more significant incentive, though, was the court's assurance that no one would suffer for turning in Ming works that contained derogatory remarks about the Manchus.[122] This was an absolute necessity, because no one could have forgotten how scores of scholars were executed two years earlier for their association with Chuang T'ing-lung's history of the Ming dynasty. In response to this second initiative by the court, Ku Ju-hua, the intendant of Shantung, suggested the establishment of a historiographical commission to oversee the work of filling in the known lacunae. He also urged the emperor to make an attempt to involve reputable scholars in this work.[123] In his two suggestions lay the germ of the idea which eventually developed into the 1679 *po-hsüeh* examination and the Ming History project.

The first directors of the compilation work were appointed in 1679 immediately following the *po-hsüeh* examination.[124] Among them were Hsü Yüan-wen and Yeh Fang-ai—both of whom, it may be recalled, had been involved in the Kiangnan tax case of 1661. In addition to the successful *po-hsüeh* candidates, other scholars served on the Ming History project or aided its work in various unofficial capacities. This latter group included a noted triumvirate of Ming loyalists who had refused to participate in the examination itself—Huang Tsung-hsi, Wan Ssu-t'ung, and Ku Yen-wu.

Huang Tsung-hsi himself did not go to Peking when he and others were invited by the emperor at the suggestion of Hsü

Yüan-wen,[125] but one of Huang's sons and several of his pupils accepted K'ang-hsi's offer and assisted in the work of compiling the Ming History. Huang, however, did submit to the board his writings on the Ming dynasty and his biographical sketches of important Southern Ming figures. In addition, he recommended to the compilers a work on late Ming rebellions by P'eng Sun-i (a cousin of P'eng Sun-yü, who placed first on the 1679 examination).[126] Wan Ssu-t'ung, unlike Huang, agreed to join the history project, but he did so on a private basis. Refusing an official appointment, he worked out of the residences of various directors. His draft history of the preceding dynasty formed the basis of the *Ming-shih* that was submitted to the throne in 1723 by Wang Hung-hsü, the chief compiler who unfairly assumed authorship for Wan's and other scholars' work.[127] Ku Yen-wu had a number of friends and a relative taking the examination and working on the Ming History project. Like Huang, Ku refused to serve on the board, but he offered advice to the compilers on what sources to consult for reliable information on the later Ming period.[128]

The only major exception to the general cooptation of loyalist scholars was Wang Fu-chih, the prominent Neo-Confucianist and historian who in 1648 had raised a local army to fight the Manchus (as had Huang Tsung-hsi and Ku Yen-wu). Curiously, no pressure seems to have been applied to Wang to participate in either the *po-hsüeh* examination or the Ming History project. At the time, Wang was in seclusion after refusing to support Wu San-kuei's cause when the latter came to Heng-yang, Wang's birthplace, to proclaim himself emperor of the Chou dynasty.[129] If Wang was still unwilling to accept the Manchu dynasty, he also was denying the legitimacy of the only possible rival claimant to the throne.

Once the compiling began, K'ang-hsi's main concern was to insure its impartiality. Extra compilers were added so that no aspect of the work would be slighted.[130] He also frequently reminded his chief compilers of the difficulty in remaining unbiased in recording recent history, but he wanted to be fair to the Ming house. To check against personal bias, the emperor asked that each compiler submit his work to other members of the project for criticism. No one's writing, not even his own, he claimed, was above criticism or not subject to change.[131] K'ang-hsi's encouragement and concern paid off in the quality of the *Ming-shih*, which is recognized by many as an excellent work.[132]

Whatever literary merit the *Ming-shih* might have, it must be emphasized that its compilation primarily served political ends. It was the pièce de résistance that tempted the most loyal Ming scholar, as I have shown. While the *po-hsüeh* examination tested and employed primarily men who already held minor positions in the Manchu government, the history project decisively ended the holdout of significant elements of the Chinese scholar-gentry class and restored their confidence in the court's commitment to respect their traditional values and prerogatives—a commitment that was not clear to many in the dark days of 1661. Together, these two imperial projects drew "learned scholars and eminent men together in great numbers" and "set the direction of intellectual interest for all of China," according to the testimony of a mid-Ch'ing scholar.[133] K'ang-hsi the exemplar and patron of the arts had bagged the scholar's heart just as K'ang-hsi the strategist had buried the soldier's hope.

Seven

CONCLUSION: K'ANG-HSI AND CONSOLIDATION

APPROPRIATELY ENOUGH, K'ANG-HSI HAD JUST TURNED THIRTY AND finished the work of consolidating Ch'ing rule in 1684, a traditionally auspicious first year (*chia-tzu*) of the sexagenary cycle. Chinese, committed as they were to cyclical development, could confidently await the arrival of a new age of peace and order. K'ang-hsi's achievements during his early reign (1661–84) would justify such expectations. The young emperor had reversed the general direction of government policy, repulsed military challenges to the new regime and moved to secure the empire's northern frontier (which, however, was soon to be threatened again by the Mongol chieftain Galdan), harnessed both Manchu and Chinese talents for government service, opened China to Western scientific knowledge, and dissipated the anti-Manchu hostility of a large group of Chinese scholar-gentry. Ch'ing rule was effectively consolidated and the foundations were laid for a Pax Sinica in Asia.

K'ang-hsi's early reign, then, was in sharp contrast to the Regency which preceded it. Oboi and his colleagues were still too committed to traditional Manchu customs and attitudes to successfully make the necessary transition from barbarian conquerors to sinified emperors, necessary if the Manchus were to establish a dynasty of long duration. The centralization and sinicization of the Manchu state, which began under Nurhaci and flourished under Abahai and Dorgon, received setbacks during the Oboi regency. The regents pursued a policy of Manchu nativism—a ready willingness to place short-range Manchu interests over long-range imperial goals. They replaced Chinese style institutions with practices familiar to Manchus—the Three Inner Courts (*nei-san-yuan*) and the bondservant system (*pao-i* or *booi*); they persecuted southeastern scholar-gentry in a number of literary and tax-evasion cases; and by 1666 Oboi had become a virtual dictator and forced an exchange of banner land and new enclosures (*ch'üan-ti*) at great inconvenience to both the bannermen involved and commoners.

Clearly, the regents were jeopardizing the earlier efforts of Manchu leaders to construct a stable, alien-dominated regime that was still capable of gaining legitimacy in the eyes of the Chinese. In the 1660s, the future direction of the Ch'ing dynasty was in doubt. The consolidation process, already underway, needed careful nurturing if it was not to wither and die. It is in this context that the contribution of K'ang-hsi and his advisers must be evaluated. They were not content to accept Oboi's rule or policies, which were a challenge to imperial supremacy and the forging of a viable Manchu-Chinese working relationship. It was not just a matter of elevating Chinese institutions over Manchu institutions—in some cases, in fact, institutions favored by the regents (e.g., the Imperial Household Agency) were retained by the emperor but used to serve his interests against the power of Manchu princes.[1] It was more a question of values and outlook. K'ang-hsi realized, as apparently the regents did not, that concessions to the Chinese elite could be made without the Manchus losing grip on the reins of power and had to be made to gain their recognition and support as the legitimate successors of the Ming order. Thus, it was in 1684 and not 1661 that Ch'ing rule was consolidated. With the Mandate of Heaven safely in place again, opposition to the Manchus had only one recourse (within the traditional Confucian framework of political behavior): to go underground and survive at a lower, semilegitimate level of operations until such time as the new order was subject again to an open challenge.

If looking back on the Oboi regency gives us a clearer understanding of the tasks confronting K'ang-hsi, then looking ahead to the zenith of Chinese power and splendor in the eighteenth century can help us assess the lasting contribution of K'ang-hsi's labors. The political and intellectual climate had changed considerably from one century to the next. In the early Ch'ing period, before consolidation was completed, the demands of Confucianism and nationalism were in open conflict. Anti-Manchu scholars had to decide whether to emphasize the distinctions between aliens and Chinese or to subordinate their nationalist sentiments to Confucian imperatives to serve legitimate rulers.[2] After K'ang-hsi's self-conscious cultivation of Chinese scholarship and scholars, the urgency of the conflict dissipated. The image and reality of K'ang-hsi as a Confucian monarch blotted out almost all consciousness of the Manchu rulers as "barbarian conquerors." By the mid-eighteenth century, the problem of Manchu-Chinese relations were just not on the minds of the scholar-official class at all.[3]

Unity, not conflict, dominated the political and intellectual world of Ch'ien-lung's China. Manchus and Chinese served together in metropolitan and provincial posts. Breaking down the ethnic barriers was one of K'ang-hsi's most important and lasting contributions. Admittedly, K'ang-hsi failed to check completely the evils of factionalism and corruption among officialdom, even being overindulgent at times in personnel management. On other occasions, the emperor was impatient and abusive, but he developed mutually productive relations with his officials and used them effectively, particularly in gathering information essential to informed and independent decision making. Even more importantly, the Manchu-controlled state and the Chinese-guarded Confucian value system were harmoniously joined. The Confucian ideal of the unity of state and knowledge, under the rule of a sage-king, seemed near realization. While K'ang-hsi's mastery of Confucian and Western knowledge is open to question. Chinese scholars compare him favorably with such illustrious emperors of the past as T'ang T'ai-tsung, Sung T'ai-tsung, and Ming Ch'eng-tsu (the Yung-lo emperor) as a great patron of literature and promoter of scholarhip.[4] K'ang-hsi also had a genuine interest in knowledge, and Li Kuang-ti, an eminent Neo-Confucian of the orthodox Ch'eng-Chu school and a tutor to K'ang-hsi, praised him as a sage-ruler in the mold of Yao and Shun of antiquity. Li predicted that "the authoritative line of the *tao* and government will again be united."[5] Many early Ch'ing scholars, sickened by what they considered the intellectual decay and wrangling of late Ming and concerned about serving alien masters, welcomed this new order and contributed to its development. David Nivison concludes that "the regime's ideological self-justification, difficult to accept at first, was by the eighteenth century a real intellectual fact, solidly founded in Confucian doctrine."[6]

Complementing this success in the ideological realm, K'ang-hsi exhibited military and political leadership that also contributed to the consolidation of Ch'ing rule. This was true in two senses. While accommodating himself to his Chinese subjects by cultivating the arts and studying Confucian literature, the emperor also appealed to his Manchu compatriots as an energetic warrior. He engaged in martial exercises such as hunting and archery because he enjoyed them but also to emphasize the desired traits of hardiness and vitality. The Southern Tours gave K'ang-hsi ample opportunity to self-consciously display these complementary virtues of Confucian sagacity and Manchu vitality: he was the "serious-minded scholar" on the first tour in 1684 and the "sensitive aesthete" in 1689, but by the third tour in 1699 he had become the hard-riding Manchu.[7] K'ang-hsi's actual military and political leadership, as opposed to the image he projected, also strengthened his claims to Chinese and Manchu loyalty. The emperor had shown great courage and political maturity while still young in seizing the reins of government from the regent Oboi and then firmly dealing with the awesome challenge to Ch'ing rule presented by Wu San-kuei and the other feudatory princes. These were impressive moves that paid handsome dividends: dynastic rule was stabilized and legitimized, and personal (imperial) rule was strengthened as well. The Manchus had restored the peace and order that neither Ming nor rebel Chinese leaders were able to provide, and they reaped the benefits. With military and political supremacy assured, K'ang-hsi moved to conciliate the Chinese elite and gain their legitimizing support of and participation in Ch'ing rule.

By breaking down the barriers between Manchus and Chinese and erecting an edifice of strong dynastic rule, K'ang-hsi had forged a unified state, politically and ethnically, that would dominate Asia and resist Western penetration for a century or more. Such an achievement has not been lost on Chinese Marxist historians, who applaud the emperor's contribution to national development while attacking him as an agent of landlord class rule.[8] Alien though he may have been, K'ang-hsi infused new life into the traditional Chinese state and empire.

In sum, K'ang-hsi personified a successful blend of *wen* and *wu*, of knowledge and action, of the accomplished scholar and the courageous strategist. The two images were really just complementary phases of a single purpose which motivated the emperor in the years between 1669 and 1684: the consolidation of Ch'ing rule over China. His strong interest in learning, competence in the basic Confucian classics, open-minded attitude toward new knowledge, and patronage and dominance of scholars and the scholarly world assuredly won for him and the dynasty the support of the Chinese; but so did his purposeful and energetic response to military challenges, thorough personal attention to details of governing, and mature judgment in political crisis. The youthful, ambitious, and capable emperor had completed the great work of his Manchu forebears: the alien conquest and rule of the great empire of China envisioned by Nurhaci and Abahai became a reality under K'ang-hsi.

ABBREVIATIONS

CHLC	*Kuo-ch'ao ch'i-hsien lei-cheng ch'u-pien,* ed. Li Huan (Hunan, 1884–90); references given to the Taiwan continuous pagination reprint (1966), with the original *chüan* and page numbers in parenthesis.
CS	*Ch'ing-shih* (Taipei, 1961); cited by page and column numbers.
CSLC	*Ch'ing-shih lieh-chuan* (Shanghai, 1928; reprinted Taipei: Chung-hua, 1962).
ECCP	*Eminent Chinese of the Ch'ing Period,* ed. Arthur Hummel (2 vols.; Washington, D.C.: Government Printing Office, 1943–44).
HCTI	*Huang-Ch'ing ming-ch'en tsou-i* (Chia-ch'ing ed.).
HTSL	*Ta-Ch'ing hui-tien shih-li* (Kuang-hsü ed.; Taipei: Ch'i-wen, 1963); citations as for *CHLC.*
IHPA	Academia Sinica (Taiwan), Institute of History and Philology, Miscellaneous Archives from the Grand Secretariat.
KHSL	*Ta-Ch'ing Sheng-tsu Jen-huang-ti* [*K'ang-hsi*] *shih-lu* (Mukden, 1937; reprinted Taipei: Hua-lien, 1964); citations as for *CHLC.*
MCSL	*Ming-Ch'ing shih-liao,* comp. Academia Sinica, Institute of History and Philology (Shanghai: Commerical Press, 1936 [Ser. III] and 1951 [Ser. IV]).
PCTC	*Pa-ch'i t'ung-chih* (1799 ed.).
SCSL	*Ta-Ch'ing Shih-tsu Chang-huang-ti* [*Shun-chih*] *shih-lu* (Mukden, 1937; reprinted Taipei: Hua-lien, 1964); citations as for *CHLC.*

When citing page numbers of *chüan*, "a" indicates recto, "b" indicates verso, and the absence of either indicates the material cited continues from recto to verso.

NOTES

Chapter One

1. *KHSL*, p. 1570(117.15a).

2. Charles O. Hucker, *The Censorial System of Ming China* (Stanford: Stanford University Press, 1966), p. 204.

3. David S. Nivison, "Ho-shen and His Accusers: Ideology and Political Behavior in the Eighteenth Century," in *Confucianism in Action*, ed. David S. Nivison and Arthur F. Wright (Stanford University Press, 1949), pp. 223–32.

4. For the Chinese texts, see James Legge, *The Chinese Classics*, vol. I, *Confucian Analects* (3d ed., Hong Kong, 1961), pp. 300, 150, and 273 respectively. These translations are mine; cf. Arthur Waley, *The Analects of Confucius* (New York: Random House, 1938), pp. 197, 91, and 177, respectively.

5. Analects XV, 22: "A gentleman does not accept men because of what they say, nor reject sayings, because the speaker is what he is" (Waley, *Analects*, p. 197).

6. Ou-yang Hsiu, "P'eng-tang lun," *Ou-yang Yung-shu-chi* (Shanghai, 1936), III, 22.

7. See William S. Atwell, "From Education to Politics: The Fu She," in *The Unfolding of Neo-Confucianism*, ed. Wm. Theodore de Bary (New York: Columbia University Press, 1975), pp. 333–67.

8. On Ming eunuchs and the Tung-lin movement, respectively, see Robert Crawford, "Eunuch Power in the Ming Dynasty," *T'oung-pao*, XLIX, no. 3 (1961), 115–48; and Charles O. Hucker, "The Tung-lin Movement of the Late Ming Period," in *Chinese Thought and Institutions*, ed. John K. Fairbank (Chicago: University of Chicago Press, 1957), pp. 132–62.

9. *HCTI*, 2.3a–7a; Feng's biography is in *ECCP*, I, 240–41. On Huang, see Wm. Theodore de Bary, "Chinese Despotism and the Confucian Ideal: A Seventeenth-Century View," in *Chinese Thought and Institutions*, (see n. 8 above), pp. 176–77.

10. Li Kuang-pi, "Ming-mo nung-min ta-ch'i-i," in *Ming-Ch'ing shih-lun ts'ung*, comp. Li Kuang-pi (Wuhan: Hupeh Jen-min, 1956), p. 114.

11. James B. Parsons, "The Ming Dynasty Bureaucracy: Aspects of Background Forces," in *Chinese Government in Ming Times: Seven Studies*, ed. Charles O. Hucker (New York: Columbia University Press, 1969), pp. 219–20.

12. Li Wen-chih, "Wan-Ming t'ung-chih chieh-chi ti t'ou-hsiang Ch'ing-ch'ao chi nung-min ch'i-i-chün ti fan-Ch'ing tou-cheng," in *Ming-Ch'ing shih-lun ts'ung*, comp. Li Kuang-pi (Wuhan: Hupeh Jen-min, 1956), p. 150.

13. David S. Nivison, *The Life and Thought of Chang Hsueh-ch'eng (1738–1801)* (Stanford: Stanford University Press, 1966), p. 4.

14. See studies of Wm. Theodore de Bary, "Individualism and Humanitarianism in Late Ming Thought," and Tadao Sakai, "Confucianism and Popular Educational Works," in *Self and Society in Ming Thought*, ed. Wm. Theodore de Bary (New York: Columbia University Press, 1970). The quoted phrase is from de Bary's study, p. 173.

15. Wm. Theodore de Bary, "Introduction," in ibid., p. 6.

16. See Weber's discussion of this theme in Lewis A. Coser and Bernard Rosenberg, eds., *Sociological Theory* (New York: Macmillan, 1957), pp. 129–34.

17. Biographies of the three men and the basic outlines of their policies are in *ECCP*, I, 594–99, 1–3, and 215–19, respectively.

18. The following discussion of this theme has been influenced primarily by Meng Shen's painstaking research in his pioneering study of the Eight Banners system, "Pa-ch'i chih-tu k'ao-shih," reprinted in his *Ch'ing-tai shih* (Taipei: Cheng-chung, 1960), pp. 20–100; see also Franz Michael, *The Origin of Manchu Rule in China* (Baltimore: Johns Hopkins Press, 1942; reprinted New York: Octagon Books, 1965), esp. chaps. 4–9; David M. Farquhar, "Mongolian versus Chinese Elements in the Early Manchu State," *Ch'ing-shih wen-t'i*, II, no. 6 (June 1971), 11–23.

19. Wei-ping Wu, "The Development and Decline of the Eight Banners" (Ph.D. diss., University of Pennsylvania, 1969), pp. 6–12; Ch'en Wen-shih, "Man-chou pa-ch'i niu-lu ti kou-ch'eng," *Ta-lu tsa-chih*, 30 Nov. 1965, pp. 314–18.

20. Meng Shen, "Pa-ch'i," pp. 23–28, shows that before 1625 there were only the four *hosoi beile* named above, and only two more were ever so honored (Jirgaling, a nephew of Nurhaci, in 1625; and Haoge in 1628 when his father, Abahai, was reigning). Afterward, the title was informally applied to all of the banner princes, and likewise the number of banner princes was not always fixed at eight; some documents list ten, or thirteen, or fifteen (e.g., ibid., pp. 38–39 and 70).

21. *ECCP*, I, 1, 214, and 597; Michael, *Origin of Manchu Rule*, pp. 85–87.

22. Meng Shen, "Pa-ch'i," pp. 33–34; slightly different versions of this instruction are found in *Ta-Ch'ing Kao-huang-ti shih-lu* (Mukden, 1937; reprinted Taipei: Hua-lien, 1964), p. 102(8.15b–16b); *Huang-Ch'ing k'ai-kuo fang-lüeh*, 1789 ed., 7.27b–28a.

23. Meng Shen, "Pa-ch'i," pp. 35–36; see also *Kao-huang-ti shih-lu*, pp. 126–27(10.16a–18b).

24. *ECCP,* I, 303; Meng Shen, "Pa-ch'i," pp. 48–49.
25. Meng Shen, "Pa-ch'i," p. 40.
26. Ibid., p. 70.
27. Ibid., pp. 42–47 and 55–56.
28. Ibid., p. 71; *ECCP,* I, 562–63.
29. Michael, *Origin of Manchu Rule,* p. 89; Piero Corradini, "Civil Administration at the Beginning of the Manchu Dynasty: A Note on the Establishment of the Six Ministries (Liu-pu)," *Oriens extremus,* IX (1962), 135.
30. Fu Tsung-mao, "Ch'ing-ch'u i-cheng t'i-chih chih yen-chiu," *Cheng-chih ta-hsüeh hsüeh-pao,* XI (May 1965), 245–51; Silas H. L. Wu, *Communication and Imperial Control in China* (Cambridge: Harvard University Press, 1970), pp. 10–13.
31. Wei-ping Wu, "Eight Banners," pp. 18–23; *ECCP,* II, 797; Liu Chia-chü, "Ch'ing-ch'u Han-chün pa-ch'i ti chao-chien," *Ta-lu tsa-chih,* 15 June 1967, pp. 338–39.
32. Liu Chia-chü, "Han-chün pa-ch'i," p. 377.
33. *HTSL,* p. 5205(11.1a). The biography of Soni, later to be regent of K'ang-hsi, states that he, his father, and his uncle served in the Literary Office during Nurhaci's time (*CSLC,* 6.14a). Perhaps it was not institutionalized until 1629.
34. Charles O. Hucker, "Governmental Organization of the Ming Dynasty," *Harvard Journal of Asiatic Studies,* XXI (1958), 27–31.
35. *HTSL,* pp. 17506(1044.1a), and 5205(11.1); Piero Corradini, "A propos de l'institution de Nei-ko sous la dynastie des Ts'ing," *T'oung-pao,* XLVIII (1960), 419–20.
36. Huang Pei, "Aspects of Ch'ing Autocracy: An Institutional Study, 1644–1735," *Tsing-hua Journal of Chinese Studies,* n.s., VI (Dec., 1967), 117–18.
37. Corradini, "Civil Administration," pp. 136–38.
38. Silas Wu, *Communication and Imperial Control,* p. 7.
39. Meng Shen, "Pa-ch'i," pp. 20–21; *ECCP,* II, 916–17.
40. *ECCP,* I, 214, 216, 280, and 443.
41. Michael, *Origin of Manchu Rule,* pp. 92, and 94.
42. See ibid., pp. 93–94; *ECCP,* I, 216–17.
43. *ECCP,* I, 217.
44. Meng Shen, "Pa-ch'i," pp. 50–55; *ECCP,* I, 217.
45. *ECCP,* I, 217–218; Meng Shen, "Pa-ch'i," pp. 49–55 and 69. Meng in his study showed that only the plain red banner remained under the control of descendants of its original chief, Daisan.
46. *Te-chih i, chih-chih nan;* memorial in 1649 of Governor-general Liu Wu-yüan, *HCTI,* 3.31a.
47. See, for instance, memorials in *HCTI,* 12.1a–4a and 17.1a–3a.
48. Wei I-chieh memorial of 1660, in *HCTI,* 15.8b.
49. Wei-ping Wu, "Eight Banners," pp. 52–56; Ma Feng-ch'en, "Manchu-Chinese Social and Economic Conflicts," in *Chinese Social History,* ed. E-tu Zen Sun and John deFrancis (Washington, D.C.: American Council of Learned Soceties, 1956), pp. 335–39; Liu Chia-chü, *Ch'ing-ch'ao ch'u-ch'i ti pa-ch'i ch'üan-ti* (Taipei: National Taiwan University,

1964), pp. 48–54.

50. Jonathan Spence, *Ts'ao Yin and the K'ang-hsi Emperor: Bondservant and Master* (New Haven: Yale University Press, 1966), p. 47; *CS*, p. 3897.4: biography of Wei Hsiang-shu.

51. The best study is Liu Chia-chü, "Shun-chih nien-chien ti t'ao-jen wen-t'i," in *Ch'ing-tsu Li Chi hsien-sheng ch'i-shih-sui lun-wen chi* (Taipei, 1967), pp. 1049–80; see also Ma Feng-ch'en, "Manchu-Chinese Conflicts," pp. 343–47.

52. *ECCP*, I, 417.

53. Such a complaint was registered in 1660 by an official of the special agency established in the Board of War to enforce the fugitive law (*MSCL*, ser. 3, vol. 10, p. 991), but the abuses continued (e.g., see *KHSL*, pp. 141[8.2], 215–16[13.22a–23a], and 217[14.2]).

54. *SCSL*, p. 1021(86.1b); *HCTI*, 7.29a–31b.

55. *SCSL*, pp. 1070–71 (90.4a–5b); for an earlier enunciation of this position, see *SCSL*, p. 1021(86.1b–2a). When Shun-chih once read a memorial reflecting a Chinese official's concern over the impoverished condition of some banner forces, he was overjoyed and rewarded the official (*CSLC*, 5.30b).

56. *SCSL*, p. 1072(90.8).

57. Liu Hsien-t'ing, *Kuang-yang tsa-chi* [comp. c. 1694] (Taipei: Shih-chieh, 1962), p. 42, reports on an isolated community in Kwangtung led by two Ming *sheng-yüan* who had not shaved their heads; the community only came under Ch'ing control in the 1680s. See also ibid., p. 77; *ECCP*, I, 54.

58. Li Hsün, *Ming-Ch'ing shih* (Peking: Jen-min, 1957), pp. 160–62; Willard J. Peterson, "The Life of Ku Yen-wu (1613–1682)," *Harvard Journal of Asiatic Studies*, XXVIII (1968), 139–40.

59. *CS*, p. 3889.7.

60. Li Hsün, *Ming-Ch'ing shih*, pp. 194–96; *ECCP*, I, 102, 166, 352, and 422; II, 671 and 817. A recently published study of Ku Yen-wu describes his role in military opposition to the Manchus as marginal (Peterson, "Ku Yen-wu," pp. 140–42 and 146–48).

61. *HCTI*, 15.26a.

Chapter Two

1. As indeed the Chinese official record would have us believe (*KHSL*, pp. 43–44[1.1a–4a]).

2. The Regency and its policies have been treated in depth by Robert Oxnam in a recent study, *Ruling from Horseback: Manchu Politics in the Oboi Regency, 1661-1669* (Chicago: University of Chicago Press, 1975). Our interpretations and conclusions generally coincide, but where we differ or he offers evidence I had not independently obtained, this will be indicated in a note. For a fuller treatment of the whole Regency, the reader, of course, is advised to consult Oxnam's book.

3. *KHSL*, p. 45(1.5a).

4. The following biographical information is taken from *ECCP*, II, 663–64; *CS*, p. 3803.1; *CSLC*, 6.14a; *CHLC*, p. 3091(41.12a).

5. On the Deliberative Council, see chap. 1 above; for the other posts and titles listed here and throughout this work, see H. S. Brunnert and V. V. Hagelstrom, *Present Day Political Organization of China* (Shanghai: Kelly and Walsh, Ltd., 1912).

6. Biographical information taken from *ECCP*, I, 218; *CS*, p. 3805.11; *CSLC*, 6.5a; *CHLC*, p. 8976(264.34a).

7. Biographical information taken from *ECCP*, I, 219–22; *CS*, p. 3806.7; *CSLC*, 6.17a; *CHLC*, p. 9088(269.41a).

8. Biographical information taken from *ECCP*, I, 599–600; *CS*, 3807.3; *CSLC*, 6.9b.

9. Ralph Linton, "Nativistic Movements," *American Anthropologist*, XLV, no. 2 (April–June 1943), 230.

10. Ibid., pp. 230–31 and 239.

11. T'ao Chin-sheng, "Chin-tai chung-ch'i ti Nü-chen pen-t'u-hua yün-tung," *Ssu yü yen*, VII, no. 6 (March 1970), 328–32.

12. Oxnam, *Ruling from Horseback*, pp. 14 and 203.

13. Ibid., p. 66.

14. These posts are discussed in chap. 6 below.

15. *ECCP*, II, 819; *CSLC*, 8.1a; *CS*, p. 3812.3.

16. *CSLC*, 10.1a; *CS*, p. 3950.3.

17. *KHSL*, pp. 44–45(1.4b–6a); *CS*, p. 3812.5.

18. *ECCP*, I, 258; Meng Shen, "Ch'ing-ch'u san-ta i-an k'ao-shih," in id., *Ch'ing-tai shih* (Taipei: Cheng-chung, 1960), pp. 457–58 and 461–63; Cheng T'ien-t'ing, *Ch'ing-shih t'an-wei* (Nanking: Tu-li, 1946), pp. 71–72.

19. *SCSL*, pp. 1695–97(144.2a–6a).

20. For example, repenting of the excessive grief expressed at the death of his favorite consort, empress Hsiao-hsien, or decrying his use of eunuchs.

21. Cheng T'ien-t'ing, *Ch'ing-shih t'an-wei*, p. 66.

22. *ECCP*, I, 216; *SCSL*, pp. 70 (6.12a), 271(22.17b), and 301(25.22b); Cheng T'ien-t'ing, *Ch'ing-shih t'an-wei*, pp. 65–66; *HTSL*, p. 19196 (1216.9b–10a).

23. *SCSL*, pp. 904–05(76.16a–18a). Two years later, in 1655, Shun-chih had erected at the thirteen yamen a metal placard with the warning not to meddle in politics engraved on it (*SCSL*, p. 1098[92.12]).

24. *KHSL*, p. 53(1.21a–22b); Cheng T'ien-t'ing, *Ch'ing-shih t'an-wei*, p. 67.

25. Cheng T'ien-t'ing, *Ch'ing-shih t'an-wei*, p. 71.

26. Ibid., p. 68; *SCSL*, pp. 913–14(77.2a–4a).

27. *SCSL*, pp. 1371(115.10b–11a), 1373(115.13b–14a), and 1385–86 (117.14b–15a).

28. *SCSL*, p. 1410(119.3b).

29. *ECCP*, I, 258; Meng Shen, "San-ta i-an," p. 463.

30. *KHSL*, p. 53(1.21a–22b).

31. Spence, *Ts'ao Yin*, pp. 12–13; Cheng T'ien-t'ing, *Ch'ing-shih t'an-wei*, pp. 78–80. See K'ang-hsi's comments on his eunuch staff in Jonathan Spence, *Emperor of China: Self-Portrait of K'ang-hsi* (New York: Alfred A. Knopf, 1974), pp. 45–46.

32. The following account of the *booi* system and its development is based mainly on Cheng T'ien-t'ing, *Ch'ing-shih t'an-wei*, pp. 59–65; see also Spence, *Ts'ao Yin*, pp. 7–11; Meng Shen, "Pa-ch'i," pp. 56–57.

33. Liu Chia-chü, "Han-chün pa-ch'i," p. 340; Li Hsün, *Ming-ch'ing shih*, p. 123.

34. An exposition of how this *t'ou-ch'ung* practice was manipulated for personal gain is found in the 1652 memorial of Board of Revenue president Liu Yü-yu, who suggested it be abolished (*HCTI*, 6.6a–8b); see also Ma Feng-ch'en, "Manchu-Chinese Conflicts," pp. 340–42.

35. Spence, *Ts'ao Yin*, p. 8, dates the formation of bondservant companies as somewhere in the period 1615–20, but Chang Te-ch'ang, "The Economic Role of the Imperial Household in the Ch'ing Dynasty," *Journal of Asian Studies*, XXXI, no. 2 (Feb. 1972), 244–45, concludes they existed by 1615.

36. Chang Te-ch'ang, "Imperial Household," pp. 245–46.

37. Ibid., pp. 249–50; Oxnam, *Ruling from Horseback*, pp. 67–69. The final form of the Imperial Household structure was defined later in K'ang-hsi's reign (see Spence, *Ts'ao Yin*, pp. 32–33).

38. See Chang Te-ch'ang, "Imperial Household," pp. 249–50, on the Imperial Household as an instrument of political and, especially, economic control over the empire.

39. *HTSL*, p. 17506(1044.1); see chap. 1 above for early development of this institution.

40. *HTSL*, pp. 5205(11.1b) and 17507(1044.2a); *SCSL*, pp. 1412(119.7), and 1423(120.13b–14a).

41. *KHSL*, p. 79(3.9); this edict is translated into French by Corradini, "Nei-ko," p. 424.

42. *KHSL*, p. 81(3.13). *HTSL*, p. 5206(11.3a) states that each bureau was to be headed by 2 Manchus and 1 Chinese, which clearly did not occur. The third Manchu position was filled within two weeks with the appointment of Itu, a member of the imperial family (*KHSL*, p. 83[3.17a]).

43. Yen Mao-kung, comp., *Ch'ing-tai cheng-hsien lei-pien* (Taipei: Shih-chieh, 1961): Table of Grand Secretaries, chap. 1.

44. *KHSL*, pp. 478(33.27a) and 486(34.13); *HTSL*, p. 17507(1044.2b–3a).

45. Oxnam, *Ruling from Horseback*, p. 69.

46. Ibid., pp. 78–81.

47. *KHSL*, p. 420(29.8b): the sixteenth offense listed.

48. Oxnam, *Ruling from Horseback*, pp. 81–84. It should be noted, however, that evaluations based on efficiency in tax collection were already in force during Shun-chih's reign (*SCSL*, pp. 1048–49[88.8b–9a]).

49. Archival records from Shun-chih's first year (1644) reveal that memorialists were exclusively recommending men from Chihli, Shantung, Honan, and Shansi for office (*Shun-chih yüan-nien nei-wai-kuan shu tsou-su* [Peking, 1931], Preface by Chu Hsi-tsu).

50. *Tseng-chiao Ch'ing-ch'ao chin-shih t'i-ming pei-lu*, comp. Fang Chao-ying and Tu Lien-che (Peking, 1941). The provincial registration of the 373 *chin-shih* was as follows: Chihli, 95; Shantung, 93; Honan, 87;

Shansi, 81; Shensi, 8; Chekiang, 4; Kiangnan, 2; Fukien, Hukuang, and Liaotung, each 1.

51. See the table of grand secretaries in Yen Mao-kung, *Ch'ing-tai cheng-hsien lei-pien*, chap. 1.

52. *ECCP*, I, 358–59; *CSLC*, 79.4a, 6a.

53. Men from these two provinces accounted for all but one of the nine first-ranked *chin-shih* in the last three examinations of the Shun-chih period (1658, 1659, 1661) (Fang and Tu, comps., *Tseng-chiao Ch'ing-ch'ao chin-shih*). For the entire period 1644–61, Kiangnan ranked first with 564 *chin-shih* or 19.4 percent of the total, and Chekiang accounted for another 301 or 10.4 percent; the four northern provinces combined total was 1,398 or over 48 percent (Ping-ti Ho, *The Ladder of Success in Imperial China* [New York: Columbia University Press, 1962], p. 228 [table 28]).

54. The judgment is Fang Chao-ying's (*ECCP*, I, 188). The brief summary of this case given below is taken, unless indicated otherwise, from the account in Luther Carrington Goodrich, *The Literary Inquisition of Ch'ien-lung*, 2d ed. (New York: Paragon Book Reprint Corp., 1966), pp. 75–76, and from Chuang's biography in *ECCP*, I, 205–6, which also was written by Goodrich and actually contains a fuller description of the case than his former account.

55. Oxnam, *Ruling from Horseback*, p. 111; Hsiao I-shan, *Chung-kuo chin-tai-shih kai-yao* (Taipei: San-min, 1963), p. 58, gave the total as 221.

56. *ECCP*, I, 206 (on Ku), and 184 (on Chu, where it is reported that his family destroyed his library in 1662 to avoid implication); Meng Shen, "Shu Ming-shih ch'ao-lüeh," in id., *Ming-Ch'ing shih lun-chi chi-k'an* (Taipei: Shih-chieh, 1961), pp. 141–42.

57. Biographies in *ECCP*, II, 606 (P'an) and 883 (Wu).

58. *ECCP*, I, 424; his biography is in *ECCP*, II, 606–7.

59. Peterson, "Ku Yen-wu," pp. 227–33.

60. See, for instance, how Yüan Mei and his wide circle of friends were periodically affected (Arthur Waley, *Yüan Mei: Eighteenth-Century Chinese Poet* [New York: Grove Press, 1958]).

61. See Ray Huang, "Fiscal Administration During the Ming Dynasty," in Hucker, ed., *Chinese Government in Ming Times*, pp. 112–28.

62. *SCSL*, pp. 1048–49(88.8b–9a).

63. *HTSL*, p. 7354(172.15b–16a).

64. *KHSL*, pp. 50–51(1.16b–17b), 57(2.1b), and 58(2.3b–4a). The government, however, did not always follow its own orders. On the same day that the first edict cited in this note was issued (27 Feb. 1661), the district magistrate of Ch'ung-ming, Ch'en Shen, was promoted to prefect despite his recent failure to collect the full amount of taxes due from his district. Extenuating circumstances were present, however, because Ch'en had earlier gained merit for his defense of Ch'ung-ming against rebels. When Ch'en died a few months later, he was posthumously awarded the post of junior secretary (*yu-ts'an-i;* translation based on Brunnert and Hagelstrom, *Political Organization of China*, no. 284) in the provincial financial commissioner's office, and one son was admitted to the Imperial academy (*kuo-tzu-chien*) to study (*KHSL*, pp. 51[1.18] and 58[2.4]). Ch'en

Shen's successor as magistrate also failed at tax collection, but again he was kept on because of his defense work (*KHSL*, p. 106[5.15b–16a]).

65. *ECCP*, I, 165; for a detailed account of the case by an anonymous sympathizer, see *Hsin-ch'ou chi-wen*, vol. 4 of Chi-tsai hui-pien (Peking, n.d.).

66. It has been said (*Hsin-ch'ou chi-wen*, p. 2b) that Chu issued an order and predated it to give the measures used by the district magistrate the appearance of legality. Chu, however, had no reason to resort to subterfuge, because the imperial edict of 27 February 1661 (*KHSL*, pp. 50–51 [1.16b–17b]) cited this same reason—military exigencies—in urging provincial officials to collect taxes on time. If edicts could reach Soochow in fifteen days (see Ssu-yü Teng and John K. Fairbank, "On the Transmission of Ch'ing Documents," *Harvard Journal of Asiatic Studies*, IV [1939], p. 27), then the governor's office might have known of the court's order by the time of the preliminary hearings. If so, then Chu Kuo-chih's actions could be perfectly legitimate and not necessarily underhanded.

67. *Hsin-ch'ou chi-wen*, pp. 3a–5a.

68. *CSLC*, 6.25b; *SCSL*, pp. 1655–56(140.2b–3a); *KHSL*, p. 67(2.21).

69. Meng Shen, "Tsou-hsiao an," in id., *Ming-Ch'ing shih-lun-chu chi-k'an*, p. 447.

70. Ibid.; *CHLC*, p. 5594(140.35b–36a).

71. *KHSL*, p. 76(3.3a).

72. *CSLC*, 6.25b; Hsiao Kung-ch'üan, *Rural China: Imperial Control in the Nineteenth Century* (Seattle: University of Washington Press, 1960), p. 127; Meng Shen, "Tsou-hsiao an," p. 443. It has been suggested that leniency might have been recommended had it not been for the action of Chin Chih-chün, one of the grand secretaries at that time (*ECCP*, I, 160–61). Some of Chin's relatives were included in the governor's list, so he quickly memorialized on their guilt to forestall any charges of covering up for them. After Chin's memorial, no one was willing to suggest leniency for the offenders (Meng Shen, "Tsou-hsiao an," p. 452).

73. Yeh Meng-chu, *Yüeh-shih pien* (Shang-hai Chang-ku ts'ung-shu ed.; Shanghai, 1936), 2.1b.

74. Meng Shen, "Tsou-hsiao an," pp. 451–52.

75. Ibid., pp. 439–41; *ECCP*, I, 275–76.

76. *ECCP*, I, 327.

77. *ECCP*, I, 431; II, 882–83; *CS*, p. 5227.6; Goodrich, *Literary Inquisition*, pp. 100–101 and 219–20.

78. *ECCP*, I, 157.

79. Meng Shen, "Tsou-hsiao an," pp. 436 and 438–39; the saying is: *t'an-hua pu-chih i-wen-ch'ien*. One source reported the amount owed to be only one *li*, which is one-thousandth of an ounce of silver (quoted in ibid., p. 438); see also *Ch'ing-ch'ao yeh-shih ta-kuan*, 5 parts (Taipei: Chung-hua, 1959), part 3, p. 13.

80. Meng Shen, "Tsou-hsiao an," p. 448.

81. Ibid., p. 439.

82. Yeh Meng-chu, *Yüeh-shih pien*, 2.1b–2a; Hu's biography is in *CHLC*, p. 7276(207.42a).

83. Hsiao Kung-ch'üan, *Rural China*, p. 127; various authors cited in Meng Shen, "Tsou-hsiao an," pp. 436 and 442.

84. Meng Shen, "Tsou-hsiao an," pp. 439 and 444; Hsiao Kung-ch'üan, *Rural China*, p. 127. There were over two hundred Kiangnan licentiates in prison whose release was effected by Wu Cheng-chih (*ECCP*, II, 863; *CS*, p. 3813.5). Wu seems to have taken a personal interest in helping the Kiangnan scholars: besides his action here in 1661, he also recommended one of the scholars involved in the tax case, P'eng Sun-yü, for the *po-hsüeh* examination in 1679.

85. *CSLC*, 6.25b; *CS*, p. 3014; Meng Shen, "Tsou-hsiao an," p. 444; *KHSL*, p. 113(6.5). Han, a Chinese bannerman, ironically was later accused of mismanagement of tax collections (*Man-chou ming-ch'en chuan*, 19.34a–38a).

86. *Hsin-ch'ou chi-wen*, p. 16b; *ECCP*, I, 165. News of Wu's revolt and of his murder of Chu is found in *KHSL*, pp. 614–15(44.12a–13a).

87. Meng Shen, "Tsou-hsiao an," p. 437. Fang served in the rebel government as a grand secretary and was summarily executed in December 1681, as Yunnan-fu, their capital, was recovered by the imperial forces (*KHSL*, p. 1312[98.1b]; Tsao Kai-fu, "The Rebellion of the Three Feudatories against the Manchu Throne in China, 1673–1681; Its Setting and Significance" [Ph.D. diss., Columbia University, 1966], p. 75). It is this Fang with whom Fang Hsiao-piao was confused—a confusion that led to the posthumous disgrace of the latter in 1711 in connection with the Tai Ming-shih literary purge (*ECCP*, I, 233; II, 701; Goodrich, *Literary Inquisition*, pp. 77–79).

88. Meng Shen, "Tsou-hsiao an," pp. 445–46 and 447–48. The Kiangsu scholar in question was Shao Ch'ang-heng (biography in *ECCP*, II, 636), who had been involved in the 1661 tax case.

89. *KHSL*, p. 164(9.23b); Meng Shen, "Tsou-hsiao an," pp. 436 and 439.

90. *CS*, p. 3951.6; Hsiao Kung-ch'üan, *Rural China*, p. 128.

91. Other campaigns of consolidation during the regency are discussed by Oxnam (*Ruling from Horseback*, pp. 127–41), who notes that they were of "lesser magnitude" (p. 139).

92. The earliest offer was made on 9 November 1652 (*SCSL*, pp. 811–12 [69.6b–7b]; MCSL, ser. IV, vol. I, p. 67), and another on 5 June 1653 (*SCSL*, pp. 886–87[75.8b–10b] and 892[75.20]; *MCSL*, ser. IV, vol. I, pp. 84–87). The history of peace negotiations between the Ch'ing court and Cheng Ch'eng-kung is fully traced by T'ung I, "Cheng-Ch'ing ho-i chih ching-wei," *T'ai-wan wen-hsien*, VI (Sept. 1955), 29–35.

93. Reported by Liu Ch'ing-t'ai, governor-general of Fukien and Chekiang (*CHLC*, p. 5889[150.20b]).

94. *MCSL*, ser. IV, vol. I, p. 91; vol. II, p. 101; *SCSL*, p. 1010 (85.3a–4a); R. A. B. Ponsonby-Fane, "Koxinga: Chronicles of the Tei Family, Loyal Servants of Ming," *Transactions and Proceedings of the Japan Society (London)*, XXXIV (1936–37), 105–6.

95. For lists of the ranks and honors received by Cheng Ch'eng-kung from the Ming court, see Chu Hsi-tsu, "Cheng Yen-p'ing-wang shou Ming kuan-chüeh k'ao," *Kuo-hsüeh chi-k'an*, III, no. 1 (1932), 87–112.

96. *SCSL*, pp. 983(83.9b), 987(83.17b–18a), 1036–37(87.6b–7a), and 1040(87.15a–16a); *HCTI*, 7.23a–25a.

97. *HCTI*, 7.22b–23a; *SCSL*, p. 1097(92.10b).

98. *MCSL*, ser. IV, vol. II, p. 155; *SCSL*, p. 1203(102.10a–11a); *HTSL*, p. 14951(776.10b–11a).

99. See, for instance, the memorials of Wei I-chieh in 1656 (*CSLC*, 5.41b), Chu Kuo-chih in 1660 (*CSLC*, 6.25b), and Chi Chen-i in 1660 (*HCTI*, 15.22a–23a).

100. Two memorials in 1659 by Wang Yü-yü, a Hanlin bachelor (*HCTI*, 12.8a–14a), and Wang Ch'i-tso, a junior metropolitan censor (*HCTI*, 12.15a–18a).

101. *MCSL*, ser. IV, vol. II, p. 257; *SCSL*, p. 1297(108.21a–22a); *CS*, p. 3886.5; Liu Hsien-t'ing, *Kuang-yang tsa-chi*, p. 146.

102. This has been studied previously by Hsieh Kuo-chen, "Removal of Coastal Population in Early Tsing Period," trans. Ch'en T'ung-hsieh, *The Chinese Social and Political Science Review*, XV (Jan. 1932), 559–96; Ura Ren'ichi, "Ch'ing-ch'u ch'ien-chieh-ling k'ao," trans. from Japanese by Lai Yung-hsiang, *T'ai-wan wen-hsien*, VI (Dec. 1955), 109–22.

103. Liu Hsien-t'ing, *Kuang-yang tsa-chi*, p. 54; William Campbell, *Formosa under the Dutch* (London: Kegan Paul, Trench, Trubner and Co., Ltd., 1903), p. 460. The most notable of the other defectors was Shih Lang (*ECCP*, II, 653).

104. Liu Hsien-t'ing, *Kuang-yang tsa-chi*, p. 145; *SCSL*, pp. 1209 (102.22), 1219(103.10b), and 1221(103.13b).

105. Sources disagree over the contents of Huang's plan. It is not even certain whether he formulated his proposals in a single memorial or in a series of documents. For what profess to be parts of his *p'ing-hai ts'e* or the plan in its entirety, see *SCSL*, pp. 1296–97(108.19b–22a) and 1300 (109.3b–4a); *CS*, p. 3886.5; Liu Hsien-t'ing, *Kuang-yang tsa-chi*, pp. 146–47; *ECCP*, I, 355; Wei Yüan, *Sheng-wu chi*, Ssu-pu pei-yao ed. (Taipei: Chung-hua, 1962), 8.4; Chiang Jih-sheng, *T'ai-wan wai-chi*, preface dated 1704 (Tainan, 1956), p. 160, trans. in Hsieh Kuo-chen, "Removal," pp. 564–66. Most sources enumerate five points, but not always the same five. I have distinguished five general areas of proposals as culled from all the sources.

106. *MCSL*, ser. IV, vol. II, p. 255; *KHSL*, p. 99(5.2a). The court had recommended execution in 1657, but the emperor reduced his sentence to exile in Ninguta and the confiscation of his possessions (*SCSL*, pp. 1296[108.19b–20b] and 1300[109.3b–4a]). The banishment order was never carried out (*CSLC*, 5.27b), but Chih-lung's position and wealth had clearly disappeared, according to Jesuit reports (Donald Keene, ed. and trans., *The Battles of Coxinga* [London: Taylor's Foreign Press, 1951], p. 64; Pierre Joseph d'Orleans, *History of the Two Tartar Conquerors of China*, trans. and ed. the Earl of Ellesmere [London: The Hakluyt Society, 1854], pp. 30–32).

107. Wei Yüan, *Sheng-wu chi*, 8.13b. When Cheng Ching (Ch'eng-kung's son and successor) captured Hai-ch'eng during the *San-fan* rebellion, he in turn desecrated Huang Wu's tomb (Liu Hsien-t'ing, *Kuang-yang*

tsa-chi, pp. 146–47).

108. *KHSL,* pp. 87–88(4.2b–3a) and 209(13.10b); *CS,* p. 3886.6; Hsieh Kuo-chen, "Removal," p. 584.

109. *SCSL,* pp. 1637–38(138.14a–15a), and 1641–42(138.22a–23a), and 1655–56(140.2b–3a); *KHSL,* p. 67(2.21).

110. *HCTI,* 12.15a–18a; Liu Hsien-t'ing, *Kuang-yang tsa-chi,* p. 147; Hsia Lin, *Hai-chi chi-yao,* T'ai-wan wen-hsien ts'ung-k'an, no. 22 (Taipei: Bank of Taiwan, 1958), p. 29.

111. *SCSL,* p. 1657(140.6); Wei Yüan, *Sheng-wu chi,* 8.6b, who mistakenly dated the incident as 1661.

112. *KHSL,* p. 91(4.10b). This was an edict of 5 October 1661 which spoke retrospectively of an order to remove coastal populations to the interior, but when such an order was issued was not stated. Wei Yüan, *Sheng-wu chi,* 8.6a, claimed that it was issued in 1660, but I have searched *SCSL, KHSL, MCSL,* and *CS* without finding it either in 1660 or in 1661.

113. Sunahai, president of the Board of War, and Ilibu, vice-president of the Board of Civil Appointments, were sent to Kiangnan, Chekiang, and Fukien (*CSLC,* 6.6b; *CS,* 3874.2), and Chieh-shan, vice-president of the Board of War, was sent to Kwangtung (*KHSL,* p. 467[33.5b–6a]).

114. *KHSL,* p. 156(9.8); *CSLC,* 78.43a.

115. *MCSL,* ser. IV, vol. III, p. 257. This document has been translated by Fu Lo-shu, *A Documentary Chronicle of Sino-Western Relations (1644–1820)* (Tucson: University of Arizona Press for the Association for Asian Studies, 1966), pp. 28–30. Shun-chih died on the 7th day of the 18th year (6 Feb. 1661), but the remainder of the year was still designated as Shun-chih's 18th year. This edict was issued on Shun-chih 18/12/18, a few weeks before the start of K'ang-hsi's first year.

116. For various edicts reinforcing the trade ban in the early K'ang-hsi period, see *KHSL,* pp. 236(15.7a–8a), 1038–39(77.12b–13a), 1095(81.18), 1100(82.4), and 1314(98.20); *K'ang-hsi hui-tien,* preface dated 1690, 99.1a–19a; *HTSL,* pp. 14951–52(775.11a–13b).

117. Hsieh Kuo-chen, "Removal," pp. 585–87. For incidence of removal in Shantung, see *KHSL,* pp. 156(9.8), 195(12.10b), and 228(14.23b–24a); for Kiangnan, see *KHSL,* pp. 119(6.17), 158(9.11a), and 915(68.2); also *CSLC,* 5.31a.

118. *CSLC,* 5.20b and 6.7; Hsieh Kuo-chen, "Removal," p. 587.

119. Hsieh Kuo-chen, "Removal," pp. 591–92; *KHSL,* pp. 326(22.20) and 398(27.16a); *CHLC,* p. 5901(151.1b–2a).

120. *KHSL,* p. 136(7.19b–20a).

121. Cecil Bowra, "Some Episodes in the History of Amoy," *The China Review,* XXI (Sept.–Oct. 1894), p. 94, quoting the Amoy gazetteer; Shen Yün, *T'ai-wan Cheng-shih shih-mo,* T'ai-wan wen-hsien ts'ung-k'an, no. 15 (Taipei: Bank of Taiwan, 1958), p. 60.

122. Hsieh Kuo-chen, "Removal," pp. 573, 580, 582–83, and 589–90; *KHSL,* pp. 978(72.19b–20a) and 1187–88(89.6b–7a); Hsia Lin, *Hai-chi chi-yao,* p. 59; Chiang Jih-sheng, *T'ai-wan wai-chi,* p. 284.

123. Emma H. Blair and James A. Robertson, eds., *The Philippine Islands, 1493–1898,* 55 vols. (Cleveland: A. H. Clark, 1903–6), XXXVI,

252, a footnote by the editors.

124. Arnoldus Montanus, *Atlas Chinensis,* trans. John Ogilby (London: Thomas Johnson, 1671), pp. 89 and 97–108. The latter fact also was reported by Chinese officials (*KHSL,* p. 119[6.18a]). The Bort expeditions were sent to China by the Dutch in 1662–64 to seek an alliance with the Manchus to drive Cheng Ching out of Taiwan (see John E. Wills, Jr., *Pepper, Guns and Parleys: The Dutch East India Company and China, 1622–1681* [Cambridge: Harvard University Press, 1974], chap. 2).

125. Adrien Greslon, *Histoire de la Chine sous la domination des Tartares* (Paris: Jean Henault, 1671), p. 239.

126. Several Western accounts give the figure of four leagues, which would be approximately twelve miles; once, in Kwangtung, the figure stated was fifty *li* (Hsieh Kuo-chen, "Removal," p. 592).

127. Ibid., pp. 583, 585–87, and 591–92; Chiang Ch'en-ying, *Hai-fang tsung-lun,* in *Chiang hsien-sheng ch'üan-chi* (1918), 1.10b–12a.

128. Domingo Navarrete, *An Account of the Empire of China,* vol. I of *Collection of Voyages and Travels,* ed. Awnsham and John Churchill, 4 vols. (London: Printed for A. and J. Churchill at the Black Swan, 1704), p. 27.

129. Hsieh Kuo-chen, "Removal," passim; Blair and Robertson, eds., *The Philippine Islands,* XXXVI, 252; G[eorge] P[hillips], "The Life of Koxinga," *The China Review,* XIII (1884–85), 73, who stated that many of these forts were still to be seen in the Amoy region at the time he wrote.

130. Hsieh Kuo-chen, "Removal," pp. 585 and 591; *KHSL,* pp. 165 (9.25a), 443(31.9b), and 915(68.2); *CHLC,* p. 5901(151.1b), IHPA command edicts (*ch'ih-yü*), *hung-tzu* 22, *lieh-tzu* 95, and an unclassified one, all dated K'ang-hsi 5/6/9.

131. Blair and Robertson, eds., *The Philippine Islands,* XXXVI, 252; Jean Pierre Guillaume Pauthier, *Chine* (Paris: Firmin Didot frères, 1839), p. 434; Jean Baptiste Du Halde, *A Description of the Empire of China,* 2 vols. (London: E. Cave, 1738–41), I, 230.

132. Navarrete, *The Empire of China,* p. 27; the other reports are quoted in Hsieh Kuo-chen, "Removal," pp. 571, 574, and 578.

133. Hsieh Kuo-chen, "Removal," pp. 578–80; *CHLC,* p. 5901(151.2a); *KHSL,* pp. 91(4.10b) and 136(7.19b–20a).

134. *KHSL,* pp. 100(5.4b), 119(6.17), 158(9.11a), 195(12.10b), 228 (14.23b–24a), 326(22.20), 978(72.19b–20a), and 1161–62(87.6b–7a); *CSLC,* 5.31a; Wang Ch'ing-yün, *Hsi-ch'ao chi-cheng* (Peking, 1902), 1.5b; *CHLC,* p. 5901(151.1b); Hsieh kuo-chen, "Removal," pp. 578, 587, 589, and 592; Fu Lo-shu, "The Two Portuguese Embassies to China during the K'ang-hsi Period," *T'oung-pao,* XLIII (1955), 86–87; Navarrete, *The Empire of China,* p. 27.

135. *ECCP,* I, 600; *KHSL,* p. 270(18.3b–4a); *HTSL,* p. 18179(1112.1a).

136. Yang Hsüeh-ch'en, "Ch'ing-tai ch'i-ti ti hsing-chih chi ch'i pien-hua," *Li-shih yen-chiu,* 1963, no. 3, p. 175; Liu Chia-chü, *Pa-ch'i ch'üan-ti,* p. 3, gives sources saying 5 or 6 *mou.*

137. Liu Chia-chü, *Pa-ch'i ch'üan-ti,* p. 54; *KHSL,* pp. 270–71(18.4, 18.5). The term used by the editors of the *shih-lu* here and in other entries

dealing with the banner land shift was *ch'eng-chih.* Up to this point, the phrase *te-chih* had always been used in referring to imperial utterances. I take the change to indicate that the editors were accusing Oboi of acting on his own in this affair.

138. *KHSL,* p. 276(18.15a–16a).

139. *KHSL,* pp. 277–78(18.18a–19b). The latitudinal and longitudinal readings are taken from G. M. H. Playfair, *The Cities and Towns of China,* 2d ed. (Shanghai: Kelly and Walsh, 1910; reprinted Taipei: Literature House, 1965).

140. *KHSL,* p. 270(18.3b–4a).

141. *KHSL,* pp. 295–96(20.10b–11b); *CSLC,* 6.7a, 7b–8a, and 9; Liu Chia-chü, *Pa-ch'i ch'üan-ti,* pp. 56–57.

142. *KHSL,* pp. 296–99(20.11b–12a, 14b–15a, 17).

143. *KHSL,* p. 299(20.17b–18a).

144. *KHSL,* pp. 296(20.12a) and 300(20.20).

145. *KHSL,* p. 306(20.7b).

146. *KHSL,* pp. 299–300(20.18b–19b).

147. *CSLC,* 5.5b–6b; Meng Shen, "Pa-ch'i," p. 55.

148. *KHSL,* p. 306(21.8).

149. Death first mentioned 12 August (*KHSL,* p. 326[22.20a]).

150. *KHSL,* p. 332(23.7a–8a).

151. *KHSL,* pp. 332–37(23.8a–18a). There is no precise date of Suksaha's death, but it must have come shortly after the charges were made.

Chapter Three

1. *SCSL,* p. 974(82.16b).

2. *ECCP,* I, 1; II, 898; Cheng T'ien-t'ing, *Ch'ing-shih t'an-wei,* pp. 18–19, notes that we cannot be sure of the pureness of the Mongol strain of Abahai's mother.

3. *ECCP,* I, 300.

4. *ECCP,* II, 796–97.

5. *KHSL,* p. 919(68.10b); Cheng T'ien-t'ing, *Ch'ing-shih t'an-wei,* p. 20.

6. See, for example, Hsüan-t'ung's plaintive comments on his relations with his father and mother (Pu Yi, *From Emperor to Citizen: The Autobiography of Aisin Gioro Pu Yi,* vol. I [Peking: Foreign Languages Press, 1964], pp. 19, 39–40, and 47–50).

7. *ECCP,* I, 257 and 301–2.

8. *KHSL,* p. 44(1.3b–4a). Biographies of the two brothers are in *ECCP,* I, 69–70 and 251–52, respectively.

9. Since girls were taken into palace service at the age of thirteen (*HTSL,* p. 19212[1218.7a]), Hsiao-k'ang conceived the future emperor not long after coming to Shun-chih's attention.

10. *ECCP,* I, 328; Orleans, *Tartar Conquerors,* p. 48.

11. See the stories about the wet-nurses of Shun-chih (*ECCP,* I, 257) and Hsüan-t'ung (Pu Yi, *From Emperor to Citizen,* pp. 71–72).

12. Spence, *Ts'ao Yin,* pp. 24–25.

13. Pu Yi, *From Emperor to Citizen,* pp. 42–43.

14. Spence, *Emperor of China,* pp. 86–87.

15. Pu Yi, *From Emperor to Citizen*, p. 64; storytelling mentioned on pp. 65–67 and passim.
16. Ibid., pp. 39–41 and 65.
17. *ECCP*, II, 898.
18. *ECCP*, I, 301.
19. Oxnam, *Ruling from Horseback*, pp. 169–70.
20. Hsiao-ch'eng was born on 4 Feb. 1654 (*ECCP*, II, 924); K'ang-hsi was born on 4 May. They were married on 16 Oct. 1665 (*KHSL*, p. 252 [16.16b]).
21. *KHSL*, p. 651(47.18a); *ECCP*, II, 924–25.
22. *CS*, pp. 3495.2–96.3. A fourth empress, the daughter of Colonel Wei-wu of the Uya clan, was only a secondary consort during K'ang-hsi's lifetime, but she was elevated to the position of empress in 1723 when her son Yung-cheng succeeded to the throne (*ECCP*, II, 302). For T'ung Kuo-wei's biography, see *ECCP*, II, 795.
23. *KHSL*, pp. 43(1.2b) and 1572(117.19b). I am indebted to Jonathan Spence for the latter reference.
24. Pu Yi, *From Emperor to Citizen*, pp. 53 and 57.
25. Orleans, *Tartar Conquerors*, p. 48; Spence, *Ts'ao Yin*, p. 27.
26. Harold Kahn, "The Education of a Prince: The Emperor Learns His Roles," in *Approaches to Modern Chinese History*, ed. Albert Feuerwerker, Rhoads Murphey, and Mary C. Wright (Berkeley: University of California Press, 1967), p. 17; Pu Yi, *From Emperor to Citizen*, p. 57. In Ch'ien-lung's case it was a younger brother.
27. *KHSL*, pp. 87(4.2a), 153–54(9.2b–3a), 324–25(22.16a–17a), 331–32 (23.6a–7a), 369(25.17a), 379(26.5b), and 414–15(28.20b–21a).
28. *KHSL*, pp. 413–14(28.18b–19b).
29. See Jonathan Spence, *To Change China* (Boston: Little, Brown and Co., 1969), pp. 3–22, for a summary account of Schall's activities. For a fuller biography, see Joseph Duhr, S. J., *Un Jésuite en Chine: Adam Schall* (Brussels: L'Edition universelle, 1936).
30. *ECCP*, II, 890; *SCSL*, pp. 77(7.1b), 134(11.19b), 314(26.19a), and 865–66(73.2b–3b); all but the second document are translated in Fu Lo-shu, *Chronicle*, pp. 4, 5, and 12–13. By January 1646, Schall was being referred to as director (*SCSL*, p. 257[21.17b]).
31. Biographical data in *ECCP*, II, 889–92. This entry by Fang Chaoying also contains the clearest exposition in English of the calendar controversy.
32. Literally, "knocking at the [palace] gate" to present a grievance—an avenue open to commoners.
33. Fu Lo-shu, *Chronicle*, pp. 36–37, translating from Yang's apologetic tract *Pu-te-i* ("I could not do otherwise").
34. Ibid., p. 37.
35. John K. Fairbank, *The United States and China*, rev. ed. (New York: Viking Press, 1962), p. 117.
36. *KHSL*, p. 230(14.27b–28a).
37. *ECCP*, II 890; Fu Lo-shu, *Chronicle*, p. 35.
38. *KHSL*, p. 230(14.28a); *ECCP*, II, 891.

39. Fu Lo-shu, *Chronicle,* p. 36.
40. *KHSL,* pp. 225(14.17), 230–31(14.28a–29a), and 233(15.1b–2a).
41. Navarrete, *The Empire of China,* p. 281.
42. *KHSL,* pp. 273(18.9b–10a), 367–68(25.14b–15a), and 384–85 (26.16b–17a). The second reference is an edict ordering a search for astronomers, but it was probably issued in response to pleas by Yang and Wu.
43. *KHSL,* pp. 384–85(26.16b–17a) and 389(26.25b–26a).
44. See, for example, *KHSL,* pp. 396(27.11b) and 399(27.18a).
45. Fu Lo-shu, *Chronicle,* pp. 42–43, translating *Hsi-ch'ao ting-an* by Verbiest and others.
46. *KHSL,* pp. 402–3(27.24, 25).
47. *KHSL,* p. 407(28.6); translated in Fu Lo-shu, *Chronicle,* p. 44.
48. *KHSL,* pp. 408–9(28.8b–9b). Neither man was punished at this time. Yang was excused from even standing trial, while Wu's sentence of death by strangulation was canceled. Later, in August, Wu was flogged for making the false claim of knowing how to construct a calendar by the Western method (*KHSL,* p. 436[30.20]). I suppose Wu was trying to go with the tide and recover his position in the Board of Astronomy.
49. *KHSL,* p. 412(28.15b–16a); *HTSL,* p. 18105(1104.1).
50. See chap. 4 below for the former and Spence, *Ts'ao Yin,* pp. 240–54, for the latter.
51. *KHSL,* pp. 440–41(31.4a–5a), translated in Fu Lo-shu, *Chronicle,* pp. 45–46. The provisions as to Schall and the five already executed Chinese astronomers were carried out a few weeks later (*KHSL,* p. 442[31.7b]).
52. A list of some of these Jesuits is given in *ECCP,* II, 892. Institutionally, the Westerners replaced the Chinese director; a Manchu director was always appointed in addition (*HTSL,* p. 18092[1103.1a]).
53. *KHSL,* p. 187(11.22), *CSLC,* 6.11a. This Fiyanggu was not the brother of Shun-chih's favorite consort (*ECCP,* I, 248–49) but an assistant chamberlain of the Imperial Bodyguards, unknown but for this incident.
54. *CSLC,* 6.12a; *KHSL,* p. 421(29.9a).
55. *CS,* p. 3809.4.
56. *CSLC,* 6.14a; *KHSL,* p. 418(29.4a).
57. On the composition of Oboi's faction, see Oxnam, *Ruling from Horseback,* pp. 175–77.
58. *KHSL,* p. 288(19.16a).
59. *KHSL,* pp. 329–31(23.2b–3a, 3b–5a). Oxnam (*Ruling from Horseback,* pp. 185–86) interprets this decision more as a move by the grand empress dowager and other supporters of the emperor to assert their power than (as I have) a move by the regents to salvage their position; our views are complementary but differ on how far the balance of power had shifted from one group to the other.
60. *KHSL,* pp. 314–15(21.24a–25a) and 317(22.1).
61. *KHSL,* pp. 329–31 (23.5, 19b, 22b, 24a).
62. *CSLC,* 6.20a and 7.38b.
63. *CSLC,* 7.48a; *ECCP,* I, 308, where the dates of his appointments are

mixed up slightly.

64. This long memorial, a summary of which is given in the next few paragraphs of the text, is found in *KHSL*, pp. 322–25(22.11b–17a).

65. Ch'eng Yi and Chu Hsi represented the Rationalist branch of Neo-Confucianism, while Lu Chiu-yüan and Wang Yang-ming formed the Idealist branch (see Fung Yu-lan, *A Short History of Chinese Philosophy*, ed. Derk Bodde [New York: Macmillan, 1960], chaps. 24–26).

66. The term used is *kuo-yung*, which might refer specifically to the Pi-yung hall within the Academy (see Brunnert and Hagelstrom, *Political Organization of China*, no. 412).

67. Composed in the Sung period by Chen Te-hsiu, a follower of Chu Hsi (*Ssu-k'u ch'üan-shu tsung-mu*, comp. Chi Yün, et al., 10 vols. [Taipei: I-wen, 1964], III, 1838–39[92.40b–42a]; Alexander Wylie, *Notes on Chinese Literature* [Shanghai: Presbyterian Mission Press, 1922; reprinted Taipei: Literature House, 1964], p. 86).

68. *CSLC*, 7.48b.

69. A body of diarists when created later in 1670 was called Ch'i-chü-chu. Hsiung was the first official to propose creating such a body (*HTSL*, p. 17610[1055.1a]).

70. *KHSL*, pp. 392–93(27.4a–5a).

71. This memorial, summarized below, is found in *KHSL*, pp. 393–94 (27.5a–7a).

72. *KHSL*, p. 394(27.7a–8a).

73. *CSLC*, 7.48b. *Te-chih* is used in the *shih-lu*, not *ch'eng-chih*.

74. *KHSL*, p. 420(29.8b); the sixteenth crime listed.

75. Actually, it was a few days off by the lunar calendar. Shun-chih died on Shun-chih 18/1/7 (5 Feb. 1661), and this incident took place on K'ang-hsi 7/1/11 (22 Feb. 1668).

76. *KHSL*, pp. 362–65(25.3b–9a), especially 5b and 6b.

77. Oxnam, *Ruling from Horseback*, pp. 192–93.

78. *CS*, p. 68.7; Hsiao I-shan, *Ch'ing-tai t'ung-shih*, 5 vols., rev. ed. (Taipei: Commercial Press, 1962–63), I, 436–37.

79. *ECCP*, II, 664; *KHSL*, p. 420(29.8).

80. Oxnam, *Ruling from Horseback*, pp. 186–88.

81. *KHSL*, pp. 418–21(29.3b–5a, 6b–10a). Despite Prince Giyesu's role in the purge of Oboi, it appears that most members of the Deliberative Council were not involved in the factional struggles of the 1660s, and the council was neither an Oboi nor anti-Oboi instrument of power (Oxnam, *Ruling from Horseback*, p. 74).

82. *KHSL*, p. 418(29.4a).

83. *KHSL*, pp. 421–23(29.10a–14a).

84. *KHSL*, pp. 430–31(31.8b–9a).

85. Oxnam, *Ruling from Horseback*, pp. 125–26. Their cases are discussed in *KHSL*, pp. 419(29.5b–6a), 423–24(29.14a–15b), 427(30.2), 429–30(30.5b–7a), and 443(31.9b–10a).

86. *KHSL*, pp. 424–25(29.16b, 18) and 443(31.10a).

87. *ECCP*, II, 600; *KHSL*, p. 424(29.16a).

88. *ECCP*, I, 200; *KHSL*, pp. 424(29.16a) and 454(32.3a). His original ducal title, which had been given to his son, was not affected.

89. *KHSL*, pp. 419(29.5a) and 424(29.16).
90. *KHSL*, pp. 425(29.18b) and 428(30.3b–4a).
91. *KHSL*, pp. 434(30.16), 437(30.21b), and 442(31.7a).
92. *KHSL*, pp. 432–33(30.12b–13b), 435–36(30.17, 19b–20a), 467(33.5b–6a), and 501(35.13); *CHLC*, p. 3229(47.6); on the Jesuits, see the previous section of this chapter.
93. *KHSL*, pp. 427–28(30.2b–3a).

Chapter Four

1. Sometimes identified as *hou* or later *San-fan* to distinguish them from the *ch'ien* (earlier) *San-fan:* the Ming pretenders Fu-wang, T'ang-wang, and Kuei-wang. For example, Yang Lu-jung's *San-fan chi-shih pen-mo*, T'ai-wan wen-hsien ts'ung-k'an, no. 149 (Taipei: Bank of Taiwan, 1962) deals with the Ming pretenders, not the three feudatories.
2. Lo Er-kang, *Lu-ying ping-chih* (Chungking: Commercial Press, 1945), pp. 1–3.
3. Tsao Kai-fu, "Rebellion," pp. 43–44; *SCSL*, pp. 513–16(44.6a–11a). All three men joined the Manchus after their commander, Mao Wen-lung, had been executed by the Ming government. For biographies, see *ECCP*, I, 435–36 (K'ung); I, 416–17 (Keng); I, 567–68 (Mao); II, 635–36 (Shang).
4. *SCSL*, pp. 704(60.7b–8a) and 116–18(10.3b–7a); *MCSL*, ser. IV, vol. VIII, pp. 701–2.
5. For details, see Tsao Kai-fu, "Rebellion," pp. 51–56.
6. It was Yang Yung-chien who suggested the shift to relieve the Kwangtung people of the burden of supporting two feudatories (*CSLC*, 6.18b). The princely title was not conferred on Keng Chi-mao until 1651 after he had proved himself in a command situation (*ECCP*, I, 415).
7. *SCSL*, pp. 1471–72(124.14b–15a); *CS*, p. 3724.3; "P'ing-ting Wu-ni lüeh," in *Hsü Yun-nan t'ung-chih kao* (Yunnan, 1901), 78.1a.
8. *ECCP*, I, 436; Meng Shen, "K'ung Ssu-chen shih-k'ao," in id., *Ming-Ch'ing shih-lun-chu chi-k'an*, pp. 455–56.
9. *SCSL*, p. 920(77.15); *KHSL*, p. 484(34.8). The use of marriage to an imperial relative as a form of hostage in Chinese history is described by Yang Lien-sheng, "Hostages in Chinese History," in id., *Studies in Chinese Institutional History* (Cambridge: Harvard University Press, 1961), pp. 54–55.
10. *ECCP*, I, 634; *KHSL*, pp. 383(26.13b–14a) and 523(37.9).
11. *ECCP*, I, 415; *KHSL*, pp. 179–80(11.6b–7a), 496(35.4), 507(36.1b), and 511(36.9a).
12. Tsao Kai-fu, "Rebellion," pp. 66–67.
13. He had 70,000 men in 1660 (*SCSL*, p. 1617[136.22a]), got approval for 1,000 more in 1662 (*KHSL*, p. 125[6.29a]), but reduced his army by 5,400 in 1665 (*KHSL*, pp. 238–39[15.12b–13a]), for a total of 65,600.
14. *KHSL*, p. 121(6.22b–23a); *MCSL*, ser. IV, vol. VIII, pp. 701–2. Earlier in 1645, he had turned down the *ch'in-wang* title (*ECCP*, II, 878).
15. *SCSL*, p. 1533(129.9b–10a).
16. Tsao Kai-fu, "Rebellion," pp. 62–63; *CSLC*, 6.26b; *KHSL*, pp. 245–46(16.2b–3a).
17. *KHSL*, pp. 138–39(7.24b–25a) and 146(8.12a).

18. *KHSL*, pp. 239(15.14), 242(15.19a), 243(15.22), and 272(18.8a).
19. *CS*, p. 3935.5–8.
20. E.g., *KHSL*, pp. 201(12.21) and 435(30.18).
21. *KHSL*, pp. 294–95(20.8b–9a).
22. Tsao Kai-fu, "Rebellion," p. 67; *SCSL*, p. 1617(136.22a); *CSLC*, 78.60a; *CS*, p. 3905.4.
23. *CS*, p. 3902.3–4; *HCTI*, 17.36a–40a and 18.44b–45a; *KHSL*, p. 346 (24.3b); *CSLC*, 8.2a.
24. *CSLC*, 8.2a; *CHLC*, p. 2216(4.6a).
25. *HCTI*, 18.44b–45a.
26. *KHSL*, p. 550(39.16b) for Yunnan; pp. 1227(92.2b), 1259(94.13b–14a), and 1407(106.1b) for the other feudatories.
27. *KHSL*, pp. 228(14.23), 320(22.7), and 329(23.2); *CSLC*, 8.2a; Wills, *Pepper, Guns and Parleys*, chap. 4, passim.
28. *ECCP*, I, 279; *CSLC*, 7.29b; *SCSL*, p. 986(83.15b).
29. *SCSL*, pp. 1681–82(142.18b–20b); *ECCP*, II, 893; *KHSL*, p. 104 (5.2). Another attack on the feudatories was made in 1659 by Censor Chu Shao-feng (*HCTI*, 12.1a–4a).
30. *CSLC*, 5.42b and 8.2a; *HCTI*, 17.1a–3a.
31. *ECCP*, I, 398.
32. *KHSL*, pp. 321–22(22.10, 11) and 348(24.8); *CSLC*, 7.46b–47a; *CS*, p. 3693.5–7.
33. *KHSL*, p. 362(25.3a).
34. Liu Hsien-t'ing, *Kuang-yang tsa-chi*, p. 164.
35. *KHSL*, p. 1320(99.8a); *CS*, pp. 3693.9–3694.0. The emperor's remarks came in 1682 after the rebellion had been crushed.
36. *KHSL*, pp. 579–80(41.17, 20b) and 581(41.21).
37. *KHSL*, pp. 592–93(42.19, 21b–22a).
38. *KHSL*, p. 595(42.26b).
39. *KHSL*, pp. 597–98(43.2b–3a).
40. Songgotu: *ECCP*, II, 664; Tuhai: *CS*, p. 3819.3–4; *KHSL*, p. 1320 (99.8a); Hsiung: *K'ang-hsi cheng-yao*, comp. Chang Shen (1910), 3.34a.
41. *ECCP*, I, 577 and 581; *CSLC*, 6.20; *CS*, p. 3826.3. Two other little-known Manchus, Sai-k'o-te and Subai, were later praised by K'ang-hsi for supporting his decision (*KHSL*, p. 1320[99.8b]). Wang Hsi's support was not mentioned by the emperor, but it is noted by a biographer (*CHLC*, p. 2223[4.19b]).
42. *KHSL*, p. 598(43.3a); *CS*, p. 3694.0.
43. *KHSL*, pp. 598–99(43.3b–4a, 5, 6a) and 601–2(43.9, 11b–12a).
44. *KHSL*, pp. 600–601(43.8b–9a).
45. *KHSL*, p. 609(44.2b).
46. *KHSL*, p. 1378(103.19); Joseph Anne-Marie de Moyriac de Mailla, *Histoire gênérale de la Chine*, 13 vols. (Paris: P.D. Pierres, 1777–85), XI, 67.
47. Wu had been approached a decade or so earlier by a Ming loyalist, who urged him to lead the fight against the Manchus, but Wu was not interested (Liu Hsien-t'ing, *Kuang-yang tsa-chi*, pp. 163–64).
48. *KHSL*, pp. 614–15(44.12a–13a, 13); *CSLC*, 6.25b–26a, 6.27, and

80.4b–5a. The subprefect, Liu K'un, while in exile wrote several works about the rebellion which formed the basis of his son's work, *T'ing-wen lu* (comp. Liu Chien; dated 1720). Liu K'un survived his exile and was rewarded for his loyalty in 1683 (*KHSL*, p. 1488[112.4b]; Chu Hsi-tsu, "Wu San-kuei Chou-wang chi-yüan shih-i," *Li-shih yü-yen yen-chiu-so chi-k'an*, II, [1930–32], 394).

49. *ECCP*, II, 664; *KHSL*, p. 1320(99.8b).

50. Orleans, *Tartar Conquerors*, p. 57.

51. *CS*, p. 3813.1; *KHSL*, p. 622(45.4).

52. Domingo Navarrete, *An Account of the Empire of China*, in *Collection of Voyages and Travels*, ed. Awnsham and John Churchill, 3d ed. (London, 1744), p. 310. It is hard to imagine how the "governor of four provinces" statement got circulated. Was it referring to the other feudatories as well? Only Keng Ching-chung in Fukien had revolted in 1674; Kwangtung was calm until 1676 when Shang Chih-hsin joined Wu.

53. He should not be confused with the real Chu Tz'u-huan, who was not fomenting any anti-Manchu rebellion (*ECCP*, I, 192).

54. *KHSL*, pp. 616(44.15a–16a) and 1232(92.11a–12a). T'ung Kuo-wei, an uncle of K'ang-hsi and in the plain blue banner, was also credited with breaking up this insurrection (*ECCP*, II, 795).

55. *KHSL*, pp. 622(45.4), 624(45.9), and 627(45.13b–14a). Someone with Yang's name was captured in 1680 by Tuhai and executed, but he was not the Yang Ch'i-lung of the 1674 plot (*CSLC*, 6.50b; *KHSL*, pp. 1232 [92.11a–12a] and 1246[93.12]).

56. Orleans, *Tartar Conquerors*, pp. 57–58. Henri Cordier, *Histoire générale de la Chine*, 4 vols. (Paris: Paul Geuthner, 1920), II, 269; Vojeu de Brunem [Joseph Jouve], *Histoire de la conquête de la Chine par les Tartares mancheaux*, 2 vols. (Lyon: Frères Duplain, 1754), II, 156–60.

57. *KHSL*, p. 617(44.17). The biography of T'ung Kuo-wei, however, does link Wu to the insurrection (*ECCP*, I, 795; *CSLC*, 11.13b).

58. *KHSL*, pp. 645–46(47.5b–7a); *ECCP*, II, 819; *CSLC*, 8.2b–3a.

59. *KHSL*, p. 615(44.14a); *CSLC*, 80.5a.

60. *KHSL*, pp. 616–18(44.16a, 18a–19b).

61. See, for example, the amnesty offers of 1677, 1678, and 1679 (*KHSL*, pp. 912[67.16], 1047–48[78.6a–8a], and 1083[80.25b–26b]), and compare them with those of 1680–81 (*KHSL*, pp. 1217[91.13b–14b] and 1247 [93.14]).

62. *KHSL*, pp. 614–17(44.12b–13a, 16b–17a), 623(45.5a–6a), 626 (45.11b–12a), and 628(45.18).

63. *KHSL*, pp. 615(44.14b), 621–22(45.2b–3a), and 636–37(46.12a–13a).

64. *KHSL*, pp. 622–23(45.4b–5a), 625–26(45.9b–10a, 12a), and 638 (46.15).

65. *KHSL*, p. 617(44.17b); Chao I, "P'ing-ting San-ni shu-lüeh," in id., *Huang-ch'ao wu-kung chi-sheng*, Ts'ung-shu chi-ch'eng ed. (Shanghai: Commercial Press, 1935), pp. 2–3.

66. *KHSL*, p. 659(48.5b–6a); Tsao Kai-fu, "Rebellion," pp. 100–101.

67. *KHSL*, pp. 623(45.6a), 638(46.16a), 651(47.17b), and 1327(99.22a); Tsao Kai-fu, "Rebellion," p. 98.

68. For brief accounts of their role in the *San-fan* rebellion, see their biographies in *ECCP*, I, 415; II, 683 and 816; also Tsao Kai-fu, "Rebellion," pp. 94, 101–11, and 113–20.

69. *ECCP*, II, 634; Tsao Kai-fu, "Rebellion," pp. 111–13.

70. *CHLC*, p. 13237(403.32b); *CS*, p. 5423.9; Etienne Balazs, *Political Theory and Administrative Reality in Traditional China* (London: University of London, School of Oriental and African Studies, 1965), p. 39.

71. *ECCP*, I, 421–25; Hellmut Wilhelm, "The *Po-hsüeh hung-ju* Examination of 1679," *Journal of the American Oriental Society*, LXXI (1951), 63.

72. *ECCP*, I, 201 and 420, respectively.

73. For details, see Tsao Kai-fu, "Rebellion," pp. 77–78 and 89–140; Hsiao I-shan, *Ch'ing-tai t'ung-shih*, I, 456–80.

74. *KHSL*, p. 643(47.1b–2a); *ECCP*, II, 879.

75. Kenneth Ch'en, *Buddhism in China: A Historical Survey* (Princeton: Princeton University Press, 1964), p. 450; Letter of Verbiest, 4 Oct. 1683, in Orleans, *Tartar Conquerors*, p. 125.

76. *ECCP*, I, 256; K'ang-hsi's first two trips to Wu-t'ai-shan in 1683 are described in *KHSL*, pp. 1429–33(107.17b–108.2a, passim) and 1491–96 (112.10b–19b, passim).

77. *KHSL*, pp. 666(48.19a–20b), 738(54.16b), and 1305–6(98.2b–3b).

78. Meng Shen, "Ch'ing kuo-shih so-wu chih Wu San-kuei p'an-shih Han-Meng-wen ch'ih-yü pa," in id., *Ming-ch'ing shih-lun-chu chi-k'an*, pp. 482–83; Edouard Chavannes, "Documents historiques et géographiques relatifs à Li-kiang," *T'oung-pao*, 2d ser., XIII (1912), 573.

79. *KHSL*, pp. 666(48.20a) and 738–39(54.16a–17b); *MCSL*, ser. IV, vol. IX, p. 815; Meng Shen, "Ch'ing kuo-shih so-wu ch'ih-yü," pp. 480–81.

80. *KHSL*, pp. 1201(90.5) and 1203(90.9b–10a).

81. *KHSL*, pp. 1282(96.11a) and 1284(96.16). This correspondence is referred to by Chavannes, "Documents historiques," p. 573.

82. *KHSL*, pp. 619(44.21), 623(45.6b), and 624(45.8a); *CHLC*, p. 3230 (47.7b).

83. *KHSL*, pp. 1375–76(103.13a–16b).

84. *ECCP*, I, 396 and 439; *KHSL*, pp. 616–17(44.16b–17a), 663(48.13a–14a), 683(49.25a–26a), 810(59.20), and 1025(76.5b).

85. Joachim Bouvet, *Histoire de l'empereur de la Chine* (The Hague: Meyndert Uytwerf, 1699; reprinted Tientsin, 1940), pp. 33–34; *KHSL*, pp. 700–701(51.7b–9b) and 1025–26(76.6a–8a).

86. *MCSL*, ser. IV, vol. IX, p. 820; *KHSL*, pp. 618(44.20), 624–45 (45.8b–9a), and 635–36(46.10b–11b).

87. For Laita, see *ECCP*, I, 410. For the cases of Chao Liang-tung and Sun Ssu-k'o, see *ECCP*, I, 77–78, and II, 682; Lergiyen, Cani, and Shang-shan were punished in December 1680 (*KHSL*, pp. 1241–43[93.2b–5a]); Yolo, Labu, and Giyesu were punished in 1683 (*KHSL*, p. 1417 [106.22]); Tuhai committed suicide in 1682 after a scolding from the emperor (*ECCP*, II, 817); Jangtai, too, was found guilty of incompetence (*ECCP*, I, 396). The merits and demerits of lesser generals were weighed throughout the first half of 1683 (*KHSL*, pp. 1415–57[106.17a–109.25b, passim]).

88. *KHSL*, pp. 834(61.9a), 860–61(63.16b–17a), and 872(64.15a–16a); Tsao Kai-fu, "Rebellion," pp. 126–30.

89. *ECCP*, II, 683. The date of his death is uncertain. It was first reported in Peking on 14 January 1677 (*KHSL*, p. 873[64.17a]), but a 1678 memorial gives it as October–November 1677 (*KHSL*, p. 989[73.9b]), as does a biography of the governor of Kwangi (*CSLC*, 6.30b).

90. *ECCP*, II, 879–80; Tsao Kai-fu, "Rebellion," pp. 134–40. The siege of Yunnan-fu began on 9 April 1681 and lasted until Wu's suicide eight months later (*KHSL*, pp. 1368[95.7] and 1312[98.15b–16b]).

91. *KHSL*, p. 1067(79.21); *CHLC*, p. 6044(156.8b).

92. *KHSL*, p. 1289(96.26).

93. *KHSL*, pp. 1332–35(100.3a–10b), records the contribution of each of the ninety-three guests.

94. *KHSL*, pp. 1323–24(99.14b–16b); *MCSL*, ser. IV, vol. X, pp. 988–90.

95. *KHSL*, pp. 1227(92.2b), 1259(94.13b–14a), and 1407(106.1b); *CS*, p. 3811.0.

96. *KHSL*, pp. 1318–19(99.3b–5b), 1321–22(99.9a–11b), 1323(99.13a–14a), and 1345(101.10b).

97. *KHSL*, pp. 1383–84(104.5a–6a, 7b–8a) and 1390(104.19). The compilers were chosen in November 1682 (*KHSL*, p. 1403[105.14]).

98. *KHSL*, pp. 1348–51(101.15a–22a). The emperor set out, with the heir apparent in tow, on 23 March 1682, and returned on 9 June (*KHSL*, pp. 1345[101.10a] and 1360[102.12b]).

99. See *KHSL*, p. 1471(111.5a) for an expression of this point of view.

100. *KHSL*, p. 640(46.19a).

101. Bowra, "History of Amoy," pp. 94–95.

102. *KHSL*, p. 649(47.14b).

103. *ECCP*, I, 111; Mailla, *Histoire gênérale*, XI, 73–75; Chu Hsi-tsu, "Wu San-kuei Chou-wang," p. 396.

104. *KHSL*, p. 672(49.4b).

105. *KHSL*, p. 1188(89.7b–8a). Cheng Ching refused to consider the government's calls for surrender (*KHSL*, pp. 957[71.5a] and 1111[83.1b–2a]).

106. *KHSL*, pp. 1064(79.15a–16a), 1066(79.19), 1074(80.7), 1143–44 (85.18a–19a), 1166–67(87.16a–17a), and 1182–83(88.23b–25a); Wills, *Pepper, Guns and Parleys*, pp. 167–87; Wei Yüan, *Sheng-wu chi*, 8.15a; Orleans, *Tartar Conquerors*, p. 68; Fu Lo-shu, *Chronicle*, pp. 51–56.

107. *KHSL*, p. 1258(94.11b–12a).

108. *KHSL*, p. 1216(91.12a); Ch'i-chü-chu draft (IHPA), entry of K'ang-hsi 19/8/3 records the discussion preceding the imperial edict.

109. *ECCP*, I, 111; *KHSL*, pp. 1283–84(96.14b–15a).

110. *KHSL*, pp. 1078–79(80.16b–17a) and 1291(96.29); *CSLC*, 9.16b.

111. *KHSL*, pp. 1258(94.11b–12a) and 1550(116.8a).

112. *CSLC*, 9.12b–13a; *KHSL*, pp. 203–4(12.26b–27a); *ECCP*, I, 474; II, 653 and 899.

113. *KHSL*, p. 1295(97.5a).

114. *KHSL*, pp. 1309–10(98.10b–11a), 1398(105.4), and 1440–41(108.16b–17a); Ch'i-chü-chu draft (IHPA), entries for K'ang-hsi 21/10/4 and

21/10/6; *ECCP*, II, 899.

115. *KHSL*, pp. 1358(102.8), 1398(105.4a), and 1367(102.26).

116. *CSLC*, 8.50a; *CS*, p. 3879.0; *KHSL*, p. 1457(109.26); Ch'i-chü-chu draft (IHPA), entry for K'ang-hsi 21/10/6.

117. *KHSL*, pp. 1465–66(110.14b–16a), 1473–74(111.9a–11a), 1480–81 (111.24a–25a), and 1485(111.33b–34b); Fu Lo-shu, *Chronicle*, p. 59.

118. *ECCP*, I, 111; *KHSL*, 1584(118.7).

119. *KHSL*, pp. 1491(112.9a–10b) and 1524(114.15b–16a); *ECCP*, II, 653–55. Yao Ch'i-sheng, on the other hand, went unrewarded for his early support and coordination of the campaign (*ECCP*, II, 899).

120. K'ang-hsi started out on 7 January 1684 and returned on the 23d (*KHSL*, pp. 1508–9)(113.11b, 14b]).

121. *KHSL*, pp. 1457(109.26) and 1496(112.20a). On the Dutch, see Wills, *Pepper, Guns and Parleys*, pp. 86–87 and 181–83.

122. *KHSL*, pp. 1480–81(111.24b–25a). On Subai's orders, see *KHSL*, pp. 1474(111.12a) and 1485(11.34).

123. Report of the court, headed by Prince Giyesu, dated K'ang-hsi 23/1/20 (IHPA, bundle 76 of K'ang-hsi *t'i-pen*); the *shih-lu* entry for the next day is not as complete (*KHSL*, p. 1519[114.5]); see also Fu Lo-shu, *Chronicle*, pp. 59–60; *CSLC*, 7.32b and 9.14b–15a.

124. *KHSL*, pp. 1534–35(115.4b–5a); *CSLC*, 9.15a.

125. *KHSL*, p. 1314(98.20); *CS*, p. 3928.9.

126. *KHSL*, p. 1498(112.23).

127. *KHSL*, pp. 1501(112.29b) and 1506(113.7b).

128. *CS*, pp. 3928.9–3939.2; *ECCP*, II, 777; Hsieh Kuo-chen, "Removal," pp. 579 and 582. The acreage figures were probably not exact, being subject to various systems of "*mou* conversion." On the problem, see Ping-ti Ho, *Studies on the Population of China, 1368-1953* (Cambridge: Harvard University Press, 1959), pp. 104–16; on the general problem of dealing with Chinese numbers and units, see Yang Lien-sheng, "Numbers and Units in Chinese Economic History," in id., *Studies in Chinese Institutional History*, pp. 75–84.

129. Fu Lo-shu, *Chronicle*, p. 61; *ECCP*, II, 777.

130. *KHSL*, p. 1535(115.6).

131. *KHSL*, p. 1458(116.3a–4a).

132. H. Bosmans, "Ferdinand Verbiest, directeur de l'observatoire de Peking (1623–88)," *Revue des questions scientifiques*, LXII (1912), 341, n.

133. *KHSL*, p. 1555(116.18).

134. Mark Mancall, "The Ch'ing Tribute System: An Interpretive Essay," in *The Chinese World Order*, ed. John K. Fairbank (Cambridge: Harvard University Press, 1968), 85–89.

135. *MCSL*, ser. IV, vol VIII, pp. 745–46; *KHSL*, pp. 1555(116.18) and 1558–59(116.24b–25a).

136. *K'ang-hsi hui-tien*, 99.19a; *KHSL*, p. 1567(117.10b).

137. Louis Daniel Le Comte, *Memoirs and Observations*, 3d ed. (London: B. Tooke, 1699), pp. 85–87; Fu Lo-shu, *Chronicle*, p. 61; José de Jesús-Maria, *Azia Sínica e Japônica*, ed. Charles R. Boxer, 2 vols. (Macao, 1950), II, 100 and 104–5.

138. Quoted in Hsieh Kuo-chen, "Removal," p. 579.

139. The phrase is from Tsao Kai-fu, "Rebellion," p. 179.

140. For the most recent treatment of pre-K'ang-hsi relations, see Mark Mancall, *Russia and China: Their Diplomatic Relations to 1728* (Cambridge: Harvard University Press, 1971), pp. 20–56. Still useful older accounts include F. A. Golder, *Russian Expansion on the Pacific, 1641–1850* (Cleveland: Arthur Clark, 1914), pp. 33–55; Joseph Sebes, S.J., *The Jesuits and the Sino-Russian Treaty of Nerchinsk: The Diary of Thomas Pereira, S.J.* (Rome: Institutum Historicum S.I., 1961), pp. 19–25 and 59–61; Vincent Chen, *Sino-Russian Relations in the Seventeenth Century* (The Hague: Martinus Nijhoff, 1966), pp. 34–58. For Russian accounts of their early embassies to China, see John F. Baddeley, ed., *Russia, Mongolia, China*, 2 vols. (New York: Burt Franklin, [1919]), II, 128–68.

141. Mancall, *Russia and China*, pp. 34–35 and 53; Eric Widmer, "'Kitai' and the Ch'ing Empire in Seventeenth Century Russian Documents on China," *Ch'ing-shih wen-t'i*, II, no. 4 (Nov. 1970), 24–32.

142. *KHSL*, p. 445(31.13); Mancall, *Russia and China*, pp. 56–59.

143. Mancall, *Russia and China*, pp. 60–62; Widmer, "'Kitai' and the Ch'ing Empire," pp. 33–35; Michel Pavlovsky, *Chinese-Russian Relations* (New York: The Philosophical Library, 1949), pp. 127–44, discusses at length the circumstances of Milovanov's mission and the letter he carried; Baddeley, *Russia, Mongolia, China*, II, 195–203; Fu Lo-shu, *Chronicle*, pp. 46 and 453, n. 73–74.

144. Mancall, *Russia and China*, pp. 62–64; Widmer, "'Kitai' and the Ch'ing Empire," pp. 35–37.

145. I am following Mancall (*Russia and China*, p. 324, n. 9).

146. Ibid., pp. 82–110; Baddeley, *Russia, Mongolia, China*, II, 242–422 (for Russian accounts); *KHSL*, pp. 832(61.3b–4a) and 842(62.3). Translation of the latter two Chinese documents are in Fu Lo-shu, *Chronicle*, pp. 49–50.

147. Sebes, *Sino-Russian Treaty*, p. 67; Pavlovsky, *Chinese-Russian Relations*, p. 119. Mancall, *Russia and China*, pp. 98–101 and 108–9, notes Verbiest's betrayal of K'ang-hsi's trust by divulging court deliberations to Milescu.

148. *KHSL*, p. 520(37.3).

149. Mancall, *Russia and China*, pp. 116–17; Robert H. G. Lee, *The Manchurian Frontier in Ch'ing History* (Cambridge: Harvard University Press, 1970), pp. 50 and 64.

150. *KHSL*, p. 1622(121.11).

151. Mancall, *Russia and China*, pp. 29–31; Sebes, *Sino-Russian Treaty*, p. 24.

152. *KHSL*, pp. 1384–85(104.8b–9b); Fu Lo-shu, *Chronicle*, pp. 56–57; Mancall, *Russia and China*, pp. 117–18.

153. *KHSL*, pp. 1414–15(106.16b–17a).

154. *KHSL*, p. 1418(106.23b–24a); Fu Lo-shu, *Chronicle*, p. 58; Mancall, *Russia and China*, p. 119.

155. *KHSL*, pp. 1448–49(109.7a–9a), translated in Fu Lo-shu, *Chronicle*, pp. 62–63; Mancall, *Russia and China*, pp. 120–23.

156. *ECCP*, II, 630; *KHSL*, p. 1500(112.28a).
157. *KHSL*, pp. 1489–90(112.6a–8a) and 1505(113.5); Mancall, *Russia and China*, pp. 122–23.
158. *KHSL*, pp. 1418(106.23b) and 1622(121.11b) for statements to this effect.
159. *KHSL*, pp. 1476–77(111.16b–17a) and 1488–89(112.4b–6a); Fu Lo-shu, *Chronicle*, pp. 64–65.
160. *KHSL*, pp. 1495(112.17b–18a) and 1507(113.9b–10a); *ECCP*, II, 631; Pavlovsky, *Chinese-Russian Relations*, pp. 154–60.
161. *KHSL*, pp. 1542–43(115.19b–21a), 1547(116.1b–2b), and 1590–91 (119.4b–6b); *CHLC*, p. 9223(275.24a); Mancall, *Russia and China*, pp. 123–25.
162. *KHSL*, pp. 1591–92(119.6b–8b); Fu Lo-shu, *Chronicle*, pp. 74–78; Mancall, *Russia and China*, p. 127.
163. *KHSL*, p. 1621(121.10); Mancall, *Russia and China*, pp. 131–33.
164. Liu Hsien-t'ing, *Kuang-yang tsa-chi*, p. 78; *KHSL*, pp. 1584(118.8) and 1591(119.5); *ECCP*, II, 621.
165. Liu Hsien-t'ing, *Kuang-yang tsa-chi*, pp. 79–80; Fu Lo-shu, *Chronicle*, pp. 78–80.
166. Mancall, *Russia and China*, pp. 134–37.
167. Ibid., pp. 137–39; *ECCP*, I, 443; II, 630–31; Fu Lo-shu, *Chronicle*, pp. 86–91.
168. Immanuel C. Y. Hsu, "Russia's Special Position in China in the Early Ch'ing Period," *Slavic Review*, XXIII (Dec. 1964), 689–92; Bouvet, *Histoire de l'empereur*, pp. 28–30; Mancall, *Russia and China*, pp. 149 and 158–59.
169. Mancall, *Russia and China*, pp. 141–62. For general accounts of the treaty, see the biography of Songgotu (the chief negotiator for Peking) in *ECCP*, II, 664–65; also Sebes, *Sino-Russian Treaty*, pp. 71–75 and 103–303; Fu Lo-shu, *Chronicle*, pp. 94–103; Vincent Chen, *Sino-Russian Relations*, pp. 86–105; Gaston Cahen, *Histoire des relations de la Russie avec la Chine sous Pierre le Grand (1689–1730)* (Paris: Félix Alcan, 1912), pp. 31–53.
170. Mancall, *Russia and China*, chaps. 2–3.
171. Ibid., pp. 160–61.
172. *CS*, p. 3819.4–5.
173. *KHSL*, pp. 739(54.18) and 743(55.1b–2b); *ECCP*, I, 305; II, 784.
174. *KHSL*, pp. 929(72.22b) and 1023–24(76.2a–3a); Mailla, *Histoire générale*, XI, 86.
175. See Galdan's biography in *ECCP*, I, 266–68; Spence, *Emperor of China*, pp. 18–22.
176. Spence, *Emperor of China*, pp. 46–47; in his valedictory edict of 1717, K'ang-hsi placed great stress on attention to detail (ibid., p. 147).
177. Chaoying Fang, "A Technique for Estimating the Numerical Strength of the Early Manchu Military Forces," *Harvard Journal of Asiatic Studies*, XIII (1950), 203 and 208–9 (table II).
178. The figures are from *K'ang-hsi hui-tien*, 82.3b–10a. On decisions to establish garrisons in these cities, see *KHSL*, pp. 1427(107.13b–14a),

1442–43(108.19b–21b), and 1455(109.21a–22a); Tsao Kai-fu, "Rebellion," pp. 141–42. A garrison was stationed at Han-chung, Shensi, but later withdrawn (*KHSL*, p. 1699[126.29b–30a]).

179. *KHSL*, pp. 1411–13(106.10a–11a, 13b–14a); letters of Verbiest, in Orleans, *Tartar Conquerors*, pp. 106–8, 121, and 130.

180. Cheng T'ien-t'ing, *Ch'ing-shih t'an-wei*, pp. 35–36; see also *KHSL*, pp. 1436–37(108.8a, 10a); Spence, *Ts'ao Yin*, pp. 36 and 52; letter of Verbiest, in Orleans, *Tartar Conquerors*, pp. 121–22.

181. Verbiest, in Orleans, *Tartar Conquerors*, p. 109. Father Pereira's account is similar (ibid., pp. 139–40).

182. Cheng T'ien-t'ing, *Ch'ing-shih t'an-wei*, pp. 36–37; Meng Shen, "Pa-ch'i," p. 21; Farquhar, "Mongolian versus Chinese Elements," pp. 14–15.

183. Letter of Verbiest, 4 October 1683, in Orleans, *Tartar Conquerors*, p. 127. Similar sentiments are expressed by Father Bouvet, *Histoire de l'empereur*, pp. 120–21.

184. Quoted in a letter of Pereira, in Orleans, *Tartar Conquerors*, p. 148. See also Father Verbiest's comments in ibid., pp. 123–24.

185. See, again, Pereira's letter of 1684 in ibid., pp. 134–35; also, Spence, *Emperor of China*, pp. 8, 12, and 22–23; Bouvet, *Histoire de l'empereur*, pp. 121–22.

186. *KHSL*, pp. 1534(115.3) and 1537–38(115.10b–11a).

187. *KHSL*, pp. 1528–31(114.23b–29b) and 1570(117.16). He repeated these contests on later tours (Spence, *Ts'ao Yin*, pp. 130–31) and on northern campaigns (Spence, *Emperor of China*, p. 18).

188. Compare *KHSL*, p. 573(41.5a–6a) with Ch'i-chü-chu entry of K'ang-hsi 12/1/20 (*Shih-hao ts'ung-k'an ch'u-pien*, comp. Lo Chen-yü, 2 vols. [Taipei: Wen-hai, 1964], I, 352).

189. *KHSL*, pp. 1453(109.18), 1456(109.23a), and 1461(110.6); *ECCP*, II, 794.

190. Lo Er-kang, *Lu-ying ping-chih*, p. 45, estimated 800,000; Li Hsün, *Ming-Ch'ing shih*, pp. 181–82, gave the higher figure. During the campaigns, about 400,000 *lu-ying* and 50,000 banner troops were used (Tsao Kai-fu, "Rebellion," p. 84, n. 40).

191. *K'ang-hsi hui-tien, chüan* 94.

192. *KHSL*, pp. 1362–63(102.15b–16a, 17b–18a) and 1379–80(103.22a–23a).

193. Lo Er-kang, *Lu-ying ping-chih*, p. 5; Li Hsün, *Ming-Ch'ing shih*, pp. 181–82; Chaoying Fang, "Numerical Strength of the Early Manchu Military Forces," pp. 208–9 (table II).

194. *KHSL*, pp. 1361(102.13) on governors, and 1381(104.4a) on governors-general.

195. *KHSL*, p. 1445(109.1b–2b).

196. Tsao Kai-fu, "Rebellion," pp. 147–48. Once, in 1680, the *lu-ying* troops in Hukuang were sent to Yunnan and given a new commander (*CHLC*, p. 3397[53.50a]), but this was probably just a wartime necessity and not a regular practice.

197. Manchus were rushed to defend Han-chung in December 1674 for

this reason (*KHSL*, pp. 692–93[50.16b–17a]).

198. *KHSL*, pp. 709(52.2a) and 831(61.1). Yolo specifically requested *lu-ying* troops for the defense of Changsha in 1675 (*KHSL*, pp. 790–91 [58.8b–9a]).

199. *KHSL*, pp. 1039(77.13a–14a) and 1200(90.3b).

200. Yang Mao-hsün, governor-general of Szechwan, praised the bravery of Manchu troops in 1679 but pointed out how inappropriate cavalry and archery were for the rugged, hilly country of his province (*CHLC*, p. 5988 [154.4a]).

201. *KHSL*, pp. 1138–39(85.8b–10a).

202. *ECCP*, I, 66–67.

203. Tsao Kai-fu, "Rebellion," pp. 137–40; *ECCP*, I, 77–78; II, 682.

204. *KHSL*, pp. 1127–29(84.5b–9a); *ECCP*, II, 682.

205. *KHSL*, pp. 1150–51(86.3, 4b–5a), 1155–56(86.14b–15a), 1172 (88.4), and 1175–76(88.10b–12b).

206. *ECCP*, I, 78. Chao in 1683 bitterly complained in a memorial of the inadequate reward he received for his efforts, but K'ang-hsi at that time ignored him (*KHSL*, pp. 1451[109.13b–14b] and 1453[109.17]).

207. See chap. 1 above, n. 60.

208. *CSLC*, 8.47b–48a; *KHSL*, pp. 900–901(66.20b–21a).

209. *Chung-hua min-kuo k'ai-kuo wu-shih-nien wen-hsien*, vol. I, book I: *Ke-ming yüan-yüan* (Taipei, 1963), pp. 270–71.

210. Franz Michael, "Military Organization and Power Structure of China during the Taiping Rebellion," *Pacific Historical Review*, XVIII (1949), 472.

Chapter Five

1. In examining the careers of fourteen high Manchu metropolitan officials of the Oboi regency, Oxnam (*Ruling from Horseback*, p. 208) concludes that most of them had earlier civil as well as military service. Still, many of them began as military men during the period of conquest, as K'ang-hsi's advisors had not.

2. *CS*, p. 2453, the date being 18 September 1669.

3. *ECCP*, II, 664.

4. Ibid., for Songgotu; *CSLC*, 6.21b for Batai.

5. For biography, see *CSLC*, 6.41a.

6. *KHSL*, pp. 419(29.5b–6a) and 447–48(31.18a–19a).

7. *KHSL*, pp. 636–37(46.12a–13a); Chu P'eng-shou, *Chiu-tien pei-cheng* (n.p., 1936), 1.12.

8. Their support is noted in their biographies. Molo: *CS*, p. 3826.3; Mingju: *ECCP*, I, 577; Mishan: *ECCP*, I, 581.

9. *CSLC*, 6.20.

10. *ECCP*, I, 579.

11. The eighth month is found in IHPA; the ninth month is published in *Shih-liao ts'ung-k'an*, I, 473–519.

12. *ECCP*, II, 784.

13. There is very little information on Batai or Duikana, although each has short biographies in *CSLC*, 6.21a and 6.24a, respectively. Duikana

died in 1675, and Batai retired after 1677 because of old age and poor health; neither, apparently, was very much involved in the leading events of his day. A final Manchu grand secretary, Ledehun, has no biography at all, although brief mention of an investigatory trip he took to Kwangsi in 1673 is mentioned in *ECCP*, II, 683.

14. Spence, *Ts'ao Yin*, pp. 87, 103–4, and 174–75; Ping-ti Ho, "The Salt Merchants of Yang-chou: A Study of Commercial Capitalism in Eighteenth-Century China," *Harvard Journal of Asiatic Studies*, XVII (June 1954), 131.

15. He served as a grand secretary in 1654–70; for his biography, see *CSLC*, 5.38a.

16. Fang Chao-ying in *ECCP*, I, 494.

17. *CS*, p. 3809.5; *CHLC*, p. 2196(3.7b–8a).

18. *CSLC*, 8.2a.

19. *CHLC*, p. 2223(4.19b).

20. *ECCP*, II, 819; *CSLC*, 8.2b–3a; *CS*, p. 3812.9.

21. John K. Fairbank, "The Manchu-Chinese Dyarchy in the 1840's and '50's," *Far Eastern Quarterly*, XII (May 1953), 265.

22. Alfred Kuo-liang Ho, "The Grand Council in the Ch'ing Dynasty," *Far Eastern Quarterly*, XI (Feb. 1952), 175; T'ung-tsu Ch'ü, *Local Government in China under the Ch'ing* (Cambridge: Harvard University Press, 1962), p. 22, table 5; Oxnam, *Ruling from Horseback*, pp. 214–15.

23. For the development of the *tu-fu* institution in the Ch'ing period, see Lawrence D. Kessler, "Ethnic Composition of Provincial Leadership during the Ch'ing Dynasty," *Journal of Asian Studies*, XXVIII (May 1969), 490–92. Most of this section dealing with the *tu-fu* is taken from this larger study by the author.

24. *KHSL*, p. 1051(78.14b).

25. IHPA, Ch'i-chü-chu (Diary of the Emperor's Movements) draft for K'ang-hsi 21/1/9 (15 Feb. 1682). Five days later, Chinese high officials were invited to the Ch'ien-ch'ing Hall to celebrate the imperial victory over the *San-fan* rebels (*KHSL*, pp. 1332–33[100.3a–5b]).

26. Spence, *Ts'ao Yin*, pp. 252–54.

27. *KHSL*, pp. 1115(83.10a) and 1123(83.24b–25a).

28. Hsiao I-shan, *Ch'ing-tai t'ung-shih*, II, 24.

29. *CS*, p. 3889.7.

30. Hsiao I-shan, *Ch'ing-tai t'ung-shih*, II, 24.

31. *KHSL*, pp. 325–26(22.17b, 18b, 20a) and 358(24.27a–28a).

32. *HTSL*, pp. 5350–51(23.8b, 10a).

33. *PCTC*, 339.1a.

34. Yen Mao-kung, *Ch'ing-tai cheng-hsien lei-pien*. Appendixes to Yen's *tu-fu* tables arranged all Ch'ing *tsung-tu* and *hsün-fu* (if not listed already as a *tsung-tu*) according to their ethno-political affiliation. These lists formed the basis of the dynastic totals given in P'an Kuang-tan, "Chin-tai Su-chou ti jen-ts'ai." *She-hui k'o-hsueh*, I (1935), 70–71. P'an's figures, in turn, were cited by Mary C. Wright, *The Last Stand of Chinese Conservatism: The T'ung-chih Restoration, 1862–74*, 2d printing with additional notes (Stanford: Stanford University Press, 1962), p. 55, note k.

35. *PCTC, chüan,* 339–40. I am indebted to Jonathan Spence for first calling my attention to the correlation between Fengtien registration and banner affiliation of prominent Ch'ing officials. His own findings on this subject are found in his book *Ts'ao Yin,* pp. 71–72, n. 119. A similar correlation between Liaotung registration and banner affiliation can also be hypothesized for the same reasons. A quick glance at the *Sheng-ching t'ung-chih,* 1736 ed. (Taipei: 1965 reprint), *chüan* 34, list of "men of distinction" (*jen-wu*) yields innumerable examples of Chinese bannermen *tu-fu* identified as *Liaotung-jen.*

36. To cite one case, Shih Wei-han of the Chinese bordered yellow banner is listed as a Shanghai native in *CS,* p. 3951.9; in *CHLC,* p. 6003 (154.33a); and in gazetteers of Fukien, Chekiang, and Shantung. None of those works mentions his banner affiliation, which is recorded in *PCTC.*

37. *ECCP, CHLC, CSLC, CS,* and local gazetteers.

38. See tables 2 and 3 in Kessler, "Provincial Leadership," pp. 497 and 500.

39. Ping-ti Ho, "The Significance of the Ch'ing Period in Chinese History," *Journal of Asian Studies,* XXVI (Feb. 1967), 191–93.

40. *KHSL,* p. 497(35.5b–6a).

41. IHPA, Ch'i-chü-chu draft for K'ang-hsi 12/4/12 (27 May 1673); the latter part of this entry is in *KHSL,* pp. 583–84(42.2b–3a).

42. *KHSL,* p. 703(51.13b); *CHLC,* p. 5976(153.37b).

43. See tables 12 and 13 in Kessler, "Provincial Leadership," p. 509.

44. A comparable difference in tenure according to ethnic affiliation also existed in local posts in the early Ch'ing period, if Soochow can be taken as a representative case. During the entire K'ang-hsi period, bannermen served an average of 4.3 years as prefect and 3 years as district magistrate, whereas Chinese only averaged 2.7 years in each post (Spence, *Ts'ao Yin,* p. 74).

45. *HTSL,* pp. 5300–5302(18.31b–36b).

46. *KHSL,* pp. 307–8(21.10b–11b) and 461–63(32.17b, 20b–21a).

47. *KHSL,* p. 1119(83.17a).

48. *HCTI,* 17.19a. This memorial was submitted in 1665 by Chao T'ing-ch'en, governor-general of Chekiang with a reputation for leniency toward surrendered rebels. For biography, see *CSLC,* 5.26a; *CS,* p. 3946.8.

49. *KHSL,* p. 1531(114.29b–30b).

50. *KHSL,* p. 1538(115.11).

51. *CSLC,* 7.49a–50b; Spence, *Ts'ao Yin,* pp. 230 and 274–75.

52. *CSLC,* 9.33a.

53. See, for example, his conversations with Hsiung Tz'u-li in 1673 (*KHSL,* p. 577[41.14]), with the newly appointed governor of Fukien in 1683 (*KHSL,* p. 1451[109.13a]), and with his entire court in 1679 (*KHSL,* p. 1123[83.25a]).

54. These two officials, with identical characters, have often been confused. Not the least obstacle to distinguishing between them is the fact that they both served as governor of Chihli, the elder Yü (1617–84) in 1680–82, the younger Yü (1638–1700) in 1686–90. Biographical information for both men is found in *ECCP,* II, 937–38. The younger Yü was a

bannerman, although the editors of *PCTC* failed to include him in their lists of bannermen officials (see *chüan* 339–40). To confuse matters further, there were at least two other Yü Ch'eng-lungs in the early Ch'ing period (Liu Hsien-t'ing, *Kuang-yang tsa-chi*, pp. 10 and 142).

55. *KHSL*, pp. 1238(92.23b) and 1258(94.11).

56. *KHSL*, pp. 1571(117.18b) and 1575(117.25a).

57. Spence, *Emperor of China*, p. 53; a full treatment of this affair is found in Spence, *Ts'ao Yin*, pp. 240–54.

58. *KHSL*, p. 1238(92.23b). Biographical data: Feng, *ECCP*, I, 243; Sung, *CS*, p. 3984.6.

59. *KHSL*, p. 1500(112.26b–27b).

60. *KHSL*, pp. 1373–74(103.10b–11a, 12a). The *shih-lu* is silent on whether or not this order was ever applied to provinces other than Chihli.

61. *ECCP*, I, 436.

62. *KHSL*, pp. 920–21(68.12b–13a); the terms used for cliques were *tang* and *men-hu*.

63. *KHSL*, p. 759(56.1b–2a). The ceremony of investiture took place on 26–27 January 1676 (*KHSL*, p. 796[58.19a, 19b–20a]).

64. *KHSL*, p. 1435(108.6a).

65. *KHSL*, pp. 1105–1106(82.14, 16b); Liu Hsien-t'ing, *Kuang-yang tsa-chi*, p. 13. A Western account inflated the casualty figures up to three or four hundred thousand (Mailla, *Histoire générale*, XI, 88–89).

66. *CS*, p. 3898.3; *CSLC*, 8.11a.

67. *KHSL*, pp. 1107–1108(82.18a–21b).

68. *CSLC*, 8.11, 12a; *KHSL*, p. 1435(108.6).

69. *CSLC*, 8.12b. For similar verbal abuse from K'ang-hsi to Li Hsü, a Chinese bannerman and confidant of the emperor, in 1712, see Spence, *Ts'ao Yin*, p. 262.

70. Seen on 26 August 1682 (*KHSL*, p. 1378[103.20b]).

71. *KHSL*, p. 1379(103.21a–22a).

72. *KHSL*, p. 1387(104.13); *CSLC*, 7.40a. There were two grand secretaries serving in the early K'ang-hsi period who were from the same district (I-tu) in Shantung—Feng P'u (grand secretary, 1671–82) and Sun T'ing-ch'üan (grand secretary, 1663–64; biography in *CSLC*, 5.43b).

73. A list of men punished in 1703 for being members of Songgotu's clique included only one Chinese (*CS*, p. 3931.4–5). None of these men have biographies, but one of them, Shao-kan, was director-general of grain transport in 1681–84.

74. Most have biographies in *ECCP:* I, 161 (Chin); I, 310 (Hsü); II, 734 (Ts'ai). These names and others in Mingju's clique were gleaned mostly from Kuo Hsiu's impeachment memorial of 1688 (*CSLC*, 8.13b–15b) and from Mingju's biography in the dynastic history (*CS*, p. 3931.6). Two other nonbannermen members of Mingju's clique were Hsiung I-hsiao (*CS*, p. 3984.9) and Chang Ch'ien (*ECCP*, I, 101).

75. *ECCP*, II, 819.

76. *CSLC*, 8.13b–14a.

77. Jonathan Spence, "The Seven Ages of K'ang-hsi (1654–1722)," *Journal of Asian Studies*, XXVI (Feb. 1967), 209.

78. For a perceptive comparison of the two emperors' attitude toward factionalism and corruption, see Silas Wu, *Communication and Imperial Control,* pp. 111–13 and 115.

79. Ibid., chap. 5; Spence, *Ts'ao Yin,* chap. 6.

80. *KHSL,* p. 439(31.1a–2a).

81. *KHSL,* pp. 112–13(6.4b–5a).

82. *KHSL,* p. 1132(84.15).

83. On other early Ch'ing institutions for gathering information and their limitations, see Silas Wu, *Communication and Imperial Control,* pp. 20–26 and 107–8.

84. One with Yü Ch'eng-lung (the elder) in 1681 (*KHSL,* p. 1298 [97.12b]), and another with Tung Wei-kuo in 1683 (*KHSL,* p. 1503 [113.1b–2b]).

85. *KHSL,* pp. 1501(112.29b) and 1506(113.7b).

86. The text of this first session is found in *KHSL,* pp. 1548–49(116.3a–6a).

87. Biographical information: Wu: *CSLC,* 9.1a; Li: *CSLC,* 72.50a; Liu: *CHLC,* p. 5901(151.1a); Lu: *CHLC,* p. 5939(152.20a). Wu was governor-general in 1682–89.

88. Yü was governor-general from 1682 until his death in the summer of 1684 (*ECCP,* I, 937).

89. For biography, see *ECCP,* I, 161–63.

90. That audience took place on 11 December 1682 (*KHSL,* pp. 1408–9 [106.4a–5b]) at a time when Chin Fu's river work was increasingly under attack.

91. The historical and ideological background of K'ang-hsi's interest in weather conditions and the prospects of harvests are briefly noted in Silas Wu, *Communication and Imperial Control,* pp. 34–35.

92. This second session is recorded in *KHSL,* p. 1550(116.8).

93. Wan's appointment came in 1679 (*KHSL,* pp. 1078–79[80.16b–17a]), and he was replaced by Shih in 1681 (*KHSL,* p. 1291[96.29]). For biographies, see *ECCP,* II, 653 (Shih); *CSLC,* 9.16b (Wan).

94. Actually, Taiwan surrendered without an invasion (as described in the preceding chapter).

95. K'ang-hsi had occasion again in 1688 to note the arrogance of Shih Lang ([Yung-cheng] *Jih-chiang-kuan chin-ch'eng kao* [IHPA], entry of [Yung-cheng] 13/6/15).

96. For example, see *KHSL,* pp. 1464–65(110.11b–13b), 1530(114.27b–28b), 1536–37(115.8b–9a), and 1539(115.13b–14b).

97. *KHSL,* pp. 66(2.20a), 540(38.24), and 568(40.20b).

98. *CHLC,* pp. 3184–85(45.14b–15a).

99. *KHSL,* pp. 1118(83.15a–16b) and 1122(83.23); *CS,* p. 3954.3; *CSLC,* 79.40.

Chapter Six

1. Oxnam, *Ruling from Horseback,* p. 116.

2. *HTSL,* p. 17535(1047.1); *Huang-ch'ao tz'u-lin tien-ku,* comp. Chu Kuei (1886 ed.), 21.5a–6a (cited as *Tz'u-lin tien-ku*).

3. *HTSL*, p. 17538(1047.6b); *Tz'u-lin tien-ku*, 21.7.

4. *KHSL*, pp. 486–87(34.12b, 13b–14a). As of September 1671, when the Ch'i-chü-chu was revived, tutors concurrently served as diarists to record the daily acts and sayings of the emperor. So their full title became *jih-chiang ch'i-chü-chu kuan* (*KHSL*, p. 514[36.15b]; *HTSL*, p. 17610 [1055.1]).

5. *KHSL*, pp. 499(35.9) and 505(35.21b).

6. A chronological listing of these officials is found in *Tz'u-lin tien-ku, chüan* 59–60. The roll of daily tutors included the name of Ke-er-ku-te as a 1665 appointee, which is inexplicable since tutoring did not begin until 1671; but it did not list Hu Mi-se who was appointed in 1671 (*KHSL*, p. 526 [37.16b]). The latter, but not the former, is included in my compilation, which represents appointments rather than personnel (some of whom were reappointed one or more times).

7. Ping-ti Ho, "Significance," pp. 192–93; Hsiao I-shan, *Ch'ing-tai t'ung-shih*, I, 993–96; Liang Ch'i-ch'ao, *Chung-kuo chin-san-pai-nien hsüeh-shu shih* (Taipei: Chung-hua, 1962), p. 103; Meng Shen, *Ch'ing-tai shih*, pp. 169–70.

8. *KHSL*, p. 453(32.2a); *ECCP*, I, 329, and 474.

9. *K'ang-hsi cheng-yao*, 16.22, citing *Tung-hua lu*.

10. See Ping-ti Ho, "Significance," p. 192, and "Salient Aspects of China's Heritage," in *China in Crisis*, vol. I: *China's Heritage and the Communist Political System*, ed. Ping-ti Ho and Tang Tsou (Chicago: University of Chicago Press, 1968), pp. 14–15.

11. *KHSL*, p. 575(41.9).

12. *KHSL*, pp. 586(42.7b) and 1579(117.33b–34a); Ch'i-chü-chu draft (*Shih-liao ts'ung-k'an*, I, 362), entry of K'ang-hsi 12/5/3.

13. E.g., Ch'i-chü-chu draft (IHPA), entry of K'ang-hsi 14/11/13. This time the tutoring stopped on 29 December 1675, and took up again on 4 March 1676; according to regulation, the layoff would have gone from 21 December to shortly after 11 April (the day of that spring's Lecture on the Classics ceremony).

14. *KHSL*, pp. 593(42.22) and 929(69.6a).

15. *KHSL*, p. 677(49.13b–14a); *HTSL*, p. 17538(1047.7).

16. *HTSL*, p. 17540(1047.10).

17. *KHSL*, p. 1477(111.18).

18. *HTSL*, p. 17540(1047.11); Bouvet, *Histoire de l'empereur*, p. 90; Jean de Fontaney to François de la Chaize, 15 Feb. 1703, in *Lettres édifiantes et curieuses*, 40 vols. (Paris: Nicolas Le Clerc, 1707–58), VII, 198–201.

19. *KHSL*, pp. 578(41.15a) and 737(54.13b–14a).

20. *KHSL*, p. 905(67.1b–2b).

21. (Silas) Hsiu-liang Wu, "Nan-shu-fang chih chien-chih chi ch'i ch'ien-ch'i chih fa-chan," *Ssu-yü-yen*, V (March 1968), 1428–34, also views the creation of the Imperial Study as a product of K'ang-hsi's disillusionment with the two formal systems of tutoring. In addition, he has traced the later development of the Imperial Study and the career of some of its famous residents.

22. Spence, "Seven Ages of K'ang-hsi," p. 206. K'ang-hsi himself admitted this on several occasions (*KHSL*, pp. 578[41.15a] and 1209 [90.21a]).

23. *KHSL*, pp. 939(69.25b) and 945(70.6a).

24. Spence, *Ts'ao Yin*, pp. 127 and 141–44; *ECCP*, II, 413.

25. Passages chosen from the Analects for explication by the tutors are given in Ch'i-chü-chu draft entries for the 5th, 10th, and 11th months of K'ang-hsi's 12th year (*Shih-liao ts'ung-k'an*, I, 361–82 and 399–450).

26. *KHSL*, p. 500(35.11b); *ECCP*, I, 309 and 327; II, 902. The work was completed in 1682 and printed in 1690.

27. *KHSL*, pp. 549(39.13b) and 576–77(41.11b–12a, 13b). On the original Sung work, see n. 67 of chap. 3 above. An extant copy of the bilingual edition, dated K'ang-hsi 11/10/16 (4 Dec. 1672), is in the Toyo Bunko (Nicholas Poppe, Leon Hurvitz, and Hidehiro Okada, eds., *Catalogue of the Manchu-Mongol Section of the Toyo Bunko* [Tokyo: Toyo Bunko, 1964; Seattle: University of Washington Press, 1964], p. 272, no. 446).

28. *KHSL*, p. 948(70.11a–12b).

29. *KHSL*, p. 862(63.20b).

30. The *Shu-ching* in 1680 and the *I-ching* in 1683 (*HTSL*, pp. 17539–40 [1047.9a, 10a] and 17577–58[1049.5b, 7a]). The Imperial prefaces to each of the tutor's expositions on the classics are found in *K'ang-hsi cheng-yao*, 17.2b–10a. The wide distribution of these works is seen in the fact that a brigade-general of the *lu-ying* forces thanked the emperor for a copy of the *Jih-chiang Shu-ching chieh-i* brought to him in 1682 (IHPA, bundle 37 of K'ang-hsi *t'i-pen:* a memorial by Wang Ch'ao-hai, dated K'ang-hsi 21/8/4).

31. *KHSL*, pp. 862–63(63.20b–21a) and 1193(89.18).

32. *ECCP*, II, 689.

33. The discussion of this topic took place on 10 and 17 November. Only part of each discussion is recorded in the *shih-lu* (*KHSL*, pp. 604–5 [43.16b, 18]), but complete versions are found in Ch'i-chü-chu draft entries dated K'ang-hsi 12/10/2 and 12/10/9 (*Shih-liao ts'ung-k'an*, I, 400–401 and 408–9).

34. Kenneth Ch'en, *Buddhism in China*, pp. 450–52.

35. This text is found in *KHSL*, pp. 748–49(55.12b–13a). The tutors on this occasion were La-sha-li, Sun Tsai-feng, and Chang Ying.

36. Fung Yu-lan, *Short History*, pp. 195–96; *Sources of Chinese Tradition*, comp. William Theodore de Bary, Wing-tsit Chan, and Burton Watson (New York: Columbia University Press, 1960), pp. 182–83.

37. Bouvet, *Histoire de l'empereur*, pp. 83–84.

38. Henri Bernard, "Les adaptations chinoises d'ouvrages européens," *Monumenta Serica*, X (1945), p. 374, no. 457.

39. It was revised by Father Sabatino de Ursis in 1615, and reprinted in 1629, 1721, 1723, 1773, 1849, 1860, 1865, 1887, 1889, and 1926 (L. Vanhee, "Euclide en chinois et mandchou," *Isis*, XXX [1939], 87–88; *Ts'ung-shu ta-tz'u-tien*, comp. Yang Chia-lo [Nanking, 1936], sec. 2, p. 49, col. 6). The last nine books of the Elements were not translated into Chinese until 1858 under the supervision of Alexander Wylie and Li Shan-lan, a noted Chinese mathematician (*ECCP*, I, 479).

40. Report of Father Sabatino de Ursis, Peking, 1 Sept. 1612, in Pasquale M. D'Elia, *Galileo in China,* trans. Rufus Suter and Matthew Sciascia (Cambridge: Harvard University Press, 1960), p. 67.

41. T. H. Tsien, "Western Impact on China through Translation—a Bibliographical Study" (Ph.D. diss., University of Chicago, 1952), pp. 219–20, tables I and II. The data presented was based on the bibliographical material found in Louis Pfister, *Notices biographiques et bibliographiques sur les Jésuites de l'ancienne mission de Chine (1552–1773),* 2 vols., Variétés Sinologiques, nos. 59–60 (Shanghai: Imprimerie de la Mission Catholique, 1932–34).

42. Chou Ch'ang-shou, "I-k'an k'o-hsüeh shu-chi k'ao-lüeh," in *Chang Chü-sheng hsien-sheng ch'i-shih sheng-jih chi-nien lun-wen-chi,* comp. Hu Shih, et al. (Shanghai: Commercial Press, 1937), pp. 413–20.

43. Bernard, "Les adaptations chinoises," p. 310. Bernard's compilation, which totals 656 titles for the period 1514–1799, was published in three installments in *Monumenta Serica,* X (1945), 1–57 and 309–88; and XIX (1960), 349–83.

44. Letter from Verbiest to Charles de Noyelle, Peking, 15 Sept. 1681, in Bosmans, "Ferdinand Verbiest," p. 389; Le Comte, *Memoirs,* pp. 368–69; *KHSL,* p. 673(49.6b).

45. *KHSL,* pp. 1206(90.15b–16a), 1308(98.7a), and 1356(102.3b); Du Halde, *The Empire of China,* I, 263; letter of Verbiest in Orleans, *Tartar Conquerors,* pp. 123–24. A detailed account of Verbiest's methods of making cannon is given in Bosmans, "Ferdinand Verbiest," pp. 393–400, which is based on the Jesuit's own account; the same work contains a letter of Verbiest to Charles de Noyelle, Peking, 15 Sept. 1681, which mentions the emperor's aiming the cannon.

46. *KHSL,* pp. 790–91(58.8b–9a), 897(66.13), 1111(83.1b), and 1243–44 (93.6a–7a).

47. *KHSL,* p. 555(39.25a–26b).

48. *KHSL,* pp. 815–16(59.30b–31a) and 831–33(61.1a, 4b–5a).

49. Bosmans, "Ferdinand Verbiest," pp. 405–6 and 444–45.

50. Virgile Pinot, *La Chine et la formation de l'esprit philosophique en France (1640–1740)* (Paris: Paul Geuthner, 1932), pp. 44–46; Jean de Fontaney to François de la Chaize, 15 Feb. 1703, in *Lettres édifiantes,* VII, 78–79. The six Jesuits were Jean de Fontaney (leader of the group), Guy Tachard (who was detained in Siam by its king), Jean-François Gerbillon, Louis Le Comte, Claude de Visdelou, and Joachim Bouvet.

51. Fu Lo-shu, *Chronicle,* p. 93, translating a Chinese work of Verbiest; Jean de Fontaney to François de la Chaize, 15 Feb. 1703, in *Lettres édifiantes,* VII, 122–25 and 132; Verbiest to François de la Chaize, 1 Oct. 1687, in Bosmans, "Ferdinand Verbiest," pp. 447–49.

52. Pfister, *Notices,* I, 425–26 and 434; Fu Lo-shu, *Chronicle,* pp. 98–99.

53. Li Yen, *Chung-kuo suan-hsüeh shih* (Shanghai: Commercial Press, 1937), p. 218.

54. The following was taken from the 1699 French edition, *Histoire de l'empereur,* pp. 84–97.

55. One of the other French Jesuits reported that Bouvet and Gerbillon every day spent two hours in the morning and two more in the afternoon

instructing the emperor. Back at their apartment, they would work late into the night preparing their lessons for the next day. When K'ang-hsi went to his summer palace several miles out of Peking, the Jesuits had to set out from the capital at 4 a.m. and did not return until late in the evening (Jean de Fontaney to François de la Chaize, 15 Feb. 1703, in *Lettres édifiantes*, VII, 198–201).

56. This statement is puzzling because presumably they knew of and had access to Verbiest's earlier translation of the Elements.

57. These instruments must have been given to the Jesuits in France before they left for China in 1685. The religious aspect of the Jesuit mission to China, while recognized, was publicly minimized in France and its scientific nature emphasized. Louis XIV gave each Jesuit the title of Royal Mathematician (Guy Tachard, *Voyage de Siam* [Amsterdam: Pierre Mortier, 1687], p. 13), made them correspondents of the Royal Academy (Académie des sciences, *Index biographique des membres et correspondants* . . . [Paris: Gauthier-Villars, 1954], p. 192), and provided them with all the mathematical and astronomical instruments necessary for the project (Jean de Fontaney to François de la Chaize, 15 Feb. 1703, in *Lettres édifiantes*, VII, 89–90).

58. Bouvet left Peking on 8 July 1693, to return to France as K'ang-hsi's personal envoy to Louis XIV (Bouvet, "The Journey of Joachim Bouvet, Jesuit, from Peking to Kanton, When Sent by the Emperor Kang-hi into Europe, in 1693," in *A New General Collection of Voyages and Travels*, vol. III [London: Thomas Astley, 1746], 540). The elided section contained a description of other instruments the Jesuits had given K'ang-hsi.

59. The identity of these two works is puzzling. Some sources refer to the work on the Elements as a revision of the Ricci-Hsü translation of the same, while others take it to be an independent work. One source even claims that the *Chi-ho yüan-pen* in the *Shu-li ching-yün* compilation of 1723 was the work of Bouvet and Gerbillon and not of Ricci and Hsü (Hsiang Ta, *Chung-hsi chiao-t'ung shih* [Shanghai: Chung-hua, 1934], p. 87). The second work on practical geometry apparently was a translation by Bouvet and Gerbillon from Pardies, *Géometrie pratique et théorique*. It is given the Chinese name of *Ying-yung chi-ho*. Neither book was found by Pfister, *Notices*, I, 437 and 449; while Bernard, in "Les adaptations chinoises," X, 365, nos. 552 and 556, found only a xylograph of the second.

60. Bouvet corresponded with the German philosopher Leibniz on the possibility of establishing a Chinese Academy, to parallel the French Academy, consisting of five or six Jesuits to gather information sought by European scientists and scholars (Bouvet to Leibniz, Peking, 4 Nov. 1701, in *Mémoirs de Trevoux*, 1704, pp. 152–53; Bouvet to Leibniz, Peking, 8 Nov. 1702, in *G. G. Leibnitii* . . . *opera omnia*, ed. Ludovici Dutens, 6 vols. [Geneva: De Tournes, 1768], IV, pt. I, 168; Donald Lach, "Leibniz and China," *Journal of the History of Ideas*, VI [1945], 436 n. 2).

61. Orleans, *Tartar Conquerors*, p. 96.

62. Bouvet, *Histoire de l'empereur*, pp. 99–107.

63. Pfister, *Notices*, I, 434. Gheradini has left an account, *Relation du*

voyage fait à la Chine sur le vaisseau l'Ampithitrite en l'année 1698 (Paris, 1700).

64. *Histoire des ouvrages des savants,* XIV (Aug. 1698), 350; *The History of the Works of the Learned,* I (June 1699), 364; *ECCP,* I, 331, quoting Ripa's *Memoirs.*

65. *KHSL,* p. 2076(154.3a).

66. Fu Lo-shu, *Chronicle,* pp. 112–13, translating Kao's *P'eng-shan mi-chi* (see *ECCP,* I, 414 on this work).

67. Wang Hao, *Sui-luan chi-en,* abstracted in Fu Lo-shu, "Sino-Western Relations during the K'ang-hsi Period, 1661–1722" (Ph.D. diss., University of Chicago, 1952), pp. 315–20. Wang was one of four *chü-jen* who served in the Imperial Study in 1703, and later that year he became a *chin-shih.* He helped compile an imperially commissioned work on botany (*ECCP,* I, 21; II, 701 and 821).

68. Two letters of Verbiest, in Orleans, *Tartar Conquerors,* pp. 104 and 115–16.

69. Spence, *Ts'ao Yin,* pp. 256–57 and 259–60.

70. Sven Hedin, *Jehol, City of Emperors,* trans. E. G. Nash (New York: E. P. Dutton, 1933), p. 141; the edict he translated is found in *KHSL,* pp. 2093–94(155.5a–7a). On the history of early-ripening rice in China and its demographic and economic effects, see Ping-ti Ho, "Early-Ripening Rice in Chinese History," *Economic History Review,* 2d ser., IX (Dec. 1956), 200–218; and the same author's *Population,* pp. 169–76.

71. Spence, *Ts'ao Yin,* pp. 278–81.

72. Li Yen, *Chung-kuo suan-hsüeh shih,* p. 222; *HTSL,* p. 18092 (1103.1b–2a). In 1675 the student quotas were reduced to 14 Chinese, plus 2 Manchus and 1 Chinese from each banner (*HTSL,* p. 18092[1103.2b]).

73. *HTSL,* p. 18087(1102.10b).

74. Bouvet, *Histoire de l'empereur,* p. 97.

75. For their biographies, see Juan Yüan, *Ch'ou-jen chuan* (1799 ed.; Shanghai: Commercial Press, 1935), *chüan* 34–42; also *CS, chüan* 505.

76. *ECCP,* I, 569–71.

77. The movement was full-blown in the nineteenth century through the efforts of Lo Shih-lin and Tai Chen (*ECCP,* I, 539–40; II, 696–97).

78. Spence, *To Change China,* chap. 1; Antonio S. Rosso, O.F.M., *Apostolic Legations to China of the Eighteenth Century* (South Pasadena: P.D. and Ione Perkins, 1948).

79. Ping-ti Ho, *Ladder of Success,* pp. 111–14 and 189 (table 22). His figures are rounded off to the nearest digit. Individual figures for nine examinations in the Shun-chih and K'ang-hsi periods are given on pp. 112–13 (table 9) of the same work. There is some indication that Ming loyalist *chü-jen* were not welcome at metropolitan examinations (Liu Hsien-t'ing, *Kuang-yang tsa-chi,* p. 166).

80. Chang Chung-li, *The Chinese Gentry* (Seattle: University of Washington Press, 1955), p. 157, table 27.

81. Ping-ti Ho, *Ladder of Success,* pp. 178–79.

82. Chang Chung-li, *The Chinese Gentry,* pp. 74–75 and 77, citing *HTSL;* a Shanghai history recorded the date of this change as 1659 and gave

slightly different figures for the new quotas: 15, 10, and 7–8 (Yeh Meng-chu, *Yüeh-shih pien*, 2.1).

83. *HCTI*, 14.13: a memorial by Yao T'ing-ch'i.

84. Yeh Meng-chu, *Yüeh-shih pien*, 2.2. Quotas varied from one province or district to another (Chang Chung-li, *The Chinese Gentry*, p. 78).

85. Spence, *Ts'ao Yin*, pp. 73–74.

86. *KHSL*, p. 200(12.19b–20a). The emperor denied their request.

87. Ping-ti Ho, *Ladder of Success*, pp. 30, 33, and 46.

88. Hsü Ta-ling, *Ch'ing-tai chüan-na chih-tu* (Peking: Harvard-Yenching Institute, 1950), p. 23; Ping-ti Ho; *Ladder of Success*, p. 30.

89. Ping-ti Ho, *Ladder of Success*, p. 179; Yeh Meng-chu, *Yüeh-shih pien*, 2.2b.

90. *CSLC*, 7.32b. Some date the origin of the sale of offices as 1675 (Hsü Ta-ling, *Chüan-na*, pp. 23–25).

91. Yeh Meng-chu, *Yüeh-shih pien*, 2.2; Ping-ti Ho, *Ladder of Success*, pp. 179–80.

92. Hsü Ta-ling, *Chüan-na*, p. 131.

93. Ibid., pp. 13–14 and 25–26; *CSLC*, 8.8b.

94. Hsü Ta-ling, *Chüan-na*, pp. 129–30; *HCTI*, 21.45a–47a; *CS*, p. 3817.9.

95. Hsü Ta-ling, *Chüan-na*, pp. 26–27. This had been done earlier (ibid., p. 23; *HCTI*, 21.18a).

96. Ping-ti Ho, *Ladder of Success*, pp. 112–13, table 9.

97. *KHSL*, p. 1526(114.19b–20b).

98. Balazs, *Political Theory*, p. 32.

99. *KHSL*, p. 960(71.11a–12a).

100. *ECCP*, I, 353 states that Huang managed to have his name excluded from the list of competitors, but he is included in the list compiled by Ch'in Ying, *Chi-wei tz'u-k'o lu* (1807).

101. Wilhelm, "*Po-hsüeh*," p. 64.

102. *ECCP*, I, 261; Meng Shen, "Chi-wei tz'u-k'o-lu wai-lu," in id., *Ming-Ch'ing shih-lun-chu chi-k'an*, pp. 499–500 and 502.

103. *KHSL*, p. 1017(75.18).

104. Meng Shen, "Chi-wei wai-lu," p. 498: "Wu sui Chou Yung, shih Shang-yung yeh."

105. *KHSL*, pp. 1067(79.22) and 1071(80.1b). The official record states that only 143 scholars took the examination; the figure of 152 is based on lists in Ch'in Ying, *Chi-wei tz'u-k'o lu*.

106. After 1675, Chinese grand secretary appointees were beginning to come from provinces other than the four northern ones that had monopolized the body previously; also, the new appointees, unlike their older colleagues, had not acquired their *chin-shih* degrees under the Ming dynasty or in the 1646 examination dominated by northerners (see the grand secretary table in Yen Mao-kung *Ch'ing-tai cheng-hsien lei-pien*; and chap. 2, n. 50, above). For the shift in top provincial posts, see Kessler, "Provincial Leadership," pp. 496–99.

107. Meng Shen, "Tsou-hsiao an," p. 450; *ECCP*, II, 863; *CS*, p. 3813.5.

108. *CSLC*, 70.34a; *ECCP*, I, 167–68; Meng Shen, "Chi-wei wai-lu," p. 510.

109. *ECCP*, II, 840; Meng Shen, "Tsou-hsiao an," p. 450; *KHSL*, p. 1568(117.12b).

110. Meng Shen, "Tsou-hsiao an," p. 442; *CSLC*, 70.45a. Six other recommendees who did not participate in the examination were similarly honored.

111. The other three were the current Chinese grand secretaries—Li Wei, Feng P'u, and Tu Li-te—who together had jointly recommended eight men for the examination (Ch'in Ying, *Chi-wei tz'u-k'o-lu*, Foreword, 2b–3a; *CSLC*, 7.39b).

112. Wilhelm, "*Po-hsueh*," pp. 63–64.

113. Peterson, "Ku Yen-wu," pp. 132 and 235–36; *ECCP*, II, 902.

114. Ch'in Ying, *Chi-wei tz'u-k'o lu*, Foreword, 3a–9a; *KHSL*, pp. 1077 (80.14) and 1089(81.5).

115. Meng Shen, "Chi-wei wai-lu," p. 496.

116. Ibid., p. 502; *CSLC*, 70.34b.

117. Meng Shen, "Chi-wei wai-lu," pp. 502–3; *KHSL*, p. 1335(100.10a).

118. *ECCP*, I, 183; II, 606; Meng Shen, "Chi-wei wai-lu," pp. 502–5.

119. Spence, *Ts'ao Yin*, pp. 50–51, 62–63, and 67–68; *ECCP*, II, 662.

120. *ECCP*, II, 909.

121. *SCSL*, p. 468(41.15b–16a).

122. *KHSL*, p. 250(16.11b–12a).

123. *KHSL*, pp. 259–60(17.2b–3a).

124. *KHSL*, p. 1090(81.8b).

125. *KHSL*, pp. 1179–80(88.18b–19a).

126. *ECCP*, I, 353; II, 615; *CSLC*, 9.35b.

127. *ECCP*, II, 802–3 and 826.

128. Peterson, "Ku Yen-wu," pp. 242–43.

129. Balazs, *Political Theory*, p. 39; *CHLC*, p. 12237(403.32b).

130. *KHSL*, p. 1370(103.3b–4a).

131. *KHSL*, pp. 1484(111.32) and 1505(113.6); Harold Kahn, "Some Mid-Ch'ing Views of the Monarchy," *Journal of Asian Studies*, XXIV (Feb. 1965), 233–34; *K'ang-hsi cheng-yao*, 17.21b–22a, 25a–26b; Spence, *Emperor of China*, pp. 88–89.

132. See the judgments of Yang Lien-sheng, Wolfgang Franke, and Paul Demiéville in separate articles in *Historians of China and Japan*, ed. W. G. Beasley and E. G. Pulleyblank (London: Oxford University Press, 1961), pp. 55, 61, and 167.

133. Nivison, *Chang Hsüeh-ch'eng*, p. 6 and note.

Chapter Seven

1. Chang Te-ch'ang, "Imperial Household," pp. 247–50.

2. For a discussion of this problem, see Mi Chu Wiens, "Anti-Manchu Thought during the Early Ch'ing," (Harvard) *Papers on China*, XXII-A (May 1969), 1–24.

3. Nivison, *Chang Hsüeh-ch'eng*, p. 6.

4. Meng Shen, *Ch'ing-tai shih*, p. 171; Fang Chao-ying in *ECCP*, I,

329–31; Liu Ta-nien, "Lun K'ang-hsi," in id., *Chung-kuo chin-tai-shih chu-wen-t'i* (Peking: Jen-min, 1965), p. 183.

5. Nivison, *Chang Hsüeh-ch'eng,* p. 18.

6. Ibid., p. 17.

7. Spence, *Ts-ao Yin,* pp. 129–30.

8. See Liu Ta-nien, "Lun K'ang-hsi," esp. pp. 183–87. This essay was originally published in *Li-shih yen-chiu,* 1961, no. 3, pp. 5–21. Liu wrote at a time when Chinese historians were reappraising China's past, giving more emphasis to national and cultural development and the persons who contributed to it, and less to theoretical history of faceless social forces (see Albert Feuerwerker, "China's History in Marxian Dress," *American Historical Review,* LXVI [Jan. 1961], 348–53). The need to promote patriotism and national heroes in face of the growing Sino-Soviet dispute undoubtedly sparked this transformation of Chinese historiography.

GLOSSARY

A-ssu-ha 阿思哈
Abahai 阿巴海
Aisin-Gioro 愛新覺羅
Ajige 阿濟格
Amin 阿敏
Ananda 阿南達
Anking 安慶
Ata 阿塔

Bahai 巴海
Bahana 巴哈納
Bambursan 班布尔善
Batai 巴泰
Becingge 白清額
booi amban 包衣昂邦
Burni 布尔尼

Cani 察尼
Chai-miu lun 摘謬論
Chang Ch'ien 張汧
Chang-chou 漳州
Chang Hsien-chung 張獻忠
Chang Kuang-ssu 張廣泗

GLOSSARY

Chang Po-hsing	張伯行
Chang So-chih	張所知
Chang Ying	張英
Chang Yung	張勇
Chang Yü-shu	張玉書
chang-yüan hsüeh-shih	掌院學士
Ch'ang-chou	常州
Ch'ang-ch'un-yüan	暢春園
Ch'ang-ning	常寧
Ch'ang-te	常德
Changsha	長沙
Chao Liang-tung	趙良棟
Chao T'ing-ch'en	趙廷臣
Ch'ao-chou	潮州
Chen-ting	真定
Ch'en Shen	陳慎
Ch'en T'ing-ching	陳廷敬
Ch'en Tzu-chuang	陳子壯
Cheng Ch'eng-kung	鄭成功
Cheng Chih-lung	鄭芝龍
Cheng Ching	鄭經
Cheng K'o-shuang	鄭克塽
ch'eng-chih	稱旨
Chenkiang	鎮江
Chi Chen-i	季振宜
Chi-ho yüan-pen	幾何原本
Chi K'ai-sheng	季開生
Chi-shih	濟世
Ch'i-chü-chu	起居注
ch'i-fen tso-ling	旗分佐領
chia-chih	家之
chia-p'ai	加派
chia-ti	家的
chia-tzu	甲子
chiang-chün	將軍
Chiang He-te	蔣赫德
Chiang-tso san-ta-chia	江左三大家

Chieh-shan 介山
chien 監
chien-cheng 監正
Chien-chou 建州
chien-fu 監副
chien-pi ch'ing-yeh 監壁清野
chien-sheng 監生
Ch'ien Ch'ien-i 錢謙益
Ch'ien-ch'ing 乾清
Ch'ien Tseng 錢曾
ch'ih-shu 勅書
ch'ih-yü 勅諭
Chin Chih-chün 金之俊
Chin Chün 金儁
Chin Fu 靳輔
Chin Jen-jui 金人瑞
Chin-men (Quemoy) 金門
Chin Pao 金寶
chin-shih 進士
Chin Shih-chien 金世鑑
Ch'in Sung-ling 秦松齡
ch'in-t'ien-chien 欽天監
ch'in-wang 親王
Ching-chou 荊州
Ching-hai 靖海
ching-lüeh 經略
Ching-nan wang 靖南王
ching-yen chiang-kuan 經筵講官
ch'ing 頃
Ch'ing-yüan 慶元
Chou Yu-te 周有德
Chou Yung 周容
Chu Ch'ang-tso 朱昌祚
Chu I-tsun 朱彝尊
Chu Kuo-chen 朱國楨
Chu Kuo-chih 朱國治
Chu San-t'ai-tzu 朱三太子

Chu Shao-feng 朱紹鳳
Chu Tz'u-huan 朱慈煥
Chu Yu-lang 朱由榔
Chuang T'ing-lung 莊廷鑨
chuang-yüan 狀元
ch'un-fen, ch'iu-fen 春分 秋分
Chung-yung 中庸
Ch'ung-ming 崇明
Chusan 舟山
chü-jen 舉人
Ch'ü Ta-chün 屈大均
chüan-na 捐納
ch'üan-ti 圈地
Ch'üan-chou 泉州
chün-tzu 君子
chün-wang 君王
Cokto 綽克託

Dadu 達都
Daisan 代善
Degelei 德格類
Dodo 多鐸
Dongge 洞鄂
Donggo 董鄂
Doni 多尼
Dorbo 多爾博
Dorgon 多爾袞
Duikana 對喀納

E-su-li 額蘇哩
Ebilun 遏必隆
Eidu 額亦都

Fan Chung-yen 范仲淹
Fang Hsiao-piao 方孝標
Fang Kuang-chen 方觀永
Fei Mi 費密

Feng Ch'üan 馮銓
Feng-jun 豐潤
Feng P'u 馮溥
feng-shui 風水
feng-wen 風聞
Fengtien 奉天
Fiyanggu 飛揚古
fu-chiang 副將
Fu-ch'üan 福全
Fu-lin 福臨
Fu Shan 傅山
Fu She 復社
fu-tu-t'ung 副都統

Gabuli 噶布拉
Galdan 噶尔丹
Gali 噶禮
gashen 嘎山
Ghantimur 根特木
Giyabuja 賈卜嘉
Giyesu 傑書
gusai ejen 固山額真
Guwalgiya 瓜尔佳

Hai-ch'eng 海澄
Hai-ch'eng kung 海澄公
hai-chin 海禁
Hai-yen 海鹽
Han-chung 漢中
Han Shih-ch'i 韓世琦
Han T'an 韓菼
Hao Yü 郝浴
Haoge 豪格
Heng-yang 衡陽
Heseri 赫舍里
Hife 希福
ho-she e-fu 和碩額駙

Ho Yu	何佑
hosoi beile	和碩貝勒
Hsi-chu	席柱
hsi-hsüan	西選
hsia-chih	夏至
Hsia-men (Amoy)	廈門
hsia wu-ch'i	下五旗
Hsiang-yang	襄陽
Hsiao-ch'eng	孝誠
Hsiao-ching yen-i	孝經衍義
Hsiao-chuang	孝莊
Hsiao-hsien	孝獻
hsiao-jen	小人
Hsiao-k'ang	孝康
Hsiao-lieh	孝烈
Hsiao-tz'u	孝慈
Hsing-kuo	興國
hsiu-ts'ai	秀才
Hsiung I-hsiao	熊一瀟
Hsiung Tz'u-li	熊賜履
Hsü Ch'ien-hsüeh	徐乾學
Hsü Kuang-ch'i	徐光啓
Hsü Yüan-wen	徐元文
Hsüan-tse i	選擇議
hsüeh-shih	學士
hsün-fu	巡撫
hu-chün t'ung-ling	護軍統領
Hu Mi-se	胡密色
Hu Shih-an	胡世安
Hu Tsai-ko	胡在恪
Huai-jou	懷柔
huang-kuei-fei	皇貴妃
Huang Tsung-hsi	黃宗羲
Huang Wu	黃梧
Hui-chou	惠州
hui-tien	會典
Hung Ch'eng-ch'ou	洪承疇

hung-i p'ao 紅夷砲
Hung-wen-yüan 宏文院
huo-ch'i-ying 火器營

i-cheng wang-ta-ch'en 議政王大臣
i hsi-yang hsin-fa 依西洋新法
I-tu 益都
Ilibu 宜里布
Ingguldai 英武尔岱

Jangtai 彰泰
Jen Wei-ch'u 任維初
jen-wu 人物
Jidu 濟度
jih-chiang kuan 日講官
Jih-chiang I-ching (Shih-ching, Shu-ching, Ssu-shu) chieh-i 日講易經(詩經,書經,四書)解義
Jih-chih lu 日知錄
Jirgalang 濟尔哈朗
ju-mu 乳母
Juchen 女真
Jung 榮

Kan Wen-k'un 甘文焜
K'ang-hsi 康熙
Kao Shih-ch'i 高士奇
Ke-er-ku-te 格尔古德
Keng Chi-mao 耿繼茂
Keng Ching-chung 耿精忠
Keng Chung-ming 耿仲明
Kiangning 江寧
Kirin 吉林
Ko-ch'u-ha 噶褚哈
K'o-ch'un 恪純
k'ou-hun 叩閽
Ku Ju-hua 顧如華
Ku Tsu-yü 顧祖禹

Ku Yen-wu 顧炎武
k'u-miao an 哭廟案
K'uai-chi 會稽
kung-sheng 貢生
Kung Ting-tzu 龔鼎孳
K'ung Yu-te 孔有德
Kuo Hsiu 郭琇
Kuo Shih-ching 郭士璟
kuo-shih-yüán 國史院
kuo-tzu-chien 國子監
kuo-yung 國雍
Kwei yang 桂陽

La-sha-li 喇沙里
Labu 喇布
Laita 賚塔
Lambu 蘭布
Langtan 郎坦
Ledehun 勒德洪
Lergiyen 勒尔謹
Li Chih-fang 李之芳
Li Ch'ing 李清
li-ch'un, li-ch'iu 立春 立秋
li-fan yüan 理藩院
Li Hsü 李煦
Li Kuang-ti 李光地
Li Shih-chen 李士楨
Li Shuai-t'ai 李率泰
Li Tzu-ch'eng 李自成
Li Wei 李蔚
Li-yang 溧陽
Li Yin-tu 李因篤
Li Yung 李顒
Liang-chou 涼州
Lien-ch'uan 練川
Lin Hsing-chu 林興珠
ling-ch'ih 凌遲

ling-sheng 廩生
Liu Chih-yüan 劉之源
Liu Ch'ing-t'ai 劉清泰
Liu Kuang 劉光
Liu K'un 劉崑
Liu Kuo-hsüan 劉國軒
Liu Pang-chu 劉邦柱
Liu Ping-ch'üan 劉秉權
liu-t'ou pu liu-fa 留頭不留髮
Liu Wu-yüan 劉武元
Liu Yü-yu 劉餘祐
Lo Shih-lin 羅士琳
Loto 羅多
Lu Hsing-tsu 盧興祖
lu-ying 綠營

Mahu 馬祜
Mai-yin-ta 邁音達
Mala 瑪喇
Manggitu 莽依圖
Manggultai 莽古尔泰
Mao Wen-lung 毛文龍
Margi 麻勒吉
Marsai 瑪尔賽
Mei Ku-ch'eng 梅轂成
Mei Wen-ting 梅文鼎
men-hu 門戶
Meng-yang-chai 蒙養齋
min-ping 民兵
Ming-i tai-fang lu 明夷待訪錄
Mingju 明珠
Mishan 米思翰
Molo 莫洛
mokun 莫昆
Murma 穆里瑪

Nan-shu-fang 南書房

Nan-t'ang 南堂
Nanchang 南昌
Nara 納喇
nei-ko 內閣
nei-ko chung-shu 內閣中書
nei-san-yüan 內三院
nei shih-san ya-men 內十三衙門
nei-wu-fu 內務府
Nikan 尼堪
Ningpo 甯波
Ninguta 寧古塔
Niohuru 鈕祜祿
niru 牛彔
niru ejen 牛彔額真
No-mo 訥莫
Nurhaci 努尔哈赤

O-er-t'ai 鄂尔泰
Oboi 鼇拜
Oja 鄂扎
Ou-yang Hsiu 歐陽修

Pa-ko 巴格
P'an Ch'eng-chang 潘檉章
P'an Chin-hsiao 潘盡孝
P'an Lei 潘耒
pao-i tso-ling 包衣佐領
pao-mu 保姆
pao-wen 報聞
P'eng Sun-i 彭孫貽
P'eng Sun-yü 彭孫遹
P'eng-tang lun 朋黨論
Pengcun 朋春
pi-shu-yüan 秘書院
Pi-yung 辟雍
p'iao 票
p'ing-hai ts'e 平海策

P'ing-hsi wang 平西王
P'ing-nan wang 平南王
po-hsüeh hung-tz'u 博學宏詞
pu-hsü 不許
Pu-te-i 不得以

Sabsu 薩布素
Sai-k'o-te 塞克德
Sai-pen-t'e 塞本特
San-fan 三藩
sao-i mu-t'ien 掃迹木天
Shan-hai-kuan 山海關
shang 晌
Shang Chih-hsin 尚之信
Shang K'o-hsi 尚可喜
shang san-ch'i 上三旗
Shang-shan 尚善
Shao Ch'ang-heng 邵長蘅
Shao-kan 邵甘
Sheng-ching 盛京
sheng-hsün 聖訓
sheng-yüan 生員
Shih Lang 施琅
Shih Wei-han 施維翰
shih-wei nei-ta-ch'en 侍衛內大臣
shou-ling 首領
shou-pei 守備
Shun-i 順義
shun shui-hsing hsiu-chih 順水性修治
Shuntien 順天
Sian 西安
Singde 性德
Songgotu 索額圖
Soni 索尼
Sose 碩色
ssu pu-i 四布衣
ssu-ta beile 四大貝勒

ssu-yeh	司業
Su-ch'ien	宿遷
Su-Sung	蘇松
Subai	蘇拜
Suksaha	蘇克薩哈
Sun Ch'i-feng	孫奇逢
Sun K'o-wang	孫可望
Sun Ssu-k'o	孫思克
Sun T'ing-ch'üan	孫廷銓
Sun Tsai-feng	孫在豐
Sun Yen-ling	孫延齡
Suna	蘇納
Sunahai	蘇納海
Sung-chiang	松江
Sung Lao	宋犖
Sung Te-i	宋德宜
Sung Wen-lien	宋文連
ta-chiang-chün	大將軍
Ta-hsüeh	大學
ta-hsüeh-shih	大學士
Ta-hsüeh yen-i	大學衍義
Tai Chen	戴震
Tai Ming-shih	戴名世
T'ai-chou	臺州
Taibitu	泰壁圖
Taiyuan	太原
t'an-hua	探花
t'an-hua pu-chih i-wen-ch'ien	探花不值一文錢
Tantai	譚泰
tang	黨
T'ang Pin	湯斌
t'ao-jen	逃人
Tatara	他搭喇
te-chih	得旨
te-chih i, chih-chih nan	得之易治之難
Te-chou	德州

t'i-tu 提督

T'ien-hsüeh chuan-kai 天學傳概

Ting-nan wang 定南王

t'ing-wang chieh-chih 聽王節制

t'ou-ch'ung 投充

Ts'ai Chang 蔡璋

Ts'ai Yü-jung 蔡毓榮

Ts'ao Fu 曹頫

Ts'ao Jung 曹溶

Ts'ao Yin 曹寅

tso-ling 佐領

tsou-hsiao an 奏銷案

tsung-kuan 總管

tsung-kuan nei-wu-fu ta-ch'en 總管內務府大臣

tsung-ping 總兵

tsung-tu 總督

Tu Chen 都臻

tu-fu 督撫

Tu Li-te 杜立德

tu-t'ung 都統

Tu Yüeh 杜越

t'uan-lien 團練

Tuhai 圖海

Tulai 圖賴

t'un-t'ien 屯田

Tuna 圖納

Tunci 屯齊

Tung Kuo-hsing 董國興

Tung-lin 東林

Tung Wei-kuo 董衛國

T'ung-an 同安

T'ung-chien kang-mu 通鑑綱目

T'ung-chou 通州

T'ung-i 佟義

T'ung Kuo-kang 佟國綱

T'ung Kuo-wei 佟國維

T'ung-shan 銅山

t'ung-shih 通事
T'ung-t'ing 洞庭
T'ung T'u-lai 佟圖賴
Tuntai 屯泰
Tzu-chih t'ung-chien 資治通鑑

Uya 烏雅

Walihu 瓦禮祜
Wan Cheng-se 萬正色
Wan Ssu-t'ung 萬斯同
Wang Ch'ao-hai 王朝海
Wang Ch'i-tso 王啓祚
Wang Chin-pao 王進寶
Wang Fu-ch'en 王輔臣
Wang Fu-chih 王夫之
Wang Hao 王昊
Wang Hsi 王熙
Wang Hung-hsü 王鴻緒
Wang Kung-chi 王公紀
Wang Lai-jen 王來任
Wang Shih-chen 王世貞
Wang Teng-lien 王登聯
Wang Wan 汪琬
Wang Yü-yü 王于玉
Wehe 倭赫
Wei Chung-hsien 魏忠賢
Wei Hsiang-shu 魏象樞
Wei I-chieh 魏裔介
Wei-wu 威武
Wen-chou 温州
Wen-hua 文華
wen-kuan 文官
wen-wu 文武
Wu Cheng-chih 吳正治
Wu Chih-jung 吳之榮
wu-ching po-shih 五經博士

Wu-hsien 吳縣
Wu Hsing-tso 吳興祚
Wu Ke-sai 吳格塞
Wu Liang-fu 吳良輔
Wu Ming-hsüan 吳明烜
Wu San-kuei 吳三桂
Wu Shih-fan 吳世璠
wu sui Chou Yung, shih Shang-yung yeh 吾雖周容實尚容也
Wu-t'ai-shan 五臺山
Wu Wei-yeh (Mei-ts'un) 吳偉業(梅村)
Wu Yen 吳炎
Wu Ying-hsiung 吳應熊
Wuchang 武昌

Ya-ssu-ha 雅思哈
Yang Ch'i-lung 楊起隆
Yang Kuang-hsien 楊光先
Yang Lien 楊漣
yang-lien 養廉
Yang Mao-hsün 楊茂勳
Yang Su-yün 楊素蘊
Yang Yung-chien 楊雍建
Yao Ch'i-sheng 姚啓聖
Yao Ti-yü 姚締虞
Yao T'ing-ch'i 姚廷啓
Yeh Fang-ai 葉方藹
Yeh Fang-heng 葉方恒
yeh han-lin 野翰林
Yen Jo-chü 閻若璩
Yen Sheng-sun 嚴繩孫
Yenchow 兗州
yin 蔭
Yin-chih 胤祉
Yin-jeng 胤礽
Ying-yung chi-ho 應用幾何
Yolo 岳樂
Yoto 岳託

yu-ts'an-i	右參議
Yung-p'ing	永平府
Yunnan-fu	雲南府
Yü Ch'eng-lung	于成龍
Yü Kuo-chu	余國柱
yü-shui	雨水
yüan	院
Yüeh-chou	岳州
Yün-t'ai-shan	雲臺山

BIBLIOGRAPHY

Chinese Primary Sources

Academia Sinica (Taiwan). Institute of History and Philology. Miscellaneous Archives from the Grand Secretariat 內閣大庫殘餘檔案.

Chao I 趙翼. "P'ing-ting san-ni shu-lüeh 平定三逆述略." *Huang-ch'ao wu-kung chi-sheng* 皇朝武功紀盛. Ts'ung-shu chi-ch'eng ed. Shanghai: Commercial Press, 1935.

Chiang Ch'en-ying 姜宸英. *Hai-fang tsung-lun* 海防總論. *Chiang hsien-sheng ch'üan-chi* 姜先生全集. Chüan 1. N.p., 1918.

Chiang Jih-sheng 江日昇. *Tai-wan wai-chi* 臺灣外記. Preface dated 1704. Tainan, 1956.

Chin Te-ch'un 金德純. *Ch'i-chün-chih* 旗軍志. Dated 1715. Hsüeh-hai lei-pien 學海類編 ed. Vol. XL. Shanghai: Commercial Press, 1920.

Ch'in Ying 秦瀛. *Chi-wei tz'u-k'o lu* 己未詞科錄. N.p., 1807.

Ch'ing-ch'ao yeh-shih ta-kuan 清朝野史大觀. 5 Parts. Taipei: Chung-hua, 1959.

Ch'ing-shih 清史. Taipei: Kuo-fang yen-chiu-yüan, 1961.

Ch'ing-shih lieh-chuan 清史列傳. Shanghai, 1928. Reprinted Taipei: Chung-hua, 1962.

Chung-hua min-kuo k'ai-kuo wu-shih-nien wen-hsien 中華民國開國五十年文獻. Vol. I, book I: *Ke-ming yüan-yüan* 革命遠源. Taipei, 1963.

Hsia Lin 夏琳. *Hai-chi chi-yao* 海紀輯要. T'ai-wan wen-hsien ts'ung-k'an, no. 22. Taipei: Bank of Taiwan, 1958.

Hsin-ch'ou chi-wen 辛丑紀聞. Chi-tsai hui-pien 紀載彙編 ed. Vol. IV. Peking, n.d.

Huang-ch'ao tz'u-lin tien-ku 皇朝詞林典故. Compiled by Chu Kuei 朱珪. Kuang-hsü 12 (1886) ed.

Huang-Ch'ing k'ai-kuo fang-lüeh 皇清開國方略. 1789 ed.

Huang-Ch'ing ming-ch'en tsou-i 皇清名臣奏議. Chia-ch'ing ed.

K'ang-hsi cheng-yao 康熙政要. Compiled by Chang Shen 章梫. Hsüan-t'ung 2 (1910) ed.

K'ang-hsi hui-tien 康熙會典. Preface dated 1690.

Kuo-ch'ao ch'i-hsien lei-cheng ch'u-pien 國朝耆獻類徵初編. Edited by Li Huan 李桓. Hunan, 1884–90. Reprinted Taipei, 1966.

Liu Hsien-t'ing 劉獻廷. *Kuang-yang tsa-chi* 廣陽雜記. [Compiled c. 1694]. Taipei: Shih-chieh, 1962.

Man-chou ming-ch'en chuan 滿洲名臣傳. N.p., n.d.

Ming-Ch'ing shih-liao 明清史料. Compiled by Academia Sinica, Institute of History and Philology. Series III and IV. Shanghai: Commercial Press, 1936, 1951.

Pa-ch'i t'ung-chih 八旗通志. 1799 ed.

Pei-chuan chi 碑傳集. Kiangsu, 1893.

Sheng-ching t'ung-chih 盛京通志. 1736 ed. Reprinted Taipei, 1965.

Shih-liao ts'ung-k'an ch'u-pien 史料叢刊初編. Compiled by Lo Chen-yü 羅振玉. 2 Vols. Taipei: Wen-hai, 1964.

Shun-chih yüan-nien nei-wai-kuan shu tsou-su 順治元年內外官署奏疏. Preface by Chu Hsi tsu 朱希祖. Peking, 1931.

Ta-Ch'ing hui-tien shih-li 大清會典事例. Kuang-hsü ed. Taipei: Ch'i-wen, 1963.

Ta-Ch'ing Sheng-tsu Jen-huang-ti shih-lu 大清聖祖仁皇帝實錄. Mukden, 1937. Reprinted Taipei: Hua-lien, 1964.

Ta-Ch'ing Shih-tsu Chang-huang-ti shih-lu 大清世祖章皇帝實錄. Mukden, 1937. Reprinted Taipei: Hua-lien, 1964.

Ta-Ch'ing T'ai-tsu Kao-huang-ti shih-lu 大清太祖高皇帝實錄. Mukden, 1937. Reprinted Taipei: Hua-lien, 1964.

Tu Chen 杜臻. *Hai-fang lüeh-shu* 海防略述. [Written c. 1684.] Hsüeh-hai lei-pien 學海類編 ed. Vol XLVI. Shanghai: Commercial Press, 1920.

Wei Yüan 魏源. *Sheng-wu chi* 聖武記. Completed in 1842. Ssu-pu pei-yao ed. Taipei: Chung-hua, 1962.

Yeh Meng-chu 葉夢珠. *Yüeh-shih pien* 閱世編. Shang-hai chang-ku ts'ung-shu ed. Ser. I. Vols. III–V. Shanghai, 1936.

Chinese Secondary and Reference Works

Chang Chin-chien 張金鑑. "Chung-kuo li-tai tsai-fu chih-tu ti yen-pien

中國歷代宰輔制度的演變." *Cheng-chih ta-hsüeh hsüeh-pao* 政治大學學報, VI (Dec. 1962), 1–24.

Ch'en Wen-shih 陳文石. "Man-chou pa-ch'i niu-lu ti kou-ch'eng 滿洲八旗牛彔的構成." *Ta-lu tsa-chih* 大陸雜誌, 15 November 1965, pp. 266–70; 30 November 1965, pp. 314–18.

Cheng Ho-sheng 鄭鶴聲. *Chin-shih chung-hsi shih-jih tui-chao-piao* 近世中西史日對照表. Taipei: Commercial Press, 1962.

Cheng T'ien-t'ing 鄭天挺. *Ch'ing-shih t'an-wei* 清史探微. Nanking: Tu-li, 1946.

Ch'ien Mu 錢穆. *Kuo-shih ta-kang* 國史大綱. Taipei: Commercial Press, 1960.

Chou Ch'ang-shou 周昌壽. "I-k'an k'o-hsüeh shu-chi k'ao-lüeh 譯刊科學書籍考略." *Chang Chü-sheng hsien-sheng ch'i-shih sheng-jih chi-nien lun-wen chi* 張菊生先生七十生日紀念論文集. Compiled by Hu Shih 胡適, et al. Shanghai: Commercial Press, 1937.

Chu Hsi-tsu 朱希祖. "Cheng Yen-p'ing-wang shou Ming kuan-chüeh k'ao 鄭延平王受明官爵考." *Kuo-hsüeh chi-k'an* 國學季刊, III, no. 1 (1932), 87–112.

———. "Wu San-kuei Chou-wang chi-yüan shih-i 吳三桂周王紀元釋疑." *Li-shih yü-yen yen-chiu-so chi-k'an* 歷史語言研究所集刊, II (1930–32), 393–401.

Chu P'eng-shou 朱彭壽. *Chiu-tien pei-cheng* 舊典備徵. N.p., 1936.

Fu Tsung-mao 傅宗懋. "Ch'ing-ch'u i-cheng t'i-chih chih yen-chiu 清初議政體制之研究." *Cheng-chih ta-hsüeh hsüeh-pao* 政治大學學報 XI (May 1965), 245–94.

Hsiang Ta 向達. *Chung-hsi chiao-t'ung shih* 中西交通史. Shanghai: Chung-hua, 1934.

Hsiao I-shan 蕭一山. *Ch'ing-tai t'ung-shih* 清代通史. 5 vols. Rev. ed. Taipei: Commercial Press, 1962–63.

———. *Chung-kuo chin-tai-shih kai-yao* 中國近代史概要. Taipei: San-min, 1963.

Hsu Ta-ling 許大齡. *Ch'ing-tai chüan-na chih-tu* 清代捐納制度. Peking: Harvard-Yenching Institute, 1950.

Li Hsün 李洵. *Ming-Ch'ing shih* 明清史. Peking: Jen-min, 1957.

Li Kuang-pi 李光璧. "Ming-mo nung-min ta-ch'i 明末農民大起義." *Ming-Ch'ing shih-lun ts'ung* 明清史論叢. Compiled by Li Kuang-pi. Wu-han: Hupeh Jen-min, 1956.

Li Wen-chih 李文治. "Wan-Ming t'ung-chih chieh-chi ti t'ou-hsiang Ch'ing-ch'ao chi nung-min ch'i-i-chün ti fan-Ch'ing tou-cheng 晚明統治階級的投降清朝及農民起義軍的反清斗爭." *Ming-Ch'ing shih-lun ts'ung* 明清史論叢. Compiled by Li Kuang-pi. Wuhan: Hupeh Jen-min, 1956.

Li Yen 李儼. *Chung-kuo suan-hsüeh shih* 中國算學史. Shanghai: Commercial Press, 1937.

Liang Ch'i-ch'ao 梁啓超. *Chung-kuo chin-san-pai-nien hsüeh-shu shih* 中國近三百年學術史. Taipei: Chung-hua, 1962.

Liu Chia-chu 劉家駒. *Ch'ing-ch'ao ch'u-ch'i ti pa-ch'i chüan-ti* 清朝初期的八旗圈地. Taipei: National Taiwan University, 1964.

———. "Shun-chih nien-chien ti t'ao-jen wen-t'i 順治年間的逃人問題" *Ch'ing-tsu Li Chi hsien-sheng ch'i-shih-sui lun-wen chi* 慶祝李濟先生七十歲論文集. Taipei, 1967.

———. "Ch'ing-ch'u Han-chün pa-ch'i ti chao-chien 清初漢軍八旗的肇建." *Ta-lu tsa-chih* 大陸雜誌, 15 June 1967, pp. 337–42; 30 June 1967, pp. 375–77.

Liu Ta-nien 劉大年. "Lun K'ang-hsi 論康熙." *Chung-kuo chin-tai-shih chu-wen-t'i* 中國近代史諸問題. Peking: Jen-min, 1965.

Lo Er-kang 羅尔綱. *Lu-ying ping-chih* 綠營兵志. Chungking: Commercial Press, 1945.

Meng Shen 孟森. "Chi-wei tz'u-k'o-lu wai-lu 己未詞科錄外錄." *Ming-Ch'ing shih-lun-chu chi-k'an* 明清史論著集刊. Taipei: Shih-chieh, 1961.

———. "Ch'ing-ch'u san-ta i-an k'ao-shih 清初三大疑案考實." *Ch'ing-tai shih* 清代史. Taipei: Cheng-chung, 1960.

———. "Ch'ing kuo-shih so-wu chih Wu San-kuei p'an-shih Han-Meng-wen ch'ih-yü pa 清國史所無之吳三桂叛時漢蒙文敕諭跋." *Ming-Ch'ing shih-lun-chu chi-k'an*. Taipei: Shih-chieh, 1961.

———. *Ch'ing-tai shih* 清代史. Taipei: Cheng-chung, 1960.

———. "K'ung Ssu-chen shih-k'ao 孔四貞事考." *Ming-Ch'ing shih-lun-chu chi-k'an*. Taipei: Shih-chieh, 1961.

———. "Pa-ch'i chih-tu k'ao-shih 八旗制度考實." *Ch'ing-tai shih.* Taipei: Cheng-chung, 1960.

———. "Shu Ming-shih ch'ao-lüeh 書明史鈔略." *Ming-Ch'ing shih-lun-chu chi-k'an.* Taipei: Shih-chieh, 1961.

———. "Tsou-hsiao an 奏銷案." *Ming-Ch'ing shih-lun-chu chi-k'an.* Taipei: Shih-chieh, 1961.

"P'ing-ting Wu-ni lüeh 平定吳逆略." *Hsü Yun-nan t'ung-chih kao* 續雲南通志稿. *Chüan* 78. Yunnan, 1901.

San-shih-san-chung Ch'ing-tai chuan-chi tsung-ho yin-te 三十三種清代傳記綜合引得. Compiled by Tu Lien-che 杜連喆 and Fang Chao-ying 房兆楹. 2d ed. Tokyo: Japan Council for East Asian Studies, 1960.

Shen Yün 沈雲. *T'ai-wan Cheng-shih shih-mo* 臺灣鄭氏始末. T'ai-wan wen-hsien ts'ung-k'an, no. 15. Taipei: Bank of Taiwan, 1958.

Ssu-k'u ch'üan-shu tsung-mu 四庫全書總目. Compiled by Chi Yün 紀昀, et al. 10 vols. Taipei: I-wen, 1964.

T'ao Chin-sheng 陶晉生. "Chin-tai chung-ch'i ti Nü-chen pen-t'u-hua yün-tung 金代中期的女真本土化運動." *Ssu-yü yen* 思與言, VII, no. 6 (March 1970), 328–32.

Tseng-chiao Ch'ing-ch'ao chin-shih t'i-ming pei-lu 增校清朝進士題名碑錄. Compiled by Tu Lien-che and Fang Chao-ying. Peking, 1941.

Ts'ung-shu ta-tz'u-tien 叢書大辭典. Compiled by Yang Chia-lo 楊家駱. Nanking, 1936.

T'ung I 童怡. "Cheng-Ch'ing ho-i chih ching-wei 鄭清和議之經緯." *T'ai-wan wen-hsien* 臺灣文獻, VI (Sept. 1955), 29–35.

Ura Ren'ichi 浦廉一. "Ch'ing-ch'u ch'ien-chieh-ling k'ao 清初遷界令考." Translated from Japanese by Lai Yung-hsiang 賴永祥. *T'ai-wan wen-hsien* 臺灣文獻, VI (Dec. 1955), 109–22.

Wang Ch'ing-yün 王慶雲. *Hsi-ch'ao chi-cheng* 熙朝紀政. Peking, 1902.

Wu Hsiang-hsiang 吳相湘. *Ch'ing-kung pi-t'an* 清宮秘譚. Taipei: Yüan-tung, 1961.

Wu Hsiu-liang 吳秀良. "Nan-shu-fang chih chien-chih chi ch'i ch'ien-ch'i chih fa-chan 南書房之建置及其前期之發展." *Ssu-yü-yen* 思與言, V (March 1968), 1428–34.

Yang Hsüeh-ch'en 楊學琛. "Ch'ing-tai ch'i-ti ti hsing-chih chi ch'i pien-hua 清代旗地的性質及其變化." *Li-shih yen-chiu* 歷史研究, 1963, no. 3, pp. 175–94.

Yang Lu-jung 楊陸榮. *San-fan chi-shih pen-mo* 三藩紀事本末. T'ai-wan wen-hsien ts'ung-k'an, no. 149. Taipei: Bank of Taiwan, 1962.

Yen Mao-kung 嚴懋功, comp. *Ch'ing-tai cheng-hsien lei-pien* 清代徵獻類編. Taipei: Shih-chieh, 1961.

Works in Western Languages

Atwell, William S. "From Education to Politics: The Fu She." *The Unfolding of Neo-Confucianism.* Edited by William Theodore de Bary. New York: Columbia University Press, 1975.

Baddeley, John F., ed. *Russia, Mongolia, China.* 2 vols. New York: Burt Franklin, [1919].

Balazs, Etienne. *Political Theory and Administrative Reality in Traditional China.* London: University of London, School of Oriental and African Studies, 1965.

Beasley, W. G., and Pulleyblank, E. G., eds. *Historians of China and Japan.* London: Oxford University Press, 1961.

Bernard, Henri. "Les adaptations chinoises d'ouvrages européens." *Monumenta Serica*, X (1945), 1–57 and 309–88; XIX (1960), 349–83.

Blair, Emma H., and Robertson, James A. *The Philippine Islands, 1493-1898.* 55 vols. Cleveland: A. H. Clark, 1903–6.

Bosmans, H. "Ferdinand Verbiest, directeur de l'observatoire de Peking (1623–88)." *Revue des questions scientifiques*, LXXI (1912), 195–273 and 375–464.

Bouvet, Joachim. *Histoire de l'empereur de la Chine.* The Hague: Meyndert Uytwerf, 1699. Reprinted Tientsin, 1940.

———. "The Journey of Joachim Bouvet, Jesuit, from Peking to Kanton, When Sent by the Emperor Kang-hi into Europe, in 1693." *A New General Collection of Voyages and Travels.* Vol. III. London: Thomas Astley, 1746.

Bowra, Cecil. "Some Episodes in the History of Amoy." *The China Review* XXI (Sept.–Oct. 1894), 80–100.

Brunnert, H. S., and Hagelstrom, V. V. *Present Day Political Organization of China.* Shanghai: Kelly and Walsh, Ltd., 1912.

Cahen, Gaston. *Histoire des relations de la Russie avec la Chine sous Pierre le Grand (1689–1730).* Paris: Félix Alcan, 1912.

Campbell, William. *Formosa under the Dutch.* London: Kegan Paul, Trench, Trubner and Co., Ltd., 1903.

Chang Chung-li. *The Chinese Gentry.* Seattle: University of Washington Press, 1955.

Chang Te-ch'ang. "The Economic Role of the Imperial Household in the Ch'ing Dynasty." *Journal of Asian Studies*, XXXI, no. 2 (Feb. 1972), 243–73.

Chavannes, Edouard. "Documents historiques et géographiques relatifs à Li-kiang." *T'oung-pao*, 2d ser., XIII (1912), 565–653.

Ch'en, Kenneth. *Buddhism in China: A Historical Survey.* Princeton: Princeton University Press, 1964.

Chen, Vincent. *Sino-Russian Relations in the Seventeenth Century.* The Hague: Martinus Nijhoff, 1966.

Ch'ü, T'ung-tsu. *Local Government in China under the Ch'ing.* Cambridge: Harvard University Press, 1962.

Cordier, Henri. *Histoire générale de la Chine.* 4 vols. Paris: Paul Geuthner, 1920.

Corradini, Piero. "A propos de l'institution de *Nei-ko* sous la dynastie des Ts'ing." *T'oung-pao*, XLVIII (1960), 416–24.

———. "Civil Administration at the Beginning of the Manchu Dynasty: A Note on the Establishment of the Six Ministries (Liu-pu)." *Oriens extremus*, IX (1962), 133–38.

Coser, Lewis A., and Rosenberg, Bernard, eds. *Sociological Theory*. New York: Macmillan, 1957.

Crawford, Robert B. "Eunuch Power in the Ming Dynasty." *T'oung-pao*, XLIX, no. 3 (1961), 115–48.

de Bary, William Theodore. "Chinese Despotism and the Confucian Ideal: A Seventeenth-Century View." *Chinese Thought and Institutions*. Edited by John K. Fairbank. Chicago: University of Chicago Press, 1957.

———, ed. *Self and Society in Ming Thought*. New York: Columbia University Press, 1970.

Dehergne, Joseph. "Un envoyé de l'empereur K'ang-hi à Louis XIV: le père Joachim Bouvet (1656–1730)." *Bulletin de l'Université l'Aurore* [Shanghai], 3d ser., IV (1943), 651–83.

Du Halde, Jean Baptiste. *A Description of the Empire of China*. 2 vols. London: E. Cave, 1738–41.

Duhr, Joseph, S. J. *Un Jésuite en Chine: Adam Schall*. Brussels: L'Edition universelle, 1936.

Elia, Pasquale M. de. *Galileo in China*. Translated by Rufus Suter and Matthew Sciascia. Cambridge: Harvard University Press, 1960.

Eminent Chinese of the Ch'ing Period. Edited by Arthur Hummel. 2 vols. Washington: Government Printing Office, 1943–44.

Fairbank, John K. "The Manchu-Chinese Dyarchy in the 1840's and '50's." *Far Eastern Quarterly*, XII (May 1953), 265–78.

———. *The United States and China*. Rev. ed. New York: Viking Press, 1962.

Fang, Chaoying. "A Technique for Estimating the Numerical Strength of the Early Manchu Military Forces." *Harvard Journal of Asiatic Studies*, XIII (1950), 192–215.

Farquhar, David M. "Mongolian versus Chinese Elements in the Early Manchu State." *Ch'ing-shih wen-t'i*, II, no. 6 (June 1971), 11–23.

Feuerwerker, Albert. "China's History in Marxian Dress." *American Historical Review*, LXVI (Jan. 1961), 323–53.

———. "From 'Feudalism' to 'Capitalism' in Recent Historical Writing from Mainland China." *Journal of Asian Studies*, XVIII (Nov. 1958), 107–15.

Franke, Wolfgang. "The Veritable Records of the Ming Dynasty (1368–1644)." *Historians of China and Japan*. Edited by W. G. Beasley, and E. G. Pulleyblank. London: Oxford University Press, 1961.

Fu Lo-shu. *A Documentary Chronicle of Sino-Western Relations (1644–1820)*. Tucson: University of Arizona Press for the Association for Asian Studies, 1966.

———. "Sino-Western Relations during the K'ang-hsi Period, 1661–1722." Ph.D. diss., University of Chicago, 1952.

———. "The Two Portuguese Embassies to China during the K'ang-hsi Period." *T'oung-pao*, XLIII (1955), 75–94.

Fung Yu-lan. *A Short History of Chinese Philosophy*. Edited by Derk Bodde. New York: Macmillan, 1960.

Golder, F. A. *Russian Expansion on the Pacific, 1641–1850*. Cleveland: Arthur Clark, 1914.

Goodrich, Luther Carrington. *The Literary Inquisition of Ch'ien-lung*. 2d ed. New York: Paragon Book Reprint Corp., 1966.

Greslon, Adrien. *Histoire de la Chine sous la domination des Tartares*. Paris: Jean Henault, 1671.

Hedin, Sven. *Jehol, City of Emperors*. Translated by E. G. Nash. New York: E. P. Dutton, 1933.

Hibbert, Eloise Talcott. *K'ang-hsi, Emperor of China*. London: Kegan Paul, Trench, Trubner and Co., Ltd., 1940.

Ho, Alfred Kuo-liang. "The Grand Council in the Ch'ing Dynasty." *Far Eastern Quarterly*, XI (Feb. 1952), 167–82.

Ho, Ping-ti. "Early-Ripening Rice in Chinese History." *Economic History Review*, 2d ser., IX (Dec. 1956), 200–218.

———. *The Ladder of Success in Imperial China*. New York: Columbia University Press, 1962.

———. "Salient Aspects of China's Heritage." *China in Crisis*. Vol. I: *China's Heritage and the Communist Political System*. Edited by Ping-ti Ho and Tang Tsou. Chicago: University of Chicago Press, 1968.

———. "The Salt Merchants of Yang-chou: A Study of Commercial Capitalism in Eighteenth-Century China." *Harvard Journal of Asiatic Studies*, XVII (June 1954), 130–68.

———. "The Significance of the Ch'ing Period in Chinese History." *Journal of Asian Studies*, XXVI (Feb. 1967), 189–95.

———. *Studies on the Population of China, 1368–1953*. Cambridge: Harvard University Press, 1959.

Hsi, Angela N. S. "Wu San-kuei in 1644: A Reappraisal." *Journal of Asian Studies*, XXXIV, no. 2 (Feb. 1975), 443–53.

Hsiao Kung-ch'üan. *Rural China: Imperial Control in the Nineteenth Century*. Seattle: University of Washington Press, 1960.

Hsieh Kuo-chen. "Removal of Coastal Population in Early Tsing Period." Translated by Ch'en T'ung-hsieh. *The Chinese Social and Political Science Review*, XV (Jan. 1932), 559–96.

Hsieh Pao-chao. *The Government of China (1644–1911)*. Baltimore: John Hopkins Press, 1925. Reprinted New York: Octagon Books, 1966.

Hsu, Immanuel C. Y. "Russia's Special Position in China in the Early Ch'ing Period." *Slavic Review*, XXIII (Dec. 1964), 688–700.

Huang Pei. "Aspects of Ch'ing Autocracy: An Institutional Study, 1644–1735." *Tsing-hua Journal of Chinese Studies*, n.s., VI (Dec. 1967), 105–48.

Huang, Ray. "Fiscal Administration during the Ming Dynasty." *Chinese Government in Ming Times: Seven Studies*. Edited by Charles O. Hucker. New York: Columbia University Press, 1969.

Hucker, Charles O. *The Censorial System of Ming China*. Stanford: Stanford University Press, 1966.

———. "Governmental Organization of the Ming Dynasty." *Harvard Journal of Asiatic Studies*, XXI (Dec. 1958), 1–67.

———. "The Tung-lin Movement of the Late Ming Period." *Chinese Thought and Institutions*. Edited by John K. Fairbank. Chicago: University of Chicago Press, 1957.

Jesús Maria, José de. *Azia Sínica e Japônica*. Edited by Charles R. Boxer. 2 vols. Macao: Imprensa Nacionel, 1941–50.

Kahn, Harold. "The Education of a Prince: The Emperor Learns His Roles." *Approaches to Modern Chinese History*. Edited by Albert Feuerwerker, Rhoads Murphey, and Mary C. Wright. Berkeley: University of California Press, 1967.

———. "Some Mid-Ch'ing Views of the Monarchy." *Journal of Asian Studies*, XXIV (Feb. 1965), 229–43.

Keene, Donald, ed. and trans. *The Battles of Coxinga*. London: Taylor's Foreign Press, 1951.

Kessler, Lawrence D. "Chinese Scholars and the Early Manchu State." *Harvard Journal of Asiatic Studies*, XXXI (1971), 179–200.

———. "Ethnic Composition of Provincial Leadership during the Ch'ing Dynasty." *Journal of Asian Studies*, XXVIII (May 1969), 489–511.

Lach, Donald F. "Leibniz and China." *Journal of the History of Ideas*, VI (1945), 436–55.

Le Comte, Louis Daniel. *Memoirs and Observations*. 3d ed. London: B. Tooke, 1699.

Lee, Robert H. G. *The Manchurian Frontier in Ch'ing History*. Cambridge: Harvard University Press, 1970.

Legge, James. *The Chinese Classics*. Vol. I: *Confucian Analects*. 3d ed. Hong Kong: Hong Kong University Press, 1960.

Lettres édifiantes et curieuses. 40 vols. Paris: Nicholas Le Clerc, 1707–58.

Levenson, Joseph T. *Modern China and Its Confucian Past.* Garden City, New York: Doubleday and Co., 1964.

Linton, Ralph. "Nativistic Movements." *American Anthropologist,* XLV, no. 2 (April–June 1943), 230–40.

Ma Feng-ch'en. "Manchu-Chinese Social and Economic Conflicts in Early Ch'ing." *Chinese Social History.* Edited by E-tu Zen Sun and John de Francis. Washington, D.C.: American Council of Learned Societies, 1956.

Mailla, Joseph Anne-Marie de Moyriac de. *Histoire générale de la Chine.* 13 vols. Paris: P. D. Pierres, 1777–85.

Mancall, Mark. "The Ch'ing Tribute System: An Interpretive Essay." *The Chinese World Order.* Edited by John K. Fairbank. Cambridge: Harvard University Press, 1968.

———. *Russia and China: Their Diplomatic Relations to 1728.* Cambridge: Harvard University Press, 1971.

Michael, Franz. "Military Organization and Power Structure of China during the Taiping Rebellion." *Pacific Historical Review,* XVIII (1949), 469–83.

———. *The Origin of Manchu Rule in China.* Baltimore: Johns Hopkins Press, 1942. Reprinted New York: Octagon Books, 1965.

Montanus, Arnoldus. *Atlas Chinensis.* Translated by John Ogilby. London: Thomas Johnson, 1671.

Navarrete, Domingo. *An Account of the Empire of China.* Vol. I of *Collection of Voyages and Travels.* Edited by Awnsham and John Churchill. 4 vols. London: Printed for A. and J. Churchill at the Black Swan, 1704.

Nivison, David S. "Ho-shen and His Accusers: Ideology and Political Behavior in the Eighteenth Century." In *Confucianism in Action.* Edited by David S. Nivison and Arthur F. Wright. Stanford: Stanford University Press, 1949.

———. *The Life and Thought of Chang Hsüeh-ch'eng (1738–1801).* Stanford: Stanford University Press, 1966.

Orleans, Pierre Joseph de. *History of the Two Tartar Conquerors of China.* Translated and edited by the Earl of Ellesmere. London: The Hakluyt Society, 1854.

Oxnam, Robert B. *Ruling from Horseback: Manchu Politics in the Oboi Regency, 1661-1669.* Chicago: University of Chicago Press, 1975.

Palafox y Mendoza, Juan de. *The History of the Conquest of China by the Tartars.* London: W. Godbid, 1671.

Parsons, James B. "The Ming Dynasty Bureaucracy: Aspects of Background Forces." *Chinese Government in Ming Times: Seven Studies.* Edited by Charles O. Hucker. New York: Columbia University Press, 1969.

Pauthier, Jean Pierre Guillaume. *Chine.* Paris: Firmin Didot frères, 1839.

Pavlovsky, Michel. *Chinese-Russian Relations.* New York: The Philosophical Library, 1949.

Peterson, Willard J. "The Life of Ku Yen-wu (1613–1682)." *Harvard Journal of Asiatic Studies,* XXVIII (1968), 114–56; XXIX (1969), 201–47.

Pfister, Louis. *Notices biographiques et bibliographiques sur les Jésuites de l'ancienne mission de Chine (1552–1773).* 2 vols. Variétés sinologiques, nos. 59 and 60. Shanghai: Imprimerie de la Mission Catholique, 1932–34.

P[hillips], G[eorge]. "The Life of Koxinga." *The China Review,* XIII (1884–85), 67–74 and 207–13.

Pinot, Virgile. *La Chine et la formation de l'esprit philosophique en France (1640–1740).* Paris: Paul Geuthner, 1932.

Playfair, G. M. H. *The Cities and Towns of China.* 2d ed. Shanghai: Kelly and Walsh, 1910. Reprinted Taipei: Literature House, 1965.

Ponsonby-Fane, R. A. B. "Koxinga: Chronicles of the Tei Family, Loyal Servants of Ming." *Transactions and Proceedings of the Japan Society (London),* XXXIV (1936–37), 65–132.

Poppe, Nicholas; Hurvitz, Leon; and Hidehiro Okada. *Catalogue of the Manchu-Mongol Section of the Toyo Bunko.* Tokyo: Toyo Bunko, 1964; Seattle: University of Washington Press, 1964.

Pu Yi. *From Emperor to Citizen: The Autobiography of Aisin-Gioro Pu Yi.* Vol. I. Peking: Foreign Languages Press, 1964.

Rocher, Émile. "Histoire des princes du Yun-nan et leurs relations avec la Chine d'après des documents historiques chinois." *T'oung-pao,* X (1899), 1–32, 115–54, 337–68, and 437–58.

Rosso, Antonio S., O.F.M. *Apostolic Legations to China of the Eighteenth Century.* South Pasadena: P. D. and Ione Perkins, 1948.

Sebes, Joseph, S. J. *The Jesuits and the Sino-Russian Treaty of Nerchinsk: the Diary of Thomas Pereira, S.J.* Rome: Institutum Histoircum S.I., 1961.

"The Share Taken by Chinese and Bannermen Respectively in the Government of China." *The China Review,* VI (1877–78), 136–37.

Sources of Chinese Tradition. Compiled by William Theodore de Bary, Wing-sit Chan, and Burton Watson. New York: Columbia University

Press, 1960.

Spence, Jonathan. *Emperor of China: Self-Portrait of K'ang-hsi.* New York: Alfred A. Knopf, 1974.

———. "The Seven Ages of K'ang-hsi (1654–1722)." *Journal of Asian Studies,* XXVI (Feb. 1967), 205–11.

———. *To Change China.* Boston: Little, Brown and Co., 1969.

———. *Ts'ao Yin and the K'ang-hsi Emperor: Bondservant and Master.* New Haven: Yale University Press, 1966.

Tachard, Guy. *Voyage de Siam.* Amsterdam: Pierre Mortier, 1687.

Teng, Ssu-yü, and Fairbank, John K. "On the Transmission of Ch'ing Documents." *Harvard Journal of Asiatic Studies,* IV (1939), 12–46.

Tsao, Kai-fu. "The Rebellion of the Three Feudatories against the Manchu Throne in China, 1673–1681: Its Setting and Significance." Ph.D. diss., Columbia University, 1966.

Tsien, T. H. "Western Impact on China through Translation—a Bibliographical Study." Ph.D. diss., University of Chicago, 1952.

Vanhee, L. "Euclide en chinois et mandchou." *Isis,* XXX (1939), 84–88.

Vojeu de Brunem [Joseph Jouve]. *Histoire de la conquête de la Chine par les Tartares mancheaux.* 2 vols. Lyon: Frères Duplain, 1754.

Wade, T. F. "The Army of the Chinese Empire." *Chinese Repository,* XX (1851), 250–80, 300–340, and 363–422.

Waley, Arthur. *The Analects of Confucius.* New York: Random House, 1938.

———. *Yüan Mei: Eighteenth-Century Chinese Poet.* New York: Grove Press, 1958.

Widmer, Eric. "'Kitai' and the Ch'ing Empire in Seventeenth Century Russian Documents on China." *Ch'ing-shih wen-t'i,* II, no. 4 (Nov. 1970), 21–39.

Wiens, Mi Chu. "Anti-Manchu Thought during the Early Ch'ing." (Harvard) *Papers on China,* XXII-A (May 1969), 1–24.

Wilhelm, Hellmut. "The *Po-hsüeh hung-ju* Examination of 1679." *Journal of the American Oriental Society,* LXXI (1951), 60–66.

Wills, John E., Jr. *Pepper, Guns and Parleys: The Dutch East India Company and China, 1622–1681.* Cambridge: Harvard University Press, 1974.

Wright, Mary Clabaugh. *The Last Stand of Chinese Conservatism: The T'ung-chih Restoration, 1862–74.* 2d printing with additional notes. Stanford: Stanford University Press, 1962.

Wu, Silas H. L. *Communication and Imperial Control in China.* Cambridge: Harvard University Press, 1970.

———. "The Memorial Systems of the Ch'ing Dynasty (1644–1911)." *Harvard Journal of Asiatic Studies,* XXVII (1967), 7–75.

Wu, Wei-ping. "The Development and Decline of the Eight Banners." Ph.D. diss., University of Pennsylvania, 1969.

Wylie, Alexander. *Notes on Chinese Literature.* Shanghai: Presbyterian Mission Press, 1922. Reprinted Taipei: Literature House, 1964.

Yang Lien-sheng. "Hostages in Chinese History." *Studies in Chinese Institutional History.* Cambridge: Harvard University Press, 1961.

———. "Numbers and Units in Chinese Economic History." *Studies in Chinese Institutional History.* Cambridge: Harvard University Press, 1961.

INDEX